COLIN BARROW

BUSINESS
SUCCESS

Starting a Business from Home

Your guide to planning your
home start-up, reaching a market
and creating a profit

3RD EDITION

KoganPage

First published in Great Britain and the United States in 2008 by Kogan Page Limited
Second edition 2011
Third edition 2017

2nd Floor, 45 Gee Street	c/o Martin P Hill Consulting	4737/23 Ansari Road
London EC1V 3RS	122 W 27th St, 10th Floor	Daryaganj
United Kingdom	New York, NY 10001	New Delhi 110002
www.koganpage.com	USA	India

© Colin Barrow, 2008, 2011, 2017

The right of Colin Barrow to be identified as the author of this work has been asserted by him in accordance with the Copyright, Designs and Patents Act 1988.

ISBN   978 0 7494 8084 4
E-ISBN   978 0 7494 8085 1

British Library Cataloguing-in-Publication Data

A CIP record for this book is available from the British Library.

Typeset by Integra Software Services, Pondicherry
Print production managed by Jellyfish
Printed and bound by CPI Group (UK) Ltd, Croydon CR0 4YY

CONTENTS

Introduction

The years since the first edition of this book in 2008 have witnessed a near collapse in world financial markets, by many standards the worst since the Wall Street crash of 1929; the first successful coalition government in the United Kingdom since the one led by Winston Churchill in 1940 to steer the country through the war years; the British decision to leave the European Union in 2016; and the election of Donald Trump, the first American President never to have held any prior political appointment since Eisenhower, a five star general Supreme Commander of the Allied Forces in Europe in WW2.

However, these macro gyrations have not daunted would-be business starters. There were approximately 5.5 million active businesses in the UK during 2016, up from 3.5 million in 2010 (www.fsb.org.uk/media-centre/small-business-statistics). The figures from around the world are similarly impressive. There are over 175 million people running their own business in the developed world. That is double the number of just two decades or so ago. GEM (www.gemconsortium.org), through their Global Entrepreneurship Monitor research programme headed up by Babson College in the United States, collect statistics across 60 economies around the world on business starters and equally importantly would-be starters.

Running your own business may seem a daunting task when you first start to gather ideas together and make tentative plans. Many would-be entrepreneurs after putting a toe in the water quickly pull back, reckoning that they don't have the skills, that their business concept is not all that compelling or that raising the money is going to be challenging, expensive and altogether too risky a proposition.

Certainly most of the people you talk to will be only too ready to pour cold water in liberal doses all over your proposed product or service. Your friends and loved ones through a sense of responsibility and perhaps even self-interest will naturally urge caution, preferring a safe regular salary to the apparent lottery of enterprise. After all, everyone knows that most new businesses fail, often causing misery and penury to founders, family, partners and anyone foolhardy enough to supply or in any way get involved.

The first useful fact to know is that the rumour of calamities awaiting most new ventures is just that – an unfounded and incorrect piece of oft-repeated misinformation. An exhaustive study of the eight-year destinations of all 814,000 US firms founded in a particular year revealed that just 18 per cent actually failed, meaning that the entrepreneurs were put out of business by their financial backers, lack of demand or competitive pressures (Bruce A Kirchhoff, 1994, *Entrepreneurship and Dynamic Capitalism*, Praeger Publishers, Westport, CT). True, some 28 per cent of businesses closed their doors voluntarily, their founders having decided for a variety of reasons that working either for themselves or for this particular type of business was just not for them.

But the majority of the businesses studied in Kirchhoff's mammoth and representative study survived and in many cases prospered. With a degree of preparation, a fair amount of perspiration and a modicum of luck you can get started and may even, as in the case examples in this book, become a millionaire to boot.

Working for yourself from home can seem a lonely business. Indeed loneliness is one of the most frequently quoted concerns cited to alarm prospective entrepreneurs. Paradoxically there are probably more people running their own business than there are members of almost any other profession or trade. There are certainly more entrepreneurs than there are doctors, surveyors, airline pilots or engineers. So whilst you may feel alone and maybe even that you are held in low esteem the reality is rather different.

You might be surprised at the number of people and organizations that appear keen to help you get your business up and running.

In Appendix 1 there is a directory of such organizations, prominent amongst which is the government. None of these would-be helpers is particularly altruistic. The government needs you, as new businesses create most of the new jobs in any economy, a fact uncovered by David Birch, a researcher at Massachusetts Institute of Technology (MIT) back in 1979 (*The Job Generation Process*, MIT, Cambridge, MA) and corroborated by dozens of other studies since then. Also of course you will pay tax on your profits and become an unpaid tax collector for VAT or sales tax on behalf of government agencies.

New businesses are also the main source of innovations, with around 60 per cent of all commercially viable inventions born in new businesses. So venture capital firms looking for superior returns need a steady flow of new businesses to back. Even conservative lending banks see those creating new businesses as being a target worthy of aiming for. Whilst home banking is still largely free, banks rely on business clients to make their money from.

Starting from home: Advantages and disadvantages

Starting a business from home gives you a number of distinctive advantages over other business start-ups. True, there are a couple of disadvantages as well, but these are more than offset by the benefits.

The advantages

Those starting a business from home have a number of distinct advantages over those plumping for premises straight away. A study by the US Small Business Administration tracking the survival rates on new businesses (**www.sba.gov/advo/research/business.html >** Redefining Business Success) concluded that starting from home significantly improved a founder's chances of succeeding. Other studies coming from organizations less impartial suggest that home-based businesses are two-thirds more likely to survive the crucial first four years of trading and so establish a firm footing.

The advantages a home-based business has over its peers that give it an edge are as follows.

Lower costs

Walk around town, any town, and you will see offices being refurbished, with new furniture being delivered, shops being fitted out and billboards being erected and painted. Telephone companies will be queuing up to install new lines; internet service providers will be licking their lips as they sign up new clients. Then of course there is the rent and other charges to pay out on business premises. You get the picture.

Starting from home saves most of the £35,000 start-up costs that the average business incurs even before it takes its first order. The chances are you have nearly everything you need to start up your business already somewhere around your home. The kitchen table worked fine for Blooming Marvellous to make their plans, pack up their first orders and do their accounts from. A garage, loft, spare bedroom or garden shed can be pressed into service for a whole host of business-related tasks from holding stock to being a dedicated office space away from the normal hustle of home life. Your computer, however old, will almost definitely work just fine, unless you are starting a business at the cutting edge of design or the internet.

Better costs

It's a curious phenomenon but for many people half the fun of starting a business is spending a fortune at the outset on new gizmos. At last there is an excuse for getting that new colour photocopier, cab-truck that can double for deliveries or a new suite of office furniture without feeling guilty. After all it's an investment in a new business, not an extravagant spending splurge. The beauty of starting from home is that you don't really have the excuse for new expenditure that starting in dedicated premises provides, and the chances are you don't have the space either.

But a valuable additional benefit from not having to spend too much money at the outset of your business is that you get to spend it more wisely later on when you see how your business shapes up. Countless business starters have 'invested' thousands in impressive offices only to find that no one has any reason to visit them. The suppliers and clients they hoped to impress only ever see their stationery or website. In fact, researching the local hotels to find those with discreet lobbies or coffee lounges would meet their rare need for a comfortable venue. Just as babies change shape very quickly, so do young businesses. Best to make do with what you have at first and see how the business shapes up.

More time

There are lots of things that money can buy but time isn't one of them. However close your business premises are, you could spend at least four hours a day travelling to and from them. I'm sure if your shop, restaurant or office is only a couple of miles away you won't believe that proposition. How on earth could it be possible to take an hour to travel just one mile? Well, there is an immutable law that says the closer your home is to your business premises the more often you travel between the two. Ergo, if you are 20 miles away you go once a day, covering 40 miles, and if you are only 5 miles away you come home for lunch and return once or twice more each week to collect things you have forgotten. Whatever the distance, the average weekly travel time is about the same.

Working from home also helps with all the other factors that encroach on your time. If a family member is ill and needs your attention you can work and look after the ill person too: no need to run back and forth or get into work late, as you are on the spot anyway. The same applies to having to put in extra hours to meet a work deadline. You can take an hour out to have dinner with your family and then get back to work afterwards.

Less stress

Commuting to work on a daily basis is stressful. In any vibrant and successful economic area roadworks, accidents, delays and traffic jams are pretty much the norm. Few of us are fortunate enough to live in a car-free area or where parking is never a problem. Even if you could find such a paradise the chances are it would be useless as a business proposition. Depopulated areas are equally devoid of customers, suppliers and people to employ. Even if you are the boss you have to get into your premises before anyone else and leave after them to lock up. Often this is a bonus, as with a bit of careful planning you can miss the worst of the traffic. But whatever the benefits this can make for a very long day.

Juggling the factors that make for a satisfactory home–work balance is another source of stress that homeworkers are less prone to suffer. After all, you have everything in one place and can deal with problems as they occur. The opportunity to shift between business-related tasks and working on housework, cooking or maintenance provides exactly the sort of variety that minimizes the chances of getting bored. Also you can work at what you feel best able to do when the conditions are right. Gardening will be more fun on a sunny morning than at dusk in the rain after a fraught drive home. And if the internet crashes you might be glad of the opportunity.

Improved productivity

Less stress + More time = Improved productivity. This is an equation that works for any business, but works best for a home-based one. It follows that if you can find a couple of extra hours a day and spend them working at something you really feel good about doing you will get more done each day. The more valuable work you do the more productive you are and hence the more income you can generate.

It's not rocket science. If you can make £20 an hour in your business then every extra hour you work is to your advantage. Spend the four hours you might have spent travelling at productive work and you have an extra £80 a day. Do that five days a week for 48 weeks and you have an extra £19,200 of productive output. That makes a home-based business around a fifth more productive than the average business is in its early years.

Unique competitive proposition (UCP)

Many small businesses see their primary initial competitive advantage as being able to sell at a lower price than bigger established competitors. In fact, as most owner-managers have little or no idea what their true costs will be or how much they will sell (see Chapter 9 where I cover break-even analysis, which shows you how to work this out), that proposition is almost always fallacious. They sell cheap and lose money more often than not. Then they struggle hard to get their prices up, losing dozens of expensively won customers on the way.

But most home-based businesses have a winning formula: Improved Productivity + Lower costs = The potential to sell cheaper and still make good money. This argument is a powerful one and it goes like this. The home-based business hasn't had to spend large sums of money on premises and rent at the outset, so those costs don't have to be recovered from every sale. Also, being more productive the home-based business gets more done and so has more to sell. Thus with more output to sell and less costs to recover, anyone running a business from home can undercut any premises-based business and still make more profit.

The usual suspects

Working your business from home also gives you all the advantages that anyone running a business anywhere will enjoy. These include:

- the personal satisfaction that comes from following your own vision of how things should be done;
- being able to make your own decisions and not always having to rely on others;
- having the potential to make as much money as you need rather than having to work set hours;

- not having to get involved in office politics or waste time in tedious bonding exercises;

- creating employment for family members, if you want, including spouse and children;

- having a business to pass on to future generations;

- creating a business that is valuable rather than just having a wage whilst making someone else's business valuable.

The disadvantages

Starting a business whether from home or elsewhere is not a one-way bet. There are disadvantages too. For a start, being your own boss means the buck stops with you. Ultimately you have to take responsibility for everything. As an employee you could reasonably lay the blame for a late delivery or faulty product on the relevant department, but as a business owner everyone blames you and looks to you to create a solution. If that means jumping in the car and doing a delivery yourself overnight, so be it. Owner-managers have the term 'overtime' deleted from their memory bank!

You are also responsible for paying back any money borrowed, keeping within the law, filing accounts, paying taxes, maintaining employment records – the list of responsibilities and obligations is onerous. Also, if you work from home you have a couple of specific disadvantages to keep in mind:

No place to hide

Whilst travelling to work every day can be stressful and is almost invariably a waste of time, it does at least give you some personal space. Also once you are at your business premises you can, for a while at least, leave your home concerns behind. Peeling paintwork, uncut grass, an empty refrigerator and a faulty bathroom tap are all problems that can be parked out of sight at the back of your mind until your return.

Working from home means that these and any other domestic crises are all too evident all day every day.

Disrupting influences

Business premises are usually cleaned before people turn up for work. Even if you are the person doing the cleaning, as you may well be in the early months and years, you won't be trying to work whilst it's being done. At home, unless you live alone, the chances are that you will have to work throughout whilst domestic chores are being carried out. Cleaning, cooking, feeding, ironing and all the other paraphernalia of home life will be going on whilst you are struggling to take a vital phone call on a less-than-perfect line from a client on another continent. The day you have set aside for laying your paperwork out as a prelude to filing will see you in competition for the same floor space.

Also, being on hand makes it difficult to park problems and issues until later in the day. It takes superhuman self-discipline not to answer the door if friends or relatives drop by unexpectedly or if your spouse makes 'As you are here would you mind?' type requests.

CASE STUDY Northern Dough

The Northern Dough Company started out making pizzas at their kitchen table in 2011. By 2016 the latest accounts filed at Companies House revealed that they were doubling in size every year. The company's debtors, the money owed by customers grew from £27,064 to £47,475 in the past year alone. (Look forward to chapter 9 if your accounting is a little rusty.) Those debtors, customers that owe money for supplies, now include 250 Waitrose stores as well as Booths Supermarkets, Ocado, Whole Foods and 130 individual farm shops, a healthy customer base by any standards.

The Lancashire-based company is the brainchild of husband and wife team Chris and Amy Cheadle. The idea for the business came after they hosted 'make your own pizza' dinner parties. 'We started the business as an alternative to dining out,' says Chris. 'Our friends were invited into the kitchen to create their own favourite recipes. They enjoyed it so much they often went home with a bagful of dough.'

Chris had something of a head start as he came from three generations of family of bakers in Lancashire. But the business idea wasn't born in an oven. It was only when he looked for an alternative at the supermarket that he saw a gap in the market for a convenient and authentic tasting product and the business was born. The idea was tested at a local food market where they sold out everything they had brought in 90 minutes.

www.northerndoughco.com

Finding the right business opportunity

THIS CHAPTER COVERS

- deciding on a product or service;
- looking for a gap in the market;
- buying into an established idea;
- going into franchising;
- using network marketing;
- sourcing business ideas.

Dependent on the type of person you are, the world is either full of business opportunities or everything worth doing is already being done very well by someone else. You may remember the story of the two salespeople sent to a seriously underdeveloped country to sell shoes. On arriving and noticing that none of the locals was wearing shoes, one salesperson e-mailed head office saying 'No market here, on next flight home.' The other's e-mail read rather differently – 'Enormous potential, no competition, send all warehouse stock out on next flight.'

The truth often lies somewhere between these polarized views of the market. But both salespeople did something right – they got out and saw for themselves. In this chapter you will see the generic ways into business and read case examples of others like yourself who have been, seen and done.

Product or service

One area of continuing confusion for would-be business starters is whether they should look for a product or a service to sell. Products often seem an easier choice, as customers can see immediately what they are getting for their money, and in any event tangible objects are easier to describe. As against this apparent advantage is a feeling that product orientation is old-fashioned, giving off an air of metal-bashing workshops under railway arches in cities that have seen better days.

Defining a product

A product is something physical that generally conveys to a buyer what it does and why it is worth paying good money for it. It could be something as dull as a garden spade, devoid of either technological content or any element of aesthetic design. Alternatively, a Porsche 911, an Apple iPhone and a Dyson vacuum cleaner are all every bit as much products as the humble spade, but clearly a lot more value has been pumped into them.

Sometimes a product needs a bit of embellishing to make sure end users understand what a privilege they are getting when they shell out their hard cash. Computer software and DVDs are a good example here. These products almost invariably come in a box large enough to pack in half a dozen more similarly sized items. After you have peeled the onion-like layers of wrapping, the physical product itself may be millimetres thick and a few centimetres in circumference. But that fact alone won't be enough to deter a supplier such as Microsoft from charging £400.

Explaining a service

A service on the other hand is something of value that has no residual physical presence. Baby sitting, dog walking and management consultancy advice, for example, are valuable activities that people are prepared to pay for that leave nothing material behind after being 'delivered'. True management consultants usually leave a report after they have carried out their task, but clients pay for insights and knowledge rather than a few sheets of typing and a chart or two.

Settling on a product/service mix

In truth all product-based businesses are a mixture of both the physical attributes and a specified level of service-based support. Indeed for many products the key differentiators may be the service support that underpins their offer. For example, KIA cars perform much as any other car in their category. You will get to your destination as certainly and quickly in a KIA as in say a Chevrolet, Hyundai or Skoda. But KIA guarantee all their cars for seven years or 100,000 miles, whichever comes first; with a Volvo or Volkswagen you would be on your own after three years or 60,000 miles.

The choice you have to consider in deciding what sort of business to go into is more about what level of service or warranty you want to offer rather than whether you will just sell a product or deliver a service. A mail order business could make itself better and different from competitors by offering a range of delivery speeds, order tracking so customers are not kept hanging on, and follow-up to ensure the product performs as specified. But if dealing with customers and offering a high level of service are not your bag, choose a business sector where that is not so important.

Classic ways into business

There are very few types of business that can't be run from home, at least from the outset. Whilst running a paint manufacturing business with toxic fumes pouring out of your chimney, 44-ton artics in the drive and a garage full of tins may cause sufficient problems with the neighbours to render it an impossibility, the key elements of such a business can be run from your front room with little or no difficulty.

Manufacture, warehousing, delivery and even invoicing and cash collection can all be outsourced. All you need to be sure of is that enough people want your paint at the price you have to sell to make a decent profit.

So the starting point for every business is a proposition. For Blooming Marvellous the business idea stemmed from the simple fact that once the founders became pregnant they could no longer be fashionably dressed. All the retailers they used before made nothing for pregnant women, and none of the outlets that specialized in maternity wear made anything that could be remotely considered as fashionable. That left the business founders with a classic route to market – an unfulfilled need.

Filling a gap in the market

The most fundamental way to spot a winning business idea is to find a gap in the market. Gaps are usually 'spaces' left behind by bigger, more established businesses that either consider meeting the needs of a particular group of customers uneconomic or have just become lazy as they got bigger. For example, Anita Roddick, founder of The Body Shop, found that she could only buy the beauty products she wanted in huge quantities. By breaking down the quantities and sizes of those products from her dining-room table she unleashed a huge new demand. Now owned by L'Oréal, Body Shop International currently has a range of 1,200 products sold through 2,605 franchised stores in 61 countries and employs 22,000 people.

Repositioning an existing product

Often with a few minor adjustments an old idea can be given a new lease of life. Monopoly enjoyed a renaissance when it was launched with Parisian rather than London street names.

Other rich veins of business ideas include looking overseas or into other markets at products and services that have worked well in the past but have not yet made the leap to your home market.

CASE STUDY Specsavers

Every once in a while an entrepreneur turns an industry on its head. Dame Mary Perkins was a perfect example when she launched a business that changed the face of optometry for good. We might be used to visiting showrooms to purchase glasses these days, trying on frames at our leisure until we find the perfect fit, with every item clearly priced, but back in the early 1980s this was not the case. Before Mary launched Specsavers, consumers had very little choice or control when purchasing eyewear. Indeed, before Specsavers came along, when you visited an optician they'd disappear out back to find a few pairs for you to try on. But Mary had a clear vision of how opticians could operate in order to deliver better value, choice and transparency to consumers. Driven by a mission of providing affordable eye care to all, she built the company around the idea of treating others respectfully. She still describes her billion-pound international company, which she founded with her husband, Doug Perkins, as 'a family-owned business, with family values'.

One of the key lessons Mary learnt early on was the importance of setting yourself apart from the competition. As a new business, there was no point in merely copying a major player – you had to offer customers something different. She identified a number of major problems with the way opticians were doing business at the time, and came up with a proposition that she felt was far more attractive to consumers. First of all, glasses were expensive. Mary believed that she would be able to bring prices down without compromising on quality by negotiating better buying terms and selling larger volumes. For example, instead of buying from wholesalers who added a significant mark-up on their prices, she went to factories directly.

From just two staff working at a table-tennis table, there are now more than 500 based at Specsavers' headquarters in Guernsey and around 26,000 worldwide. The company has more than 1,390 stores across the Channel Islands, the UK, Ireland, the Netherlands, Scandinavia, Spain, Australia and New Zealand. Mary believes that much of her success has been driven by the preservation of the founding culture and ideals, and a focus on giving consumers real value and choice.

Blue-skies thinking

Inventions and innovations are perhaps the most risky way into business. True, if you get it right you can make a pile of money, but most don't. Less than 1 per cent of patents filed in the United States result in a commercially viable business proposition. That adds up to a lot of wasted money on filing patents. (See Chapter 4, where the legal aspects of intellectual property are covered.)

Getting inventions to market can be an expensive and time-consuming business, as James Dyson is only too eager to confirm. It took five years and 5,127 prototypes before the world's first bagless vacuum cleaner arrived on the scene. Mark Saunders, like Dyson, studied at the Royal College of Art in London, where he designed the innovative Strida folding bike (**www.strida.com**). Saunders originally planned to make the product himself, but some rudimentary product costing convinced him to subcontract out the manufacturing process and keep working from home on design and development.

Using the internet

The internet is a classic route to market for the home-based business starter. All you need is a computer, an internet connection and a winning idea. The sting in the tail lies in the last word. The first generation of internet businesses had little unique about their propositions other than being on the 'net', which was thought exciting enough. Businesses were floated on stock markets the world over at values unheard of for firms with no sales revenue and in some cases no products. Failures abounded and, whilst a handful – Amazon and Lastminute.com, for example – prospered, most failed, dragging world stock markets down with them.

All the basic rules of business apply whatever the route to market, and route to market is really all the internet is.

Employing other people's ideas

You don't have to have a business idea of your own to get into business. A large number of people have entrepreneurship thrust upon them by external factors. An event such as inheriting money, having to move when a partner changes jobs, having to give up full-time work through pregnancy or illness, being made redundant or having to make ends meet in retirement can trigger the desire to go into business.

These are some of the ways in which you can piggyback on proven business concepts. Whilst you may lose some elements of the independence running with your own idea provides, you will at least be surer of some success.

Franchising from home

Franchising is a marketing technique used to improve and expand the distribution of a product or service. The franchisor supplies the product or teaches the service to the franchisee, who in turn sells it to the public. In return for this, the franchisee pays a fee and a continuing royalty, based usually on turnover. The franchisee may also be required to buy materials or ingredients from the franchisor, giving the latter an additional income stream. The advantage to franchisees is a relatively safe and quick way of getting into business for themselves, but with the support and advice of an experienced organization close at hand.

Franchisors can expand their distribution with the minimum strain on their own capital and have the services of a highly moti-vated team of owner-managers. Franchising is not a path to great riches, nor is it for the truly independent spirit, as policy and profits will come from the franchisor.

Recruitment, travel and leisure, bookkeeping, photography, pet foods, jewellery, greeting cards, magazine publishing, internet services, education and dating agencies are just a handful of the 1,500 franchise systems on offer around the world. The average cost of a home-based franchise is £15,000 including franchise fee, working capital, equipment and fittings, stock and materials. But you can set a home-based franchise for as little as £4,500.

Before deciding on a particular franchise it is essential that you consult your legal and financial advisers. Franchisees must also ask franchisors some very searching questions to prove their competence. You will need to know if they have operated a pilot unit in the UK –

an essential first step before selling franchises to third parties. Otherwise, how can they really know all the problems and so put you on the right track? You will need to know what training and support are included in the franchise package, the name given to the start-up kit provided by franchisors to see you successfully launched. This package should extend to support staff over the launch period and give you access to back-up advice. You will need to know how substantial the franchise company is. Ask to see its balance sheet (take it to your accountant if you cannot understand it). Ask for the track record of the directors (including their other directorships).

You can find out more about franchise opportunities and the rules and regulations in each country at the World Franchise Council website (**www.worldfranchisingcouncil.net**). On this site you will also find links to the various country franchise associations who can provide detailed information on the relevant local proceedings.

Network marketing

Companies such as Amway, Avon, Betterware, The Body Shop at Home, Herbal Life and Kleeneze are amongst a host of household names providing full- or part-time profitable business opportunities that can be run from home. The business model is varyingly called network marketing, multilevel marketing and referral marketing. They are differentiated from pyramid selling, which is focused almost entirely on recruiting new members rather than selling products and services. If a company offers substantial profits for little work, asks you to make an enormous investment in stock or doesn't offer to buy back unsold stock, which is in itself illegal in most countries, then avoid it like the plague. Pyramid selling is illegal in the UK. Check out the characteristics at www. dsa.org.uk/consumer-advice/illegal-schemes – and steer clear.

There are hundreds of sound businesses out there, so there is no need to be lured into a bad deal. Check if the firm you are considering is a member of the Direct Selling Association (**www.dsa.org.uk**), the Direct Marketing Association (**www.dma. org.uk**), or the Multi-Level Marketing International Association (**www.mlmia.com**).

The pros and cons of network marketing

Pros

- Start-up costs are low and indeed the law generally prohibits investments of over £200. This also means that you can usually store all the product you need in a car boot, garage or spare bedroom.

- The business model is proven, having been around for close on a century.

- There is plenty of support and advice on offer, making being home based less of a lonely proposition.

- The business is ideal to run from home as no specialist equipment or storage is needed.

- There is the potential to scale up, and as there are no territory or geographic restrictions you can sell anywhere in the world and use the internet for global reach.

Cons

- You may find some negative vibes, as people may associate your product or service with pyramid selling.

- You need to be comfortable selling to friends and associates and be a net worker par excellence.

- You are heavily dependent on the success of the parent organization. If that goes belly up so do you. Cabuchon grew spectacularly as a jewellery networking company aimed primarily at women and failed owing to quality problems and the management's inability to control a bigger business. You could even find that a change in philosophy, such as occurred when Dorling Kindersley Family Learning was closed by its new owners, Pearson, could pull the rug from under your feet.

Buying a business

Taking out a franchise or getting into a network marketing chain has a number of attractions over starting up from scratch, as we have already seen. Perhaps the most valuable advantage is that in an established business many of the unknowns of the business world are eliminated: who your first customers will be; how much they will pay; how you will find reliable suppliers; what equipment you will need; and how much your costs will be. All these issues and more have already been considered, and all you need bring is energy, enthusiasm and a modest amount of cash.

True, neither franchising nor network marketing is a one-way street; things can and do go wrong. But one weakness of both these routes to starting a business is that at no point will you ever truly *own* the business concerned. It will always be fundamentally the property of the franchisor or network firm concerned. You could view the situation much as if you were subletting a property at a profit. You rent from the landlord at one price and with the landlord's consent take in tenants who pay you more than you pay out. Nevertheless at the end of the day the capital asset belongs to the landlord, and the landlord, not you, enjoys any uplift in value.

One way to square this circle is to buy a business that is already up and running. In that way you can get into business taking fewer market risks and keep all the gains if and when they arise.

Advantages and disadvantages of buying a business

Buying a business has a number of advantages and disadvantages. Advantages of buying a business include:

- Much of the uncertainty of starting up has been eliminated, so you should have fewer costly mistakes.

- You inherit relationships with customers, suppliers and perhaps even financial institutions that would otherwise take years of hard work to build.

- You may be able to pay yourself a living wage from the outset.

- You eliminate one competitor. If there are already two car-cleaning businesses in the small area in which you live, both have been around for years and yet you have decided that this is the business for you, then buying one out may make economic sense. That way you could get 50 per cent of the market rather than the third you could aim for with three players in the game.

Disadvantages of buying a business include:

- Valuing a private business is difficult (see the next section).

- Finding a business and negotiating a purchase price can take time and may require several attempts before you succeed.

- You will need costly professional advice from lawyers and accountants as safeguards to ensure that you don't end up taking on hidden liabilities for tax owed, or responsibilities to past and present employees.

Valuing a business

When you buy a business you are in essence buying an established stream of profits. True, the business may have tangible assets such as stock, computing equipment or machinery. But the value of these hard items will be insufficient to compensate the previous owner for the accumulated time and effort that he or she has spent growing the business to its present state. The price/earnings ratio (P/E) is used estimate the value of a business. If a business has earnings (profits) of £50,000 and is in a sector where the usual P/E is 10, the value would be 10 × £50,000 = £500,000.

Arriving at a multiple is far from an exact science and the main guideline is what is being paid for shares on stock market. Vodafone for example has a current P/E of 39 while Marks and Spencer which operates in a more mature and established sector trades on a P/E of 9.

Private companies have a P/E about a third lower than similar public companies; that is, those on a stock market. This is a reflection of the fact that the shares are harder to buy and sell.

You can find P/Es in any paper that lists shares.

Finding a business to buy

These organizations can help you find a business to buy:

- BizBuySell (**www.bizbuysell.com**). This site lists 45,000 businesses for sale, covering the United States by state, and by country, including: Africa, Asia/Pacific; Australia/New Zealand; Canada; Caribbean; Mexico/Central America; Europe and South America.

- WorldBusinessforSale.com (**www.worldbusinessforsale.com**). This site claims to have listings of businesses for sale from 1237 countries, updated daily.

CASE STUDY Money Supermarket

On the 16 March 2016, Simon Nixon, who founded the price comparison site Moneysupermarket.com. sold the final tranche of some 6.9% of the company's shares for £124 million.

Founded in a bedroom by Simon Nixon and Duncan Cameron in 1999, Money Supermarket grew to have revenues in excess of £100 ($160/€118) million barely a decade later. Nixon was a drop-out from an accounting course at Nottingham University, leaving half way through the second year. He initially worked as a self-employed financial consultant and persuaded Cameron, a computer geek and his girlfriend's brother, to give up a computer studies course at Liverpool University to write the software programs that were crucial to the launch of the venture.

By the summer of 2007, on the eve of its stock market float, it was valued at around £1 billion, more than 30 times its previous year's profits. As the name would suggest, the business is an internet-based price comparator that started out in the financial services sector and now covers a myriad of other sectors including utilities, travel and general shopping. The value proposition is that Money Supermarket saves you hours surfing the net yourself. But despite some fairly complicated technology the business model is little more than the tried and tested role of the intermediary or broker doing the sums for their client that Nixon started out with when he started his first business, Mortgage 2000.

Key jobs to do

- Can you see any gaps in the market for your product or service?

- If you can see a gap, why do you think it hasn't been exploited yet?

- Research for any franchise, network marketing or business for sale available in the sectors you are considering.

- If any such opportunities are available, would one of these be a better proposition for you either from an investment, risk, skill or speed-to-market perspective?

Picking the right business for you

Your market research should put you at the point where you can define your business proposition in a few short sentences; in business jargon this is called a 'mission statement'. Large companies may spend long weekends at country mansions wrestling with the fine print of their mission statements; in principle the task facing the home-based business owner should be less daunting.

The mission statement has two key attributes. First, the mission should be narrow enough to give direction and guidance to everything you do or plan to do. This concentration is the key to business success because it is only by focusing on specific needs that a small business can differentiate itself from its larger competitors. Nothing kills off a new business faster than trying to do too many different things at the outset. Second, the mission should open up a large enough market to allow the business to grow and realize its potential.

Above all, mission statements must be realistic, achievable – and brief. McKinsey's mission reads: 'As management consultants, to help our clients make distinctive, lasting, and substantial improvements in their performance and to build a great firm that attracts, develops, excites and retains exceptional people'.

CASE STUDY

Blooming Marvellous is a company formed by two young mothers, who, while attending an enterprise programme, developed the following mission statement:

> Arising out of our experiences, we intend to design, make and market a range of clothes for mothers-to-be that will make them feel they can still be fashionably dressed. We aim to serve a niche missed out by Mothercare, Marks & Spencer, etc, and so become a significant force in the mail order fashion for the mothers-to-be market.
>
> We are aiming for a 5 per cent share of this market in the Southeast, and a 25 per cent return on assets employed within three years of starting up. We believe we will need about £25,000 start-up capital to finance stock, a mail order catalogue and an advertising campaign. Some two decades later Mothercare paid some £3m for the brand. www.mothercare.com/maternity

Armed with a mission you can now talk succinctly about your business to anyone and hopefully galvanize them with your enthusiasm and commitment and perhaps even win over some potential customers. Three tasks remain before you can commit to the venture. Two are the subject of this chapter and they both concern you, the business founder. The third is to do with the financial viability of your business, which will be covered when you prepare your business plan and make your financial projections.

Do you have what it takes?

To launch a new home-based business successfully, you have to be the right sort of person. The typical business founder is frequently seen as someone who is always bursting with new ideas, highly enthusiastic, hyperactive and insatiably curious. But the more you try to create a picture of the typical entrepreneur, the more elusive he or she becomes.

That said, there are certain characteristics that successful newcomers to running their own business do have in common:

- *Self-confident all-rounder.* Entrepreneurs are rarely geniuses. There are nearly always people in their business who have more competence, in one field, than they could ever aspire to. But they have a wide range of ability and a willingness to turn their hands to anything that has to be done to make the venture succeed. They can usually make the product, market it and count the money, but above all they have self-confidence that lets them move comfortably through uncharted waters.

- *Resilient.* Rising from the ashes of former disasters is also a common feature of many successful entrepreneurs. Henry Ford had been bankrupted twice before founding the Ford Motor Corporation with a loan of $28,000 in his fortieth year.

- *Innovative.* Almost by definition, entrepreneurs are innovators who either tackle the unknown or do old things in new ways. It is this inventive streak that allows them to carve out a new niche, often invisible to others.

- *Results orientated.* Successful people set themselves goals and get pleasure out of trying to achieve them. Once a goal has been reached, they have to get the next target in view as quickly as possible. This restlessness is very characteristic. Sir James Goldsmith was a classic example, moving the base of his business empire from the UK to France, then the United States – and finally into pure cash, ahead of a stock market crash.

- *Careful risk taker.* The high failure rate shows that small businesses are faced with many dangers. An essential characteristic of someone starting a business is a willingness to make decisions and to take risks. This does not mean gambling on hunches. It means carefully calculating the odds and deciding which risks to take and when to take them.

- *Total commitment.* You will need complete faith in your idea. How else will you convince all the doubters you are bound to meet that it is a worthwhile venture? You will also need single-mindedness, energy and a lot of hard work to get things started; working 18-hour days is not uncommon. This can put a strain on relationships, particularly within your family, so they too have to become involved and committed if you are to succeed.

CASE STUDY

At the age of 18, when his contemporaries were going off to university, Darren Saunders chose the route of the inventor. In pursuit of his 'mad idea' of the Cyberquin – a highly realistic, moving mannequin for display in shop windows and exhibitions – he spent six months in a fruitless search for development cash. 'I must have spoken to 150 people', he says. 'They all thought I was trying to achieve the impossible.' Finally, he clinched a government innovation grant; his father agreed to an overdraft with his bank to secure the remainder.

Saunders got help with the patents from a local patent agent, and took a short course in exporting at the Cardiff Chamber of Commerce. After three long years of development, he succeeded in creating a mannequin that would work 24 hours a day without a hitch, needed no maintenance, and could be easily shipped and effortlessly set up anywhere in the world. It took another 18 months of hard graft to get the product accepted, and it was all funded on a shoestring.

'Everyone advised me to stick to the UK', says Saunders, 'but, I thought, the British never try anything new.'

He was right to follow his instincts. His budding company concentrated on visiting big shop-fittings exhibitions, including Euroshop in Düsseldorf, the biggest of them all. Here, the sight of a dynamic, lifelike mannequin attracted the crowds. The orders – despite a £5,000 price tag – came flooding in.

The Cyberquin, now re-branded more descriptively as Moving Mannequins (www.movingmannequins.co.uk), has been exported to some fifty countries and used by companies as diverse as Harrods, Mitsubishi, Disney, Puma and Lego.

Remaining self-sufficient

Working from home means that you will have minimum contact with other people. If you have until now worked in a large organization and enjoyed the collegiate atmosphere that goes with it, then being alone may be something of a challenge – it will certainly be a change. Some people can only thrive when they have others to bounce ideas off, and all business owners complain that loneliness, the lack of someone to share problems with and the absence of external stimuli are serious worries. Of course if you plan to start a business as an events organizer or masseur, for example, then you will constantly be working with people and may well be more productive working for yourself than as part of a big business.

If you are happier curled up with a book than at a party then chances are that you have a strong streak of self-sufficiency and will be comfortable running your business from home. Look on the positive – no office gossip!

Retaining focus

You will be surrounded by distractions when based at home. Family pressures, noise and above all the people around you are not at work. That's quite different from going out to an office or to business premises where everyone, theoretically at least, is there for a common purpose – work.

So you will need to be able to focus on the task in hand, despite continuous distractions and without generating too much ill will. You will need an armoury of strategies to ensure you can ring-fence the critical time you have to devote exclusively to working on your business.

Scoring your home business ability

All too often, budding entrepreneurs believe themselves to be the right sort of people to set up a business. Unfortunately, the capacity for self-deception is enormous. When a random sample of male adults were asked recently to rank themselves on leadership ability, 70 per cent rated themselves in the top 25 per cent; only 2 per cent felt they were below average as leaders. In an area in which self-deception ought to be difficult, 60 per cent said they were well above average in athletic ability and only 6 per cent said they were below.

A common mistake made in assessing entrepreneurial talent is to assume that success in big business management will automatically guarantee success in a small business.

Rate yourself against the characteristics in Table 2.1 and see how you stack up as a potential home business starter. A score of over 30 suggests you have what it takes, and less than 20 should be treated as a warning signal. Get a couple of people who know you well to rate you too, so you get an unbiased opinion.

You can find out more about your likely strengths and weaknesses as an entrepreneur by taking one or more of the many online entrepreneurial IQ-type tests. A couple of sources are listed below, but an entry in Google will produce a small torrent!

Table 2.1 Home business starter attribute check

	Attribute score (0–5, where 0 indicates having none of the attribute and 5 rating highly)
Self-confident all-rounder	
Ability to bounce back	
Innovative skills	
Results orientated	
Professional risk taker	
Total commitment	
Self-sufficient	
Self-disciplined	
Total	

- Psychometric Tests: A collaborative open resource run by Warwick, Durham and Southampton Universities (www.psychometrictest. org.uk/entrepreneur-test)

- Entrepreneurial Aptitude Test (EAT): A tool drawing on hundreds of surveys and interviews with business-builders around the globe (www.hsgl.com).

Is the business right for you?

If you started reading this book with a business idea in mind, the first couple of chapters should have helped you get a clearer idea of how your concepts can be brought to fruition. If you are still casting around for an idea, then you will find a directory of home business opportunities in Appendix 2. In any event you should have at least a couple of prospective ventures in mind, as the process of comparison helps to reveal the strengths and weaknesses of a proposition that might otherwise lie dormant.

Deciding what you want

The first step in the process is to decide exactly what you are looking for in a business proposition. This is not too much different from looking for a new home. You rarely start with a completely blank sheet of paper. Rather you start with a budget of how much you are able or prepared to spend, a geographic area or radius around a town, the number of bedrooms required, proximity to public transport, local shopping and garage/parking arrangements. To these essentials you will then add some desirable features such as garden space, a patio and a conservatory. You need to do something similar with your business idea. Table 2.2 shows how you can do this for your ideas. First, decide what the important criteria for you are. In the example in Table 2.2, six are listed. Then give each of those criteria a weighting from 1 to 3 to reflect their relative importance. In the example, 'Low investment', 'Flexible hours' and 'Small space needed' are all very important and so are given the top rating

Table 2.2   Rating your business idea

Criteria	Weighting	Idea 1		Idea 2	
		Score	Weighted score	Score	Weighted score
Low investment	3	3	9	1	3
Flexible hours	3	2	6	2	6
Small space needed	3	3	9	1	3
Use all my skills	2	3	6	2	4
Need no new skills	2	3	6	1	2
No travel required	1	1	1	3	3
Total weighted score			37		21

of 3. The next two criteria, 'Use all my skills' and 'Need no new skills', being less important are given a weighting of 2. Finally, 'No travel required' being relatively unimportant is weighted only 1.

Ranking your options

Now each business idea can be assigned a score between 0 and 3. If the idea meets the criterion perfectly, score it 3, and if it fails completely score it 0. In the example in Table 2.2 you can see that Idea 1 scores 3 for 'Low investment' as it needs little cash, whilst Idea 2, which needs more upfront money, scores only 1. Next the scores are multiplied by the weighting factor to produce a weighted score. As 'Low investment' is an important criterion it is given a higher weighting than 'No travel required'. You can see that, although Idea 1 scores 3 for 'Low investment' and Idea 2 scores 3 for 'No travel required', the weighted scores are 9 and 3 respectively to allow for the difference in their importance.

The weighted scores for each idea are totalled and show in this example that Idea 1, with a score of 37, is well ahead of Idea 2, scoring just 21.

You will of course have different criteria with different levels of importance, but the basic method will work even with many more criteria and a weighting system that gives a wider spread than just 0 to 3. Having said that, adding to the number of criteria greatly may only confuse matters. As with buying a house, in the end it all comes down to a handful of critical factors.

Key jobs to do

- Take the home business start-up attribute check and see if this seems a good career choice for you.

- Cross-check that outcome by taking at least one other similar test.

- Weigh up the alternative business ideas you are considering and rank them using the weighting scheme in Table 2.2. Make any modifications to the criteria you consider relevant to you and your needs.

Researching the market

You need information on customers, competitors and any other influencers in the chain that links buyers to sellers. For example, if you are selling to another business it could be useful to know something of who their end customers are, as your future is going to be influenced by how they perform as well as by your initial customer. You may also find that not all your customers respond to the same marketing messages. For example, one client for a book-keeping service may just need someone to do the grunt and groan of data entry, whilst another may want the data analysed and interpreted. The purpose of gathering the market research data is to help you decide on the right marketing strategy when it comes to such factors as setting your price, deciding on service and quality levels and choosing where and how much to advertise.

Obviously the amount of time and money to be spent depends on the capital outlay required. If you need £1,000 to get into business, spending more than that on gathering information looks like overkill.

Understanding customers

Without customers no business can get off the ground, let alone survive. Some people believe that customers arrive after a business 'opens its doors'. This is a serious and often fatal misconception. You need a clear idea in advance of who your customers will be, as they are a vital ingredient in a successful business strategy, not simply the passive recipients of a new product or service.

Knowing something about your customers, what they need, how much they can 'consume' and whom they buy from now, seems such elementary information it is hard to believe so many people could start without those insights – and yet they do.

There is an old business maxim that says that the customer is always right. But that does not mean that the customer is necessarily right for you. So as well as knowing whom to sell to you also need to know the sorts of people that trying to interest will be a waste of scarce resources on your part.

Recognizing needs

The founder of a successful cosmetics firm, when asked what he did, replied: 'In the factories we make perfume. In the shops we sell dreams.'

Those of us in business usually start out defining our business in physical terms. Customers on the other hand see businesses having as their primary value the ability to satisfy their needs. Even firms that adopt customer satisfaction, or even delight, as their stated maxim often find it a more complex goal than it at first appears. Take Blooming Marvellous, the case study given in the Introduction, by way of an example. They made clothes for the mother-to-be, sure enough: but the primary customer need they were aiming to satisfy was not either to preserve their modesty or to keep them warm. The need they were aiming for was much higher: they were ensuring their customers would feel fashionably dressed, which is about the way people interact with each other and how they feel about themselves. Just splashing on say a tog rating showing the thermal properties of the fabric, as you would with say a duvet, would cut no ice with Blooming Marvellous's potential market.

Until you have clearly defined the needs of your market you cannot begin to assemble a product or service to satisfy it. Fortunately, help is at hand. The US psychologist Abraham Maslow demonstrated in his research that 'all customers are goal seekers who gratify their needs by purchase and consumption'. He then went a bit further and classified consumer needs into a five-stage pyramid he called the hierarchy of needs:

1 *Self-actualization.* This is the summit of Maslow's hierarchy, in which people are looking for truth, wisdom, justice and purpose. It's a need that is never fully satisfied and, according to Maslow, only a very small percentage of people ever reach the point where they are prepared to pay much money to satisfy such needs. It is left to the like of Bill Gates and Sir Tom Hunter to give away billions to form foundations to dispose of their wealth on worthy causes. The rest of us scrabble around further down the hierarchy.

2 *Esteem.* Here people are concerned with such matters as self-respect, achievement, attention, recognition and reputation. The benefits customers are looking for include the feeling that others will think better of them if they have a particular product. Much of brand marketing is aimed at making consumers believe that, by conspicuously wearing the maker's label or logo so that it can be seen by others, it will earn them 'respect'. Understanding how this part of Maslow's hierarchy works was vital to the founders of Responsibletravel.com (**www.responsibletravel.com**). Founded six years ago with backing from Anita Roddick (of Body Shop) by Justin Francis and Harold Goodwin in Francis's front room in Brighton, the company set out to be the world's first to offer environmentally responsible travel and holidays. They were one of the

first companies to offer carbon offset schemes for travellers, and they boast that they turn away more tour companies trying to list on their site than they accept. They appeal to consumers who want to be recognized in their communities as being socially responsible.

3 *Social needs.* The need for friends, belonging to associations, clubs or other groups and the need to give and get love are all social needs. After 'lower' needs have been met these needs that relate to interacting with other people come to the fore. Hotel Chocolat (www.hotelchocolat.co.uk), founded by Angus Thirlwell and Peter Harris in their kitchen, is a good example of a business based on meeting social needs. They market home-delivered luxury chocolates but generate sales by having tasting clubs to check out products each month. The concept of the club is that you invite friends round and use the firm's scoring system to rate and give feedback on the chocolates.

4 *Safety.* The second most basic need of consumers is to feel safe and secure. People who feel they are in harm's way either through their general environment or because of the product or service on offer will not be over-interested in having their higher needs met. When Charles Rigby set up World Challenge (**www. world-challenge.co.uk**) to market challenging expeditions to exotic locations around the world with the aim of taking young people up to around 19 out of their comfort zones and teaching them how to overcome adversity, he knew he had a challenge of his own on his hands: how to make an activity simultaneously exciting and apparently dangerous to teenagers, whilst being safe enough for the parents writing the cheques to feel comfortable. Six full sections on their website are devoted to explaining the safety measures the company takes to ensure that unacceptable risks are eliminated as far as is humanly possible.

5 *Physiological needs.* Air, water, sleep and food are all absolutely essential to sustain life. Until these basic needs are satisfied, higher needs such as self-esteem will not be considered.

You can read more about Maslow's hierarchy of needs and how to take it into account in understanding customers on the Net MBA website (**www.netmba.com** > Management > Maslow's Hierarchy of Needs).

Table 3.1 Example showing product features, benefits and proofs

Features	Benefits	Proofs
Our maternity clothes are designed by fashion experts.	You get to look and feel great.	See the press comments in fashion magazines.
Our bookkeeping system is approved by HM Revenue & Customs.	You can sleep at night.	Our system is rated No. 1 by the Evaluation Centre (**www. evaluationcentre.com**, Accounting software).

Features, benefits and proofs

Whilst understanding customer needs is vital, it is not sufficient on its own to help put together a saleable proposition. Before you can do that you have to understand the *benefits* customers will get when they purchase. *Features* are what a product or service has or is, and benefits are what the product does for the customer. When Nigel Apperley founded his business Internet Cameras Direct, now Internet Direct (**www.internetcamerasdirect.co.uk**), whilst a student at business school he knew there was no point in telling customers about SLRs or shutter speeds. These are not the end product that customers want; they are looking for the convenience and economy of buying direct and good pictures. He planned to follow the Dell direct sales model. Within three years Apperley had annual turnover in excess of £20 million and had moved a long way from his home-based beginnings.

Table 3.1 shows examples of product features and benefits, and has been extended to include proofs showing how the benefits will be delivered. The essential element to remember here is that the customer only wants to pay for benefits, whilst the seller has to pick up the tab for all the features whether the customer sees them as valuable or not. Benefits will provide the 'copy' for a business's advertising and promotional activities.

Who will buy first?

Customers do not sit and wait for a new business to open its doors. Word spreads slowly as the message is diffused throughout the various customer groups. Even then it is noticeable that generally it is the more adventurous types who first buy from a new business. Only after these people have given their seal of approval do the 'followers' come along. Research shows that this adoption process, the product/service adoption cycle as it is known, moves through five distinct customer characteristics, from innovators to laggards, with the overall population being different for each group:

Innovators	2.5 per cent of the overall market
Early adopters	13.5 per cent of the overall market
Early majority	34.0 per cent of the overall market
Late majority	34.0 per cent of the overall market
Laggards	16.0 per cent of the overall market
Total market	100 per cent

Let's suppose you have identified the market for your internet gift service. Initially your market has been confined to affluent professionals within five miles of your home to keep delivery costs low. So if market research shows that there are 100,000 people who meet the profile of your ideal customer and they have regular access to the internet, the market open for exploitation at the outset may be as low as 2,500, which is the 2.5 per cent of innovators.

This adoption process, from the 2.5 per cent of innovators who make up a new business's first customers, through to the laggards who won't buy from anyone until they have been in business for 20 years, is most noticeable with truly innovative and relatively costly goods and services, but the general trend is true for all businesses. Until you have sold to the innovators, significant sales cannot be achieved. So, an important first task is to identify these customers. The moral is: the more you know about your potential customers at the outset, the better your chances of success.

One further issue to keep in mind when shaping your marketing strategy is that innovators, early adopters and all the other sub-segments don't necessarily use the same media, websites, magazines and newspapers or respond to the same images and messages. So they need to be marketed to in very different ways.

Segmenting markets

Having established that customers have different needs, we need to organize our marketing effort so as to address those individually. However, trying to satisfy everyone may mean that we end up satisfying no one fully. The marketing process that helps us deal with this seemingly impossible task is market segmentation. This is the name given to the process whereby customers and potential customers are organized into clusters or groups of 'similar' types.

For example, a carpet/upholstery cleaning business has private individuals and business clients running restaurants and guest houses. These two segments are fundamentally different, with one segment being more focused on cost and the other more concerned that the work is carried out with the least disruption to their business. Also, each of these customer groups is motivated to buy for different reasons, and your selling message has to be modified accordingly.

Worthwhile criteria

Useful rules to help decide if a market segment is worth trying to sell into include:

- *Measurability.* Can you estimate how many customers are in the segment? Are there enough to make it worth offering something 'different'?

- *Accessibility.* Can you communicate with these customers, preferably in a way that reaches them on an individual basis? For example, you could reach the over-50s by advertising in a specialist 'older people's' magazine with reasonable confidence that young people will not read it. So if you were trying to promote Scrabble with tiles 50 per cent larger, you might prefer that young people did not hear about it. If they did, it might give the product an old-fashioned image.

- *Open to profitable development.* The customers must have money to spend on the benefits that you propose to offer.

- *Size*. A segment has to be large enough for it to be worth your while exploiting it, but perhaps not so large as to attract larger competitors.

- *Endurance*. Does the segment look like having a reasonably long life?

One example of a market segment that has not been open to development for hundreds of years is the sale of goods and services to retired people. Several factors made this a particularly unappealing segment. First, retired people were perceived as 'old' and less adventurous; second, they had a short life expectancy; and finally, the knockout blow was that they had no money. In the last decade or so that has all changed: people retire early and live longer and many have relatively large pensions. The result is that travel firms, housebuilders, magazine publishers and insurance companies have rushed out a stream of products and services aimed particularly at this market segment.

Segmentation is an important marketing process, as it helps to bring customers more sharply into focus, classifies them into manageable groups and allows you to focus on one or more niches. It has wide-ranging implications for other marketing decisions. For example, the same product can be priced differently according to the intensity of customers' needs. The first- and second-class post is one example, and off-peak rail travel another.

It is also a continuous process that needs to be carried out periodically, for example when strategies are being reviewed.

Analysing competitors

Researching the competition is often a time-consuming and frustrating job, but there are important lessons to be learnt from it. Some of the information that would be of most value to you will not be available. Particularly hard to find is information relating to the size and profitability of your competitors. Businesses, and particularly smaller businesses, are very secretive about their finances. Because of this, you may have to make estimates of the size and profitability of various firms.

The presence of competitors is not all bad news; in the first place it gives you the comfort of knowing that there is a base of customers out there who want what you plan to offer. If there are already dozens of businesses selling your product or service then you will have to have a better or different offering to woo them away from their existing supplier. The difference doesn't always have to be big, but it does have to be important to the customer. For example, a one-person gardening service stole a march on competitors by taking away all garden refuse rather than leaving it for the customer to remove. This meant having a slightly larger van than competitors, but it was sufficiently compelling as an advantage to win enough business to allow more staff to be recruited.

The task for research is to understand who your competitors, both direct and indirect, are, as well as their strengths and weaknesses. Direct competitors are those already actively operating in a market. So for the gardening business, other similar firms are its direct competitors. Indirect competitors would be businesses hiring out lawnmowers, hedge cutters and the like, to allow homeowners to do their own gardening.

Naming names

If your market is very confined then a Google search of the area concerned with a basic business description may have all the information you need to list out your competitors. If you have to look further to cover a wider geography, including overseas, there are numerous directories that list businesses by trade, area and size.

Aside from the names and basic contact details you will need to find out some facts about your competitors: what they do, how they are organized, what their turnover, profit and financial structure are and whether or not they are privately owned or part of a larger group of businesses. You need this information to see both how to compete and whether or not the business area looks profitable.

The sources that will provide much of the background data on the businesses that operate in your market and other relevant market data are included in Appendix 3.

Understanding strengths and weaknesses

The easiest way to find out what your competitors are doing right or wrong is to try them out. Even if you don't actually buy or even need what they sell there is nothing in the rules that says you can't enquire. Suppose, for example, you intend to set up a bookkeeping service. First search out local small businesses, using if necessary one of the sources described above. Then 'enquire' about their services with a list of questions, some of which you may find answers to in their leaflet or on their website.

The probing questions either to ask or to find out by research should include the following:

- What exactly is the range of services they offer? For example, do they just prepare the accounts? Do they help with tax returns? Do they offer advice on what the figures reveal about their client's business? Do they handle tax enquiries? Do they advise on sources of finance?

- What are their prices and when do they require to be paid?

- How long have they been in business?

- How many clients do they have? You may find some background information on their website, where businesses often list satisfied clients. Also, you can make an estimate by finding their turnover from their own accounts (see Appendix 3) and dividing that by the price they charge. So, if their last year's turnover was £400,000 and they charge £4,000 a year to do the books for one business, they have around 100 clients.

- How profitable are they? This once again is information that can be obtained from organizations listed in Appendix 3.

- How many people do they employ? You can estimate this by visiting their offices.

- Do they have other branches?

- Where do they advertise? This might give you some pointers when planning your own promotion strategy.

Deciding on advantage

The outcome of your research into customers and competitors is a clear idea of the market niche you are going to sell into first and what will be different or better about your product or service. For a business planning to offer a local gardening service the outcome of their research should allow them to make the following analysis:

We have two local competitors:

- Thompson's, with six employees, have been around for 10 years and have a small number of larger domestic clients but mostly do work for schools and business premises. They charge £20 an hour, for a minimum of four hours a week, and don't take away garden refuse from homes. They cover the whole county.

- Brown is a one-man band who has been operating for three years, but he offers a limited service – he doesn't do hedge trimming or tree pruning or take away garden refuse. He charges out at £12 an hour, with no minimum. He claims to cover a radius of 20 miles, but doesn't seem to want to go more than 5.

My initial strategy will be to concentrate on larger domestic clients within 5 miles who need hedges trimmed and trees pruned and would appreciate having their garden refuse removed for them. I will set out to make these clients feel important in a way that Thompson's does not, as they appear to only take on domestic customers as a 'favour'. I will charge out at £15 an hour, with a minimum of two hours a week per client, and will target a limited number of quality areas with high-value houses. My goal will be to get at least two clients in an area and stick to areas that are easily accessible from my home.

Carrying out DIY research

The purpose of do-it-yourself (DIY) market research is to ensure you have sufficient information on customers, competitors and markets so that your market entry strategy is at least on the target, if not the bull's-eye itself. In other words, enough people want to buy what you want to sell at a price that will give you a viable business. If you miss the target completely, you may not have the resources for a second shot.

You do not have to start a business to prove there are *no* customers for your goods or services; frequently some modest DIY market research beforehand can give clear guidance as to whether your venture will succeed or not.

The purpose of practical DIY market research for entrepreneurs investigating or seeking to start a new business is, therefore, twofold. First, it is to build *credibility* for the business idea. The entrepreneur must demonstrate to his or her own satisfaction, and later to outside financiers, a thorough understanding of the marketplace for the new product or service. This will be vital if resources are to be attracted to build the new venture. Second, it is to develop a *realistic* market entry strategy for the new business, based on a clear understanding of genuine customer needs and ensuring that product quality, price, promotional methods and the distribution chain are mutually supportive and clearly focused on target customers.

Otherwise, 'Fools rush in where angels fear to tread'; or, as they say in the army, 'Time spent in reconnaissance is rarely time wasted.' The same is certainly true in starting a business, where you will need to research in particular:

- Your customers – who will buy your goods and services? What particular customer needs will your business meet? How many of them are there?

- Your competitors – which established companies are already meeting the needs of your potential customers? What are their strengths and weaknesses?

- Your product or service – how should it be tailored to meet customer needs?

- What price should you charge to be perceived as giving value for money?

- What promotional material is needed to reach customers? Which newspapers and journals do they read?

- Is your home satisfactorily located to reach your customers most easily, at minimum cost?

Seven steps to successful market research

Researching the market need not be a complex process, nor need it be very expensive. The amount of effort and expenditure needs to be related in some way to the costs and risks associated with the business. If all that is involved with your business is getting a handful of customers for products and services that cost little to put together, then you may spend less effort on market research than you would for, say, launching a completely new product or service into an unproven market that requires a large sum of money to be spent up front.

However much or little market research you plan to carry out, the process needs to be conducted systematically. These are the seven stages you need to go through to make sure you have properly sized up your business sector:

1 *Formulate the problem.* Before embarking on your market research you should first set clear and precise objectives, rather than just set out to find interesting general information about the market. So, for example, if you are planning on selling to young fashion-conscious women, among others, your research objective could be: to find out how many women aged 18 to 28, with an income of over £35,000 a year, live or work within your catchment area. That would give you some idea whether the market could support a venture such as this.

2 *Determine the information needs.* Knowing the size of the market, in the example given above, may require several different pieces of information. For example, you would need to know the size of the resident population, which might be fairly easy to find out, but you might also want to know something about

people who come into the catchment area to work or stay on holiday or for any other major purpose. There might, for example, be a hospital, library, railway station or school nearby that also pulled potential customers to that particular area.

3 *Establish where you can get the information.* This will involve either desk research in libraries or on the internet, or field research, which you can do yourself or get help in doing. Some of the most important of these areas were covered earlier in this chapter. Field research, that is getting out and asking questions yourself, is the most fruitful way of gathering information for a home-based business.

4 *Decide the budget.* Market research will not be free even if you do it yourself. At the very least there will be your time. There may well be the cost of journals, phone calls, letters and field visits to plan for. At the top of the scale could be the costs of employing a professional market research firm. Starting at this end of the scale, a business-to-business survey comprising 200 interviews with executives responsible for office equipment purchasing decisions cost one company £12,000. Twenty in-depth interviews with consumers who are regular users of certain banking services cost £8,000. Using the internet for web surveys is another possibility, but that can impose too much of your agenda on to the recipients and turn them away from you. Check out companies such as Free Online Surveys (**http://free-online-surveys.co.uk**) and Survey Monkey (**www.surveymonkey.co.uk**) that provide software that lets you carry out online surveys and analyse the data quickly. Most of these organizations offer free trials, and Survey Monkey, for example, lets you ask up to 10 questions, collect 100 responses and analyse the data. After that, unlimited surveys using their Gold plan cost around £300 a year. Doing the research yourself may save costs but may limit the objectivity of the research. If time is your scarcest commodity, it may make more sense to get an outside agency to do the work. Using a reference librarian or university student to do some of the spadework need not be prohibitively expensive. Another argument for getting professional research is that it may carry more clout with investors. Whatever the cost of research, you need to assess

its value to you when you are setting your budget. If getting it wrong would cost £100,000 £5,000 spent on market research might be a good investment.

5 *Select the research technique.* If you cannot find the data you require from desk research, you will need to go out and find the data yourself. The options for such research are described on pages 51–52, under 'Field research'.

6 *Construct the research sample population.* It is rarely possible or even desirable to include every possible customer or competitor in your research, so you have to decide how big a sample you need to give you a reliable indication of how the whole population will behave.

7 *Process and analyse the data.* The raw market research data need to be analysed and turned into information to guide your decisions on price, promotion and location, and the shape, design and scope of the product or service itself.

Desk research

There is increasingly a great deal of secondary data available in published form and accessible either online or via business sections of public libraries to enable new home business starters both to quantify the size of market sectors they are entering and to determine trends in those markets. In addition to information on populations of cities and towns (helping to start quantification of markets), libraries frequently purchase Mintel reports, involving studies of growth in different business sectors. Government statistics, showing trends in the economy, are also held (Annual Abstracts for the economy as a whole and Business Monitors for individual sectors).

If you plan to sell to companies or shops, Kompass (**www.kompass.co.uk**) lists all company names and addresses (including buyers' telephone numbers). Many industrial sectors are represented by trade associations, which can provide information (see Trade Association Forums – **www.taforum.org/members**), while chambers of commerce are good sources of reference for import/export markets. See Appendix 3 for more on sources of information.

Using the internet

The internet can be a powerful research tool. However, it has some particular strengths and weaknesses that you need to keep in mind when using it.

Strengths of the internet include:

- Access is cheap and information is often free.
- It helps you gather good background information.
- You can access information quickly.
- It covers a wide geographic scope.

Weaknesses of the internet include:

- The bias is strongly towards the USA.
- Coverage of any given subject may be patchy.
- Authority and credentials are often lacking.

It would be a brave or foolhardy entrepreneur who started up in business or set out to launch new products or services without at least spending a day or two surfing the internet. At the very least, this surfing tells you whether anyone else has taken your business idea to market. At best, it may save you lots of legwork around libraries, if the information you want is available online.

You can gather market research information on the internet in two main ways:

- Use directories, search engines or telephone directories to research your market or product.
- Use blogs, bulletin or message boards, newsgroups and chat rooms to elicit the data you require.

See Appendix 3 for home business information resources.

Field research

Most fieldwork carried out consists of interviews, with the interviewer putting questions to a respondent. We are all becoming accustomed to it, whether being interviewed while travelling on a train or resisting the attempts of enthusiastic salespeople posing as market researchers on doorsteps ('sugging', as this is known, has been illegal since 1986). The more popular forms of interview are currently:

- personal (face-to-face) interviews: 45 per cent (especially for the consumer markets);
- telephone, e-mail and web surveys: 42 per cent (especially for surveying companies);
- post: 6 per cent (especially for industrial markets);
- test and discussion groups: 7 per cent.

Personal interviews, web surveys and postal surveys are clearly less expensive than getting together panels of interested parties or using expensive telephone time. Telephone interviewing requires a very positive attitude, courtesy, an ability not to talk too quickly and listening while sticking to a rigid questionnaire. Low response rates on postal services (less than 10 per cent is normal) can be improved by accompanying letters explaining the questionnaire's purpose and why respondents should reply, by offering rewards for completed questionnaires (small gifts), by sending reminder letters and, of course, by providing pre-paid reply envelopes. Personally addressed e-mail questionnaires have secured higher response rates – as high as 10–15 per cent – as recipients have a greater tendency to read and respond to e-mail received in their private e-mail boxes. However, unsolicited e-mails ('spam') can cause vehement reactions: the key to success is the same as with postal surveys – the mailing should feature an explanatory letter and incentives for the recipient to 'open' the questionnaire.

These are the basic rules for good questionnaire design, however the questions are to be administered:

- Keep the number of questions to a minimum.
- Keep the questions simple! Answers should be 'Yes/No/Don't know' or offer at least four options.
- Avoid ambiguity – make sure the respondent really understands the question (avoid 'generally', 'usually' and 'regularly').
- Seek factual answers; avoid opinions.

Table 3.2 How accuracy increases with the size of the sample

Size of random sample	No. of percentage points within which 95% of surveys are right
250	6.2
500	4.4
750	3.6
1,000	3.1
2,000	2.2
6,000	1.2

- Make sure at the beginning you have a cut-out question to eliminate unsuitable respondents (eg those who never use the product/ service).

- At the end, make sure you have an identifying question to show the cross-section of respondents.

The size of the survey undertaken is also important. You frequently hear of political opinion polls taken on samples of 1,500–2,000 voters. This is because the accuracy of your survey clearly increases with the size of sample, as Table 3.2 shows.

So if, on a sample size of 600, your survey showed that 40 per cent of women in the town drove cars, the true proportion would probably lie between 36 and 44 per cent. For small businesses, we usually recommend a minimum sample of 250 completed replies.

Creative Research Systems (**www.surveysystem.com**) has an easy-to-use sample size calculator. This company also provides an introduction with many useful dos and don'ts on survey design as well as on a statistical technique known as correlation that can tell you if two variables are related.

Testing the market

The ultimate form of market research is to find some real customers to buy and use your product or service before you spend too much time and money in setting up. The ideal way to do this is to sell into a limited area or small section of your market. In that way if things don't quite work out as you expect you won't have upset too many people.

This may involve buying in a small quantity of product, as you need to fulfil the order in order to test your ideas fully. Once you have found a small number of people who are happy with your product, price, and delivery or execution and have paid up then you can proceed with a bit more confidence than if all your ideas are just on paper.

Pick potential customers whose demand is likely to be small and easy to meet. For example, if you are going to run a bookkeeping business select 5 to 10 small businesses from an area reasonably close to home and make your pitch. The same approach would work with a gardening, babysitting or any other service-related venture. It's a little more difficult with products, but you could buy a small quantity of similar items in from a competitor or make up a trial batch yourself.

Key jobs to do

- Carry out a features, benefits and proofs review of your main products and services.

- Review your present method of segmenting the market or introduce segmentation if you don't now do so.

- Assess your key competitors and your relative strengths and weaknesses.

- Appraise your current market intelligence and identify any important gaps in your knowledge about customers and competitors.

- Determine and implement an appropriate market research study to fill in any gaps in your knowledge.

- Design a short questionnaire to find out more about what customers really expect of the product or service you plan to offer.

04

Business ownership and title issues

THIS CHAPTER COVERS

- choosing an ownership structure;
- deciding on a business name;
- protecting domains;
- registering intellectual property title;
- licensing of rights.

Even before you start selling your wares there are a number of important decisions to make. You have a range of ownership options that could be worth exploring even if you are going to own the business outright with no one else involved.

You may also have valuable assets such as inventions or designs that you are bringing into the business or other valuable pieces of business property such as a domain or business name that you wish to register or protect once your business gets started.

Deciding on ownership

Before you start trading you will need to consider what legal form your business will take. There are a number of legal forms that a business can take and they are never universal around the world.

The one you choose will depend on a number of factors: commercial needs, financial risk and your tax position.

Each of these forms is explained briefly below, together with the procedure to follow on setting it up. Advice and information on business ownership and title issues is available from the organizations listed in Appendix 3. You can change your ownership status later as your circumstances change, so whilst this is an important decision it is not a final one.

Sole trader

As a sole trader (personaline imone in Lithuania and empresário em nome individual in Portugal) there is no legal distinction between you and your business – your business is one of your assets, just as your house or car is. It follows from this that if your business should fail, your creditors have a right not only to the assets of the business, but also to your personal assets, subject only to the provisions of the local bankruptcy laws. Over 80 per cent of businesses start up as sole traders and indeed around 55 per cent of all businesses employing less than fifty people still use this legal structure. It has the merit of being relatively formality free.

The capital to get the business going must come from you – or from loans. There is no access to equity capital, which has the attraction of being risk-free. In return for these drawbacks you can have the pleasure of being your own boss immediately, subject only to declaring your profits on your tax return.

Partnership

Partnerships (Offene Gesellschaft (OG) in Austria and verejná obchodná spoloènost' in Slovakia) are effectively collections of sole traders and, as such, share the legal problems attached to personal liability. There are very few restrictions to setting up in business with another person (or persons) in partnership, and several definite advantages. By pooling resources you may have more capital; you will be bringing, hopefully, several sets of skills to the business; and if you are ill the business can still carry on.

There are two serious drawbacks that you should certainly consider. First, if your partner makes a business mistake, perhaps by signing a disastrous contract, without your knowledge or consent, every member of the partnership must shoulder the consequences. Under these circumstances your personal assets could be taken to pay the creditors even though the mistake was no fault of your own. Second, if your partner goes bankrupt in his or her personal capacity, for whatever reason, his or her share of the partnership can be seized by creditors. As a private individual you are not liable for your partner's private debts, but having to buy him or her out of the partnership at short notice could put you and the business in financial jeopardy. Even death may not release you from partnership obligations and in some circumstances your estate can remain liable. Unless you take 'public' leave of your partnership by notifying your business contacts and legally bringing your partnership to an end, you could remain liable. Partnerships generally require that:

- All partners contribute capital equally.
- All partners share profits and losses equally.
- No partner shall have interest paid on his capital.
- No partner shall be paid a salary.
- All partners have an equal say in the management of the business.

It is unlikely that all these provisions will suit you, so you would be well advised to get a 'partnership agreement' drawn up in writing by a lawyer at the outset of your venture.

Limited liability partnership (LLP)

Your LLP has to be registered at Companies House and you must tell them about any changes to the registered name or address or members or any other important facts about the venture.

One possibility that can reduce the more painful consequences of entering a partnership is to form a limited partnership (Kommanditgesellschaft – KG in Austria and komanditná spoloènost' in Slovakia) combining the best attributes of a partnership and a company. There must be one or more general partners with the same basic rights and responsibilities (including unlimited liability) as in any general partnership, and one or more limited partners who are usually passive investors and are only committed to the amount of their investment.

Limited company

A limited company (Sabiedriba ar ierobežotu atbildibu in Latvia and Socitatea cu Raspundere Limitata in Romania) has a legal identity of its own, separate from the people who own or run it. This means that, in the event of failure, creditors' claims are restricted to the assets of the company. The shareholders of the business are not liable as individuals for the business debts beyond the paid-up value of their shares. This applies even if the shareholders are working directors, unless of course the company has been trading fraudulently. Other advantages include the freedom to raise capital by selling shares.

Disadvantages include the cost involved in setting up the company and the legal requirement in some cases for the company's accounts to be audited by a chartered or certified accountant. Usually it is only businesses with assets approaching £3 million that have to be audited but if, for example, you have shareholders who own more than 10 per cent of your firm they can ask for the accounts to be audited.

A limited company can be formed by two shareholders, one of whom must be a director. A company secretary must also be appointed, who can be a shareholder, director, or an outside person such as an accountant or lawyer.

The company can be bought 'off the shelf' from a registration agent, then adapted to suit your own purposes. This will involve changing the name, shareholders and articles of association, and will cost about £250 ($361/€288) and take a couple of weeks to arrange. Alternatively, you can form your own company, using your lawyer or accountant. This will usually double the cost and take six to eight weeks.

Cooperative

A cooperative is an enterprise owned and controlled by the people working in it. Once in danger of becoming extinct, the workers' cooperative is enjoying something of a comeback. There are functioning cooperatives in some 90 countries employing over 800 million people worldwide. The International Co-operative Alliance (**http://ica.coop**) represents agriculture, banking, fisheries, health, housing, industry, insurance, tourism and consumer cooperatives and is the largest non-governmental organization in the world.

Naming your venture

Your business name is almost always the first way people get to hear about your venture, and it should convey quickly and clearly what you do. Once you have to start explaining what you do the job of communicating gets harder. As you are going to have to put some effort into creating this name and that of your web presence (domain name) if you plan to have one, it makes good sense to take some steps to protect your investment.

Business names

Your company name can, in effect, be the starting and sustaining point in differentiating you from your competitors and, as such, should be carefully chosen, be protected by trademarks where possible and be written in a distinctive way. It follows therefore that the main consideration in choosing a business name is its commercial usefulness.

When you choose a business name, you are also choosing an identity, so it should reflect:

- who you are;
- what you do;
- how you do it.

Given all the marketing investment you will make in your company name, you should check with a trademark agent whether you can protect your chosen name (you are not normally allowed to do so for descriptive words, surnames and place names except after long use).

Second, all businesses that intend to trade under names other than those of their owner(s) must state who does own the business and how the owner can be contacted. So, if you are a sole trader or partnership and you only use surnames with or without forenames or initials, you are not affected. Companies are also not affected if they simply use their full corporate name.

Generally, if any name other than the 'true' name is to be used, then you must disclose the name of the owner(s) and an address to which business documents can be sent. This information has to be shown on all business letters, orders for goods and services, invoices and receipts, and statements and demands for business debts. Also, a copy has to be displayed prominently on all business premises. If you are setting up as a limited company you will have to submit your choice of name to the relevant Companies Registration Office along with the other documents required for registration. It will be accepted unless there is another company with that name on the register or the Registrar considers the name to be obscene, offensive or illegal.

Changing your name

It's not the end of the world if you decide after a year or so that your business name is not quite right, but you will have largely wasted any earlier marketing effort in building up awareness.

A good name, in effect, can become a one- or two-word summary of your marketing strategy; Body Shop, Toys R Us and Kwik-Fit Exhausts are good examples. Many companies add a slogan to explain to customers and employees alike 'how they do it'.

Cobra Beer's slogan 'Unusual thing, excellence' focuses attention on quality and distinctiveness. The name, slogan and logo combine to be the most visible tip of the iceberg in your corporate communications effort.

Spending time initially on trying to get your name and slogan right could pay off in the long term.

Registering domains

If you plan to have an internet presence you will need a domain name, that is a name by which your business is known on the internet that lets people find you by entering your name into their browser address box. Ideally you want a domain name that captures the essence of your business neatly so that you will come up readily on search engines and is as close as possible to your business name.

If your business name is registered as a trademark (see page 65) you may (as current case law develops) be able to prevent another business from using it as a domain name on the internet.

Registering a domain name is simple, but as hundreds of domain names are registered every day and you must choose a name that has not already been registered you need to have a selection of domain names to hand in case your first choice is unavailable. These need only be slight variations, for example Cobra Beer could have been listed as Cobra-Beer, CobraBeer or even Cobra Indian Beer, if the original name had not been available. These would all have been more or less equally effective in terms of search engine visibility.

Once you have decided on a selection of domain names, your internet service provider (ISP), the organization that you use to link your computer to the internet, can submit a domain name application on your behalf. You can obtain free domain names along with free web space by registering with an internet community. These organizations offer you web pages within their community space as well as a free domain name, but most communities only offer free domain names that have their own community domain tagged on the end – this can make your domain name rather long and hard to remember.

Intellectual property matters

Aside from deciding on an ownership structure, a further legal issue to tackle is ensuring that you have ownership of any intellectual property (IP) that is central to your business. Even if your business is not highly technical or stashed full of innovations, if your logo, your slogan or the design of your product is part of the uniqueness that differentiates you from others in the market you will want to make sure some newcomer can't step in and purloin your valuable asset.

CASE STUDY

When Mark Zuckerberg, then aged 20, started Facebook from his college dorm back in 2004 with two fellow students, he could hardly have been aware of how the business would pan out. Facebook is a social networking website on which users have to put their real names and e-mail addresses in order to register; then they can contact current and past friends and colleagues to swap photos, news and gossip. Within three years the company was on track to make $100 million sales, partly on the back of a big order from Microsoft, which appears to have its sights on Facebook as either a partner or an acquisition target.

Zuckerberg, in jeans, Adidas sandals and a fleece, looks a bit like a latter-day Steve Jobs, Apple's founder. He also shares something else in common with Jobs. He has a gigantic intellectual property legal dispute on his hands. For three years he has been dealing with a lawsuit brought by three fellow Harvard students who claim, in effect, that he stole the Facebook concept from them.

You should investigate the four categories of protection: patenting, which protects 'how something works'; copyright, which protects 'work on paper, film and DVD'; design registration, which protects 'how something looks'; and trademark registration, which protects 'what something's called'.

The Intellectual Property Office (www.gov.uk/government/organisations/intellectual-property-office) is the definitive source of information on all matters in this area.

They all have one thing in common, though: in the event of any infringement your only redress is through the courts, and going to law can take time and money, whether you win or lose, so you should consider insuring against such eventualities.

Patents

A patent can be regarded as a contract between an inventor and the state. The state agrees with the inventor that if he or she is prepared to publish details of the invention in a set form and if it appears that he or she has made a real advance, the state will then grant the inventor a 'monopoly' on the invention for 20 years: 'protection in return for disclosure'. The inventor uses the monopoly period to manufacture and sell his or her innovation; competitors can read the published specifications and glean ideas for their research, or they can approach the inventor and offer to help to develop the idea under licence.

However, the granting of a patent doesn't mean the proprietor is automatically free to make, use or sell the invention him- or herself, since to do so might involve infringing an earlier patent that has not yet expired.

A patent really only allows the inventor to stop another person using the particular device that forms the subject of the patent. The state does not guarantee validity of a patent either, so it is not uncommon for patents to be challenged through the courts.

What you can patent

What inventions can you patent? The basic rules are that an invention must be new, must involve an inventive step and must be capable of industrial exploitation.

You can't patent scientific or mathematical theories or mental processes, computer programs or ideas that might encourage offensive, immoral or anti-social behaviour. New medicines are patentable but not medical methods of treatment. Neither can you have just rediscovered a long-forgotten idea (knowingly or unknowingly).

If you want to apply for a patent, it is essential not to disclose your idea in non-confidential circumstances. If you do, your invention is already 'published' in the eyes of the law, and this could well invalidate your application.

Stages in the patent process

There are two distinct stages in the patenting process: from filing an application up to publication of the patent; and from publication to grant of the patent. Two fees are payable for the first part of the process and a further fee for the second part. The whole process takes some two and a half years. Forms and details of how to patent are available free from the Patent Office.

Alternatives to using the patent yourself

What can you do with your inspired invention if you don't have the resources, skill, time or inclination to produce it yourself? You can take one of three courses once the idea is patented:

1 *Outright sale.* You can sell the rights and title of your patent to an individual or company. The payment you ask should be based on a sound evaluation of the market.

2 *Sale and royalty.* You can enter into an agreement whereby you assign the title and rights to produce to another party for cash but under which you get a royalty on each unit sold.

CASE STUDY   Not on the High Street

10 years ago, from around a little kitchen table Holly Tucker and Sophie Cornish launched their online retail venture knowing they were innovators. Their business, Not on the High Street, puts hundreds of personalized and unique gifts, gold rings, linen shawls, organic scented candles, overnight bags and more all on the one website. Rather than trudging round dozens of shops or scouring the internet, the pair has brought a near inexhaustible choice of gifts under the umbrella of a single online shopping mall. In fact, the collections of gifts they offer are unlikely to feature on many high streets, now almost exclusively the domain of big multiples with standardized product ranges. The flood of charity shops that fill up vacant slots left by the growing band of failed retailers are unlikely to appeal to the discerning gift buyer either.

The pair knew from the outset that protecting their intellectual property was essential to both survival and prosperity. Not only have they protected all their IP, they assert those rights unambiguously on their website – 'We own, or are the licensee to, all right, title and inter-est in and to the Service, including all rights under patent, copyright, trade secret or trademark law, and any and all other proprietary rights, including all applications, renewals, extensions and restorations thereof. You will not modify, adapt, translate, prepare derivative works from, decompile, reverse-engineer, disassemble or otherwise attempt to derive source code from the App or any other part of the Service.'

It's hardly surprising then that the business hit £6.4 million turnover in year two and in 2010 they reached £14 million. The business hired Jason Weston, formerly of Amazon, as COO and Mark Hodson from PayPal in 2011. The company's latest accounts filed in March 2016 show turnover had reached £38,664,535.

3 *Licensing*. You keep the rights and title but sell a licence for manufacturing and marketing the product to someone else. The contract between you and the licensee should contain a performance clause requiring the licensee to sell a minimum number of units each year or the licence will be revoked.

Whichever option you select, you need a good patent agent or lawyer on your side (see Appendix 3).

Copyright

Copyright gives protection against the unlicensed copying of original artistic and creative works – articles, books, paintings, films, plays, songs, music and engineering drawings. To claim copyright the item in question should carry this symbol: © (author's name) (date). You can take the further step of recording the date on which the work was completed for a moderate fee with the Registrar at Stationers' Hall. This, though, is an unusual precaution to take and probably only necessary if you anticipate an infringement.

Copyright protection lasts for around 70 years after the death of the person who holds the copyright, or 50 years after publication if this is later.

Copyright is infringed only if more than a 'substantial' part of your work is reproduced (ie issued for sale to the public) without your permission, but since there is no formal registration of copyright the question of whether or not your work is protected usually has to be decided in a court of law.

Designs

You can register the shape, design or decorative features of a commercial product if it is new, original, never published before or – if already known – never before applied to the product you have in mind. Protection is intended to apply to industrial articles to be produced in quantities of more than 50. Design registration applies only to features that appeal to the eye, not to the way the article functions.

To register a design, you should apply to the Country Design Registry and send a specimen or photograph of the design plus a registration fee. The specimen or photograph is examined to see whether it is new or original and complies with other registration requirements. If it does, a certification of registration is issued, which gives you, the proprietor, the sole right to manufacture, sell or use in business articles of that design.

Protection lasts for a maximum of 25 years. You can handle the design registration yourself, but, again, it might be preferable to let a specialist do it for you. There is no register of design agents, but most patent agents are well versed in design law. See Appendix 3 for sources of help and advice on all matter relating to intellectual property.

Trademarks and logos

A trademark is the symbol by which the goods or services of a particular manufacturer or trader can be identified. It can be a word, a signature, a monogram, a picture, a logo or a combination of these.

To qualify for registration the trademark must be distinctive, must not be deceptive and must not be capable of confusion with marks already registered. Excluded are misleading marks, national flags, royal crests and insignia of the armed forces. A trademark can apply only to tangible goods, not services (although pressure is mounting for this to be changed).

To register a trademark you or your agent should first conduct preliminary searches at the trademarks branch of your country's

Intellectual Property Office (see Appendix 3) to check there are no conflicting marks already in existence. You then apply for registration on the official trademark form and pay a fee.

Registration is initially for 10 years. After this, it can be renewed for periods of 10 years at a time, indefinitely.

It isn't mandatory to register a trademark. If an unregistered trademark has been used for some time and could be construed as closely associated with a product by customers, it will have acquired a 'reputation', which will give it some protection legally, but registration makes it much simpler for the owners to have recourse against any person who infringes the mark.

Key jobs to do

- Review your present or proposed trading structure to assess its appropriateness or otherwise.

- Look again at your business and domain names to see if they properly reflect what you do.

- Assess if you have taken or plan to take appropriate measures to safeguard your intellectual property.

- If you have significant IP assets consider whether licensing them to another firm may not be a better route to market, eg faster and less costly.

05

Operating from home

THIS CHAPTER COVERS

- assessing out space requirements;
- checking available space;
- handling health and safety;
- getting kitted out;
- motivation matters.

Starting up your business at home certainly presents some unique challenges and opportunities. Without some careful planning much of the time you save not having to travel to work can be used up in necessary and unnecessary distractions.

You need to dispel any impression that friends, neighbours or family may have that you are doing anything other than 'being at work' during the whole of the time you designate as working time. Achieving that calls for meticulous planning in terms of space, resources, equipment and above all the way in which you operate. Creating a businesslike environment and modus operandi is half the battle.

Sizing up your space needs

The first and most obvious factor to consider is where exactly in your home you will carry out your business and how much space you will require. Clearly if you live in a cul-de-sac at the end of a narrow lane surrounded by other houses you are unlikely to be allowed to manufacture using hazardous chemicals and have articulated vehicles delivering and collecting in the middle of the night. You will also have to consider how your neighbours will be affected, even if you are legally allowed to operate your business.

You don't, of course, have to carry out every activity related to your business yourself, nor do you have to do it all on your premises. If you think about it you will see that no business does everything itself.

Assessing space needs

As a first step make out a list of all the activities involved in getting your business to the point where it has something to sell. If you are going to run a bookkeeping service this could be quite a short list. You will need a computer, some software and perhaps a leaflet setting out your prices and the range of services on offer. If you are going to repair musical instruments, say, you may need much more space: a workshop space about the size of a garage, some equipment including a grinding wheel, lathe, a gas torch for repairing soldered parts and a range of small hand tools.

Use Table 5.1 to calculate how much space you will need, whether you need it all the time or just during your working day, whether or not the activity will be noisy enough to disturb others in your home and whether or not it will get dirty. If an area will get dirty you will not want others moving through that area and carrying dirt elsewhere in the house: not at any rate if you want to preserve harmony.

You can use space planning software such as InstantPlanner (**www.instantplanner.com**), Autodesk (**www.autodesk.com**) or plan3D (**www.plan3D.com**), all of which have free or very low-cost tools for testing out your space layout.

Table 5.1 Calculating your space needs

Item	Space needed	Permanent (P) or temporary (T)	Noisy	Dirty
Desk	1 sq m	P	No	No
Filing cabinet	0.25 sq m	P	No	No
Computer	0 sq m	P	No	No
Lathe	0.75 sq m	P	Yes	Yes
Meeting area	2.00 sq m	T	Yes	No
Other item				
Other item				
Other item				
Total space	**4.00 sq m**			

Make or buy, the first decision

The most important choice at the outset of planning how much space you will need when starting a business from home is to decide what you will do in-house and what you will buy. The process of getting others to do work for you rather than simply supplying you with materials for you to work on is called 'outsourcing'. There is little in terms of business functions that can't be outsourced.

So how much space do you really need?

Now with outsourcing in mind go back over the information you put together in Table 5.1 and recalculate your space needs. You can read up on the sorts of activities a small home-based business can outsource, how to choose outsourcing partners and how to draw up a supply agreement with outsource suppliers on the Deloitte website at **www.deloitte.co.uk**/makeconnections/assets/pdf/the-outsourcing-handbook-a-guide-to-outsourcing.pdf.

Auditing your home space

Once you know how much space you need for your business and what you will be doing in that space you can start to scour your home and garden for space to convert to business use. The Rules and Regulations described below vary from time to time, region to region and from country to country. You should consider them as areas to review rather than permanent facts. The list below is not exhaustive, but just enough ideas to kick-start your thinking.

Using the garage   The most obvious discrete space that is separate from the house and likely to be free of family traffic is your garage (if you have one). You can move cars on to the drive or a neighbouring street, subject to your insurance company being happy with that arrangement. According to the RAC Foundation, whilst 71 per cent of motorists have a garage only 41 per cent use it to park their car. Most people use it as storage for junk or are too lazy to open the garage doors.

Only 11 per cent of people who park on the street have arguments with their neighbours, so any inconvenience will be a small price to pay for what could be the ideal workspace, and the only drawback may be the lack of natural light: that can be solved by putting a window in the door, with a Venetian blind on the inside to restrict the view from outside. Garage Conversion Company (**www. garageconversion.com** > Garage Conversion Ideas > Home Office) have sample plans and information on any possible restrictions that may apply.

Parking space   This area and any private drive could be used for a caravan-based office, although you need to keep in mind that visitors, suppliers and of course you and your family still need to get access to your home.

If you do think that a caravan is worth considering check out that your house deeds allow you, as covenants were introduced into the title deeds of new properties from the 1960s onwards to prevent people keeping caravans at home. Even if you are legally allowed to keep a caravan at home you should consider any possible impact on your neighbours and discuss your plans with them. Caravans that could be used as home offices, though probably not as touring caravans, sell for upwards of £1,000.

Using the garden: sheds, conservatories and Portakabins You can install a shed up to 4 metres square without planning consent under certain circumstances. The exact rules are a little complicated. For example, the shed can't be bigger than 50 per cent of your garden, and you will only be permitted to install one if you are not in a conservation area and your title deeds don't expressly prohibit you. Great Little Garden (**www.greatlittlegarden.co.uk**) and Leisure Buildings (**www.leisurebuildings.com**) both offer advice on planning issues and have sections on using garden sheds as home offices. Sheds that could be used for home office purposes sell at garden centres for £800 upwards.

You could also consider adding a conservatory to one end of your home, if space allows. This would be significantly more expensive than a garden shed and, unlike the situation with a shed, in all probability you will have to negotiate your way around other family rooms.

A further option, if space allows, is to rent or buy a portable 'room'. Portakabin (**www.portakabin.co.uk**) or Foremans Relocatable Building Systems (**www.foremansbuildings.co.uk**) have new and a selection of second-hand cabins for rent and sale.

Attics Converting an attic to usable space is likely to be an expensive option and something to consider later once your business is up and running: £10,000 is the entry-level price, including a ladder and a window. Double that if you want to include a WC, plastered walls and a power supply. You may not need planning permission, but as with garden sheds the rules are complicated. Econoloft (**www.econoloft.co.uk/planning-permission-faq**) has information on the rules and much else besides.

Doubling up the spare room If you do have a spare or underutilized room then your search for office space is probably over. It will have heat, light and power and may also be out of the way of general family traffic. If it is currently a bedroom you could get the best of both worlds by putting in a sofa bed and desk with locked drawers. In that way occasional guests can still use the room and you can have it for most of the time. Though far from ideal this can be a low-cost option that can be implemented quickly. Space 2 Inspire (**www.space2inspire.com** > Home Office Furniture) offers ideas on furnishing options.

Guidelines for using space at home

Keep these factors in mind when deciding on an area of your home to work from:

- The room or area needs to be well lit, warm in winter and cool in summer.
- The space shouldn't be claustrophobic, as you could be in it 12 hours a day.
- Somewhere you can close the door and shut your business off from normal family life will be a great asset.
- Allow room for some modest expansion. You should try to anticipate what your business might look like a year out and make sure the space you allocate can accommodate that. Moving is disruptive, time-consuming and expensive.
- You will need power, a telephone line and access to the internet.

Meeting your public

Even though you may be working on your own, perhaps with a member of your family involved too, there will be occasions when you need to meet suppliers, customers or potential employees. This will mean either inviting relative strangers into your home or finding somewhere congenial to meet outside.

Carving out a corner

You could use the area of your home that you have chosen as a workspace, or if meeting 'outsiders' is to be an infrequent event you could use your smartest and most presentable room. But whatever happens you need an area that is not in the general traffic thoroughfare and is free from noise and any other potential interruption. Remember also that your house will have odours and sounds that you take for granted. Your visitors may not find these as unobtrusive as you do and may even find them offensive.

Using hotels and coffee bars

For little more than the price of a couple of cups of coffee you can find a coffee bar or hotel lobby with a businesslike atmosphere and a degree of privacy in which to conduct business meetings. Certainly, you will have to pick your time carefully and avoid 'rush hours', but you will probably find WiFi and other business-friendly facilities on tap.

Renting an office suite

If you want certainty or you need to impress you can always consider renting a meeting room in a hotel or short-term office suite. Global Office Search (**www.globalofficesearch.biz**) and Regus (**www.regus.co.uk/meeting rooms**) have between them several thousand facilities listed around the world where you can rent offices by the hour, half-day, day or week at prices from £3.50 per person per day.

Checking out the rules

Whatever business you plan to run from home and whether the space used is inside or outside your property there will be a number of important rules and regulations to check up on before you start up.

Planning consent and building regulations

The extent to which the use of your home and the land it stands on changes will determine whether or not you need planning consent or to consider building regulations. Any structural alterations, an increase in traffic, noise or smells, anything such as operating unreasonable hours or any disturbance that could affect your neighbours may need permission.

You can find out informally from your local council before applying. You can also get details of most of the organizations involved in the planning area at http://planninghelp.cpre.org.uk/ resources as well as guides to the planning system.

Health, safety and hazards

If you will be working with materials that are flammable, toxic or corrosive or give off fumes you should check on the website of the Health and Safety Executive (**www.hse.gov.uk** > Businesses > Small businesses > Topics > Hazardous substances), where you will find detailed guidance and advice.

There is no such thing as a risk-free business so you should undertake a health and safety risk assessment to see if anything you plan to do could cause harm and if so what precautions you should take. The Health and Safety Executive (**www.hse.gov.uk**) gives detailed information on the things you must do to assess risk properly.

Also check out the European Agency for Safety and Health at work (**https://osha.europa.eu/en**), United States Department of Labour, Occupational Safety and Health Administration (**http://osha.gov/**).

Insurance and financial considerations

Your home insurance policy will not cover any business activity so you must inform your insurer what you plan to do from home. You can find out more about whether or not what you plan to do from home needs special insurance cover and where to find an insurance company on websites such as Go Compare (www.gocompare.com/home-insurance/working-from-home).

Mortgage and related matters

Unless you own fully the freehold of your property some other party such as a mortgage lender, landlord or freeholder may need to give permission for you to run a business from home. Even as a freeholder you could find that a covenant has been included in your title deeds to prevent certain activities being operated from your home.

Business rates

Whilst you currently pay council tax on your home, once you start using part of it or your grounds for business purposes you could be liable to pay business rates on the part of the property you use for work. Some types of small business, particularly those in rural areas providing products or services of particular benefit to the community, are exempt from paying business rates. Details of business rates when working from home can be found on the government website at **www.gov.uk/introduction-to-business-rates/working-at-home.**

Capital gains tax implications

Any increase in the value of your main home is usually free of capital gains tax (CGT) when you sell. However, if you set aside a room or particular area solely for working in you may be liable for CGT on that proportion of any gain.

However if you expect to use a large (over 10 per cent) part of your home for business you should take professional advice from your accountant and check the government website www.gov.uk/capital-gains-tax-businesses for more information on CGT and how to calculate any possible liability. See Appendix 3 for information on the possible tax implications around the world.

Cleaning

You may have to allow something in your budget for any additional cleaning needed for the business activities, over and above what is required for purely domestic activities. This may not be a major issue but it is one that can cause domestic disharmony if not taken into account.

Refuse collection

If your business will create additional or different refuse from that of a normal domestic nature then you should check your local council's policy on collecting business refuse. You should also check on NetRegs (**www.netregs.gov.uk**), the government website that provides free environmental guidance for small businesses in the UK, what your responsibilities are for disposing of waste and hazardous substances.

Keeping the neighbours onside

Once you have satisfied yourself that you are complying with all the relevant rules and regulations you would still be prudent to advise your immediate neighbours of your plans. They may be concerned when they see any unusual comings and goings from your home, and a timely word will set their minds at rest. Talking with them will be especially important if you are doing building work. Citizens Advice (www.citizensadvice.org.uk/housing/problems-where-you-live/neighbour-disputes) has some useful pointers on what might cause problems with neighbours and how to resolve such issues.

Equipping for work

Next comes the task of getting the tools you need to do the job. If you need specific machinery, for example if you are going to repair musical instruments, then you need to find specialist suppliers. However, the general principle applies: you should buy as little as possible as inexpensively as possible, as there is one certain fact about a new business. After a few weeks or months of trading it will resemble less and less the business you planned to start. That in turn means that your initial investment in equipment could be largely wasted when you find you need to re-equip.

Getting furnished

Aside from operating equipment everyone in business needs a desk, chairs, filing cabinets, good lighting and perhaps a sound-proof screen as a barrier between domestic banter and business discussions.

Creating an image

If you will not be having business visitors then skip this section. If you are, then one factor that might override sheer economics is the need to create a professional image. This can dispel any idea that you are 'playing' rather than serious. Look around and see what conditions others in your line of work operate in and see how, with a limited investment, you can create a similar impression.

Making do

You don't need to buy anything much to get into business. You already have somewhere to sit, a table to work at and somewhere to put books, papers and so forth. Some basic shelving won't break the bank, and in terms of the facilities needed to 'administer' your business you don't have to have much more.

Buying in

If you do have to buy in either office furniture or equipment to make a product there are plenty of sources offering good quality at a low cost. For new furniture supplied to most European countries and around the world check out Amazon (**www.amazon.co.uk**) and IKEA (**www.ikea.com/gb/en**). For second-hand office furniture search Wantdontwant.com (**www.wantdontwant.com**), Green-Works (**www.green-works.co.uk**), which has outlets around the UK, and kings office Furniture (http://kingsofficefurniture.co.uk); between them you could fit out a basic office for less than £50.

For machinery and equipment you should use a trade magazine. Alternatively Friday-Ad (**www.friday-ad.co.uk** > For Sale > DIY & Tools) and Machinery Locator (**www.machinerylocator. com**) have second-hand machinery and tools of every description for sale.

Office ergonomics

There is not much point in setting up a business from home with a view to making your life better and then ending up working in an uncomfortable environment. A chair that leaves you with an aching back or a desk that makes using a keyboard difficult is ergonomically a hazard that can reduce your efficiency and output by as much as 20 per cent. That's like missing out on one working day a week.

You should give some thought to the way your workspace is organized. For example:

- Don't have your chair so high that your feet dangle; they should be flat on the floor.

- Your chair seat should reach from the base of your spine to your knees to ensure satisfactory circulation.

- When you are seated your elbows should be at right angles, with your forearm parallel to the desk.

- Lighting needs to be neither too bright nor too dim; 500 lux is comfortable and 800 is verging on high for office work. Bad lighting can cause migraine, fatigue, stress and anxiety.

Office Ergonomics Training (**www.office-ergo.com**) has information on the sorts of problems poor ergonomics can cause, how to avoid problems, and ergonomic products.

Finding suppliers

Finding suppliers is not too difficult; finding good ones is less easy. Business-to-business directories, such as Kompass (**www.kompass.co.uk**) and Applegate (**www.applegate.co.uk**), between them have global databases of over 2.4 million industrial and commercial companies in 190 countries, listing over 230,000 product categories. You can search by category, country and brand name.

You should check:

- the supplier's terms of trade;
- the supplier's level of service;
- who else they supply, getting feedback from their customers;
- what guarantees and warranties are on offer;
- the price, making sure they are competitive;
- finally, that you will enjoy doing business with them.

Other buying options

Aside from searching out suppliers through directories and word of mouth, consider one or more of the following strategies.

Bartering online

You can save using up your cash by bartering your products and services for those of other businesses. Organizations that can help you get started with bartering include Bartercard (tel: 0800 840 6333; website: **www.bartercard.co.uk**) and **SWAPZ.co.uk**).

Buying online

There are over 200 price comparison websites, covering computer hardware and software, phones, travel, credit cards, bank accounts, loans, utilities, electrical goods, office products including printer supplies and a few thousand more items a business might purchase. Paler.com, a quirky website run by Petru Paler (**www.paler.com** > UK Price Comparison Sites), has a directory listing these sites, with brief explanations and a helpful comment page where users have inserted more sites and additional information. There is a similar directory for international supplier comparison sites (**www.paler.com** > UK Price Comparison Sites > US/International). This is further split into United States and international.

Insuring essentials

Insurance is a form of protection against the unexpected happening. Now, whilst no one knows exactly what could go wrong, experience tells us the areas in which the problems are most likely to occur. Statistics from the insurance industry show that one in every six people with car insurance make a claim for damage each year; tens of millions are claimed each day for damage to business property, for accidents at work, professional and product liabilities and injuries to the public on business premises.

Checking out home cover

It is unlikely that your existing home insurance policy will extend to running a business. As you will in all probability now have business assets such as equipment, stock and furniture at home these too need to be protected from theft and damage. If others will be working with you or anyone will be visiting you at home for business purposes you will need to include an element of public liability in your insurance.

Covering your travel and related risks

If you will be travelling either at home or abroad, with or without business assets, your laptop for example, you will need to insure against the usual hazards of travel: missed planes, lost baggage, stolen wallets and documents and motor breakdowns.

Extending car insurance

If you are not carrying or delivering your products in your car then adding an element of business use to your present insurance should be possible. Otherwise you may need to change insurer or policy. In any event you must notify your current insurer of your changed circumstances if you are using your car for any business purpose, including visiting clients and suppliers.

Sources of help and advice with insurance matters

- Simply Business (www.simplybusiness.co.uk), where you can get an expert rundown explaining which covers you might need if you work from home.
- The British Insurance Brokers Association (**www.iib-uk.com >** Find an IIB Member) is the industry's professional body. You can find a regulated broker in the Institute's directory of members at this web link.

Planning your daily life

Working from home can mean that personal and business life blur into one homogeneous lump. Just because you don't have a boss or an office to go to doesn't mean that you can give up on personal planning altogether.

Organizing yourself

You are the primary business resource and, all other things being equal, the more of your time and energy that can be devoted to the business commensurate with retaining your sanity the more successful you will be. Small business owners like to say: 'You work 24 hours a day, but at least you get to choose which 24.' That entrepreneurs work hard is not in dispute. But how many work smart as well?

Most bosses have a false impression of how they use their time and how it affects their performance. There is a strong body of opinion that suggests that the typical boss of a home-based business could improve output by upwards of 15 per cent and save time by as much as 20 to 30 per cent. That in effect means that with good organization you could have an eight- or nine-day week at your disposal, but only have to work for six of them: a prize surely worth having for only a modest change in working methods.

Setting goals

Your business plan sets out the direction you want to take but that needs fleshing out with some tactical tasks. These could include getting your workspace ready for business, reaching break-even point, negotiating a bank loan or finding a reliable supplier. Whatever the goals are they should:

- be challenging in that they stretch you to aim high;
- be realistically attainable in that you can see such goals have been attained by others, though perhaps not by everyone;

- be measurable, as what gets measured gets done whilst other activities get fudged;

- have a timescale attached in that they need completing by a specific date. For complex or major tasks 'eat your elephant a bite at a time'. In other words break the task down. So getting your first order by September could be preceded by calling 20 prospects by July and getting five quotes out by August.

Deciding on working hours and routine

Despite perhaps having left the rat race of corporate life behind or even if you are still congratulating yourself for never having joined it, to succeed in a home-based business you are going to have to at least be on nodding acquaintance with big business methods.

High on the list will be to establish when your working day starts and finishes. It may not be entirely within your control to make that decision: customers, other people you work with and family or home commitments will have a part to play. Certainly, if you are a morning person you can shift the balance in that direction, but your family and anyone else living at home with you will find it easier to respect your business space if you work to a routine.

Managing your time effectively

There are many time management systems on the market, but you can realize many of the benefits yourself with nothing more elaborate than a paper diary by following these guidelines:

- *Step 1: Have a daily and weekly 'to-do' list.* Without a clear set of objectives backed up with a method of assigning priority between tasks, then you are being ruled by the incoming post, telephone calls, visitors or chance meetings. Having measurable goals to achieve within set timescales is the motivating force that drives entrepreneurs on to achieve exceptional results.

- *Step 2: Establish the key priorities.* Not all tasks are equally important or equally urgent. The first task in time management is to establish the priority and hence when a task has to be done and how much time should be devoted to it:

- 'A' priorities are those essential activities that must be completed or progressed substantially.

- 'B' priority tasks are those less essential activities that can be deferred either because the time element is less critical or because the impact on the business is likely to be less.

- 'C' priorities are non-essential activities that could be screened out, handled by someone else or handled in low-priority times.

- 'X' priorities are activities that require immediate attention, even though in themselves they may not be important or vital. So you can have 'AX', 'BX' or even 'CX' priorities.

- *Step 3: Review how you spend your time.* The Pareto, or 80/20 rule states that in 20 per cent of your time you will achieve 80 per cent of the results that matter. The remaining 20 per cent of results will come from 80 per cent of your efforts. The task is to reallocate your time towards those tasks that matter and either cut back or eliminate time spent on less essential matters:

  - Calculate how much time you spend on each activity in a given time period.

  - Assign an ABCX priority to each.

  - Work out how much time, as a proportion, was spent on each activity, eg 10 per cent on A priority activities, 20 per cent on B and 70 per cent on C.

- Once this is done you will be in a good position to look for areas of improvement in time management.

Motivating yourself

Motivating is something that you expect to have done to you. In an organization, managers rush around appraising, praising, rewarding and holding morale-boosting corporate events with prizes and applause in abundance. But as a one-person operation it's down to you to motivate yourself. Setting and achieving your business goals and being passionate about what you do should make the task easier. You should also:

- *Reward yourself.* As well as goals and targets you need rewards for success. So when you succeed in a task give yourself anything from a pat on the back to a lunch out, depending on the scale of the victory. If you take your partner or family out for that lunch you can bask in their praise as well as get them to appreciate why you need the space in the house that you have carved out for your business.

- *Make time to network.* The main complaint owner-managers have, especially if they work alone, is that they have no one to share the load with or to swap war stories with about business successes and failures. Consider joining your local chamber of commerce (**www.britishchambers.org.uk**) or attending business-to-business networking events organized by Networking4business (**www.networking4business.com**) or The Glasshouse (**http://theglasshouse.net**), where you can meet many other businesspeople informally and with no set agenda. Also check the associations listed in Appendix 1, which can help you build your network.

- *Get trained up.* Training is a classic big business motivational tool. Nothing makes people feel better about themselves than if someone is prepared to invest time and money in helping them to up their game. So if handling your finances, closing a sale, negotiating a supply contract or building a website is a skill you need but don't have, find a training programme. You can find a training course or programme to upgrade your skills from Learn Direct (www.learndirect.com) or Findsources (www.findcourses.co.uk), a search engine dedicated to business training and further education.

Dealing with the family, friends and other visitors

You might be inclined to slop around just because you are working at home. The dangers here are twofold. You will give out the wrong

```
       #61   12-13-2019 03:24PM
Item(s) checked out to OSTERRIEDER, SCOT

TITLE: Descent : my epic fall from cycli
BARCODE: 38101005303765
DUE DATE: 01-03-20

TITLE: Starting a business from home : y
BARCODE: 31812055754700
DUE DATE: 01-03-20

TITLE: A dog in a hat : an American bike
BARCODE: 34567020304919
DUE DATE: 01-03-20

TITLE: WordPress all-in-one
BARCODE: 33635003475476
DUE DATE: 01-03-20

TITLE: Wordpress : the missing manual :
BARCODE: 33081102613404
DUE DATE: 01-03-20
```

signals to everyone around you. As far as they can see you are just 'at home' and as such available for more or less anything that they would usually expect in a domestic environment. Secondly, you may not feel as though you are at work yourself. The operative word here is 'appropriate'. That doesn't have to mean a suit and tie, but 'smart casual' is a good yardstick and certainly a notch up from what you wear around the house normally, say at weekends.

Whilst dress is a powerful way of sending signals to those around you that you are 'at work', here are some other tools to help harmonize business and personal life whilst you work.

Negotiate with your spouse

Spouses, partners or housemates, whether or not they have a part to play in your business, will be affected and expect to be consulted on how you plan to make use of what they probably see as their premises. This will be doubly so if they are picking up the financial slack until your business gets going. These measures will help keep them onside:

- Tell them about your business ideas early on and why you think these ideas will succeed without disrupting home life unreasonably.

- Discuss the space you need and why you need it and if necessary 'trade' space. If you have to have one of the bedrooms or, as happened in one rather dramatic case of a boat builder, all of the downstairs rooms for 12 months to build a prototype, see what you can offer as compensation. In the case of the boat builder, he agreed to build a patio and conservatory the year his first boat sold.

- See if you can provide a 'quick win' for everyone in your home. For example, if you need broadband internet offer access to everyone either by setting time aside on your computer or by providing another wireless-enabled computer. Or if you are painting and redecorating your office, get other rooms done too.

- Explain the upside potential of what success will mean for everyone in your family when your business gets established: more money; part-time employment for those who want it; and eventually a move to a dedicated business premises.

Handling children

One of the advantages of starting your business from home is that you can adopt a great work balance from the outset. You can take the kids to school, be at home when they get back, share meals with them and handle emergency trips to the doctor and dentist yourself, rather than having to call in favours from relatives and friends. Few working more conventionally in an office an hour or more's commute away can look after family matters with such relative ease.

Pre-school children who are going to be at home when you need to work are a different matter altogether. There will be times when they are asleep or resting when you will be free to work at will. Otherwise you have two options. The simplest is to have a childminder to cover your peak working hours. Make sure the childminder knows you are working and find somewhere in the house where any noise won't disturb you. Alternatively find a crèche nearby.

One interesting statistic is that the most common defining characteristic of a successful business starter is to have a parent or sibling who has his or her own business. So take any appropriate opportunity to involve children in the business: explain what you are doing; show them you have to work to get results; and expose them to the range of problems and pitfalls as they arise. There are plenty of tasks children of most ages can help with, from filling envelopes with leaflets and mail-outs to loading images and text on to your website. Even a run down to the post office could save you some valuable time and make them feel useful and involved. And of course some extra pocket money won't go amiss.

Pet problems

Pets can't be easily persuaded to help out with your business nor can they be completely ignored. Cats look after themselves and are not noisy, but the sound of a dog barking in the background does not create a professional business image whilst on the telephone or to visitors.

Animals can cause problems for asthmatics and those with other allergies. If the first experience of clients in coming to see you is marred by their being adversely affected by your pet they have a choice: tell you and expose their weakness or phobia and perhaps incur your displeasure; continue and suffer in silence; or take their business elsewhere. You can be reasonably certain that a large proportion will settle for the last option.

Vanquishing visitors

You may live in an area besieged by Jehovah's Witnesses, itinerant door-to-door salespeople, over-friendly neighbours who now know you are working from home, or politicians after your vote. You can be certain that no one will be calling uninvited to discuss business. Dealing with an unwanted visitor may only take a couple of minutes, but the interruption to your work flow may add as much as 20 minutes to that wasted time. Three visitors a week and you have lost an hour's output, mounting up to nearly seven work days over the year. That's probably equivalent to half the amount of holiday you will be able to take in your first year or so in business so you need to find a way to isolate yourself from such distractions.

Signs saying 'No Hawkers' won't cut much ice, and if you just ignore the bell visitors may just keep ringing, annoying you and interrupting your work still more. If this is a serious problem the easiest way to deal with it is to have a video entryphone so you can see who is there and then decide whether or not to answer. These systems cost around £200. A much cheaper option, costing around £50 is to install a wireless video camera at the door so you can see who is there and then decide whether to answer or not.

Key jobs to do

- Calculate how much space you need to work with.
- Review the space inside and around your home to identify the best areas to adapt.
- Assess what equipment you will need and find a source of supply.
- Take stock of how you will work day to day and the likely impact on family life.
- Find out about health, safety, insurance and any other regulatory or legal matters that will affect your working from home.

06

Keeping the communication lines open

THIS CHAPTER COVERS

- reviewing telephone options;
- using e-mail;
- understanding postal options;
- specifying a computer system;
- assessing software needs;
- installing communications security.

With the exception of retail businesses, customers, and suppliers for that matter, have their first experience of almost every other type of business on the phone, by post or e-mail or on the internet. Often that 'moment of truth', as this initial contact experience is known, is the clincher that decides whether or not to go on and do business with the business concerned.

Injecting an element of professionalism at this stage can make your business both stand out and stand tall.

Telephone systems

Unless your business is intended as a hobby that just makes 'pin money' you will need a telephone line separate from that used by the rest of your family. If you decide on having a broadband internet connection you will in effect get three telephone lines into your house: one for internet and two more. That would be sufficient as a bare minimum.

If you will be working full time at your business and want to exude professionalism then having broadband internet, a business phone number and a spare line for a fax/answer machine would be a good starting specification. Obviously, if your business is in telemarketing you may need a much more substantial provision.

BT (**https://business.bt.com**) and Vonage (**www.vonage.co.uk**) both have a good range of products aimed at this market.

Mobile phones

Mobile phones have two valuable uses. Firstly, they let you operate your business from anywhere: the car, train and even an increasing number of aeroplanes. Secondly, they give you an additional 'landline' facility at home, for example if your main line is handling a fax or being used by someone working with you.

The cost of mobile services is ever changing, with a mass of bundling of landlines, internet and TV making comparisons difficult. That is particularly the case if you expect to be making or receiving many international calls. Money Supermarket (**www. moneysupermarket.com**) and Mobile Phone Checker (**www. mobilephone checker.co.uk**) are price comparison websites that give tariff and cost details based on the information you provide on your likely usage – calls, texts, video, internet usage and so forth. (See also Paler, above.)

VoIP (Voice over Internet Protocol)

Increasingly it is becoming possible to use the internet as a connection route for making telephone calls. This gives you instantly as many 'lines' as you need at zero or very little cost. Companies such as Skype (**www.skype.com**) provide a free piece of software that, once installed, allows all users to speak free anywhere around the world. Aside from speech, text, landline and mobile phone calls and message answering services can be added for a modest cost. To find out what developments there are in this field go to **www. voip-news.com.**

Freephone numbers

Customers are three times more likely to call a freephone number than make a standard paid-for call.

Free numbers come in all shapes and sizes, ranging from totally free from anywhere to the price of a local call from anywhere. Calls from mobile phones will be variable dependent on the network either you or your customer is using.

Operating at home

Companies such as Planet Numbers (**www.planet-numbers.co.uk**) and Call Ready (**www.callready.co.uk**) provide a mass of services, claiming that you need pay only a few pence (cents) for every call received. You can use your own landline number or a mobile phone or pick your own phone number from a menu of options. You can change the destination number of the incoming call so you can receive calls anywhere you happen to be.

Creating a global presence

You can get a private phone number in almost any country in the world, giving you a 'local' presence in that country, and have those calls redirected to your business landline or mobile phone. The caller in the country in question can get the call free or at local call rates, with you picking up the balance. Callagenix (**www.callagenix.com**) and either of the two companies listed above can provide you with international phone numbers and supporting services.

Absent answering

Just because you are away from home or immersed in tasks from which you don't want to be interrupted doesn't mean that customers, suppliers and others you work with don't want to contact you by phone. The classic way to handle this is to have some form of automated answering system that can either take a message or give a message such as: 'I am away until 11 am; call my mobile number or leave a message and I'll get back to you later today.'

Whatever system you use the cardinal rules are to let callers know your message is relevant (for example, 'You are through to Instant Interiors. It is Thursday 5 September and I am away from my desk or in meetings until 3.30 pm. I will return your call after then') and to call them back as arranged.

Answerphone options

Simplest and cheapest is to buy an old-fashioned answering machine. For around £20 you can get a machine that will do everything a small business could reasonably require, including being able to access and change messages from anywhere. Your telephone company will be able to offer a similar service without involving any hardware at your end. The most basic of these services, such as BT's Answer 1571 Free, takes up to 20 messages, but does nothing else. For more facilities expect to pay around £5 a month.

Voicemail

An answering machine uses your phone line, so when someone calls no one else can get through and you can't call out. Voicemail can handle at least 10 simultaneous calls, even when you are checking the messages. You can call in and pick up messages or get texts or e-mails, with an MP3 file attachment so you can hear the calls from any computer or internet café.

Voicemail has progressed since its introduction in the late 1970s and besides recording and playing sounds you can:

- receive voicemail messages from several callers simultaneously;
- forward voicemail messages to other mailboxes;
- add a voice introduction to the message you are forwarding;
- broadcast voice messages to many users at the same time;
- store voice messages indefinitely;

- be notified of the arrival of a voicemail by e-mail and mobile phone;
- deliver multiple greetings to different users.

Providers include the companies listed previously in this chapter and Verizon (**www.verizonwireless.com**), Soho (**http://soho66. co.uk**) and Switchboard Free (**www.switchboardfree.co.uk**).

Using an answering service

The systems described so far take and give messages but don't involve a 'warm body' response. You can get a live person to answer your phone without having them in your home. This could be a valuable service if the calls you will be receiving are complicated, for example asking for one of several information packs, asking for visit or placing an order. It could also be useful if you are expecting a large volume of high-value calls in a short period of time or if you need 24/7 cover to support your product or service.

Direct Response www.drltd.com) has service plans from £300 per month and Office Answers (**www.office-answers.co.uk**) charges £25 to set up a services followed by a subscription charge of £20 per month and receptionist time is charged at 85p per minute.

Fax facts

The fax machine still has a part to play in business life when you want to transmit pictures, diagrams and complex text such as price lists, or if the recipient doesn't have a computer. You will get best value if you buy the fax as part of an answer machine or printer combination package, but in any event the cost will be minimal. Expect to pay upwards of £30, with the most sophisticated costing around £100. Amazon (**www.amazon.co.uk**) has over 500 fax machines listed.

E-mail options

E-mail is now more or less universal and can be used as the host for almost any communication system, including being a basic telephone (VoIP), sending and receiving faxes and other documents and providing an answering service. E-mail has a number of key advantages for business users:

- If you have broadband internet connection e-mails are more or less free.

- E-mailing can save time, as you can send as many copies of the same message as you like all at the same time.

- You can do e-mail when it suits you best, whereas phone calls can interrupt the day.

- You have a written record, unlike with any telephone-based message, which should reduce the possibilities of confusion or error.

- You can e-mail from anywhere.

Your internet service provider (ISP) will almost certainly bundle in a dozen or more e-mail addresses free with their service. Hotmail (**www.hotmail.com**), Google Mail (**www.google.co.uk** > more > Google Mail) and Yahoo (**www.yahoo.com** > Free mail) all offer free e-mail services with masses of free storage – 2 GB up to 8 GB. See also Chapter 8, 'Choosing an internet service provider (ISP)'.

Accessing your diary and data remotely

Most e-mail services include the option of managing your diary and address book online. This means that when you are away from home you can access any information that you would normally have to hand, without having to carry oodles of paper with you. You can also e-mail yourself files that you may need to refer to and so have them on tap anywhere any time.

Finding an internet café or WiFi hotspot

Free WiFi is now close to ubiquitous. World 66 (**www.world66. com/netcafeguide**) has all the information you need about internet cafés all around the world and it is delivered in open content format which means that anyone can edit it and copy it. WifiMapper (www.wifimapper.com) is a free app that claims to have mapped 500 million free WiFi hotspots worldwide. It also has historical information about the quality of the signal at each hotspot, so you find one with the best quality.

Mailroom matters

Whilst technology has helped business communications it has not supplanted the good old-fashioned 'snail mail' arriving at the letterbox. However, the system that works for your home may not work when you start a business from home if the volume of post rises sharply or if the size of letters and packages gets too big for your letterbox. The easy option is to make a bigger opening or put a locked mailbox on your door. If these are not viable then consider one of the following.

Collecting your post or using a mailbox

The US Postal Service (**www.usps.com**), the Post Office (**www.postoffice.co.uk**) and most other national postal services have a number of services to make life easier for those running a business from home. Keepsafe, a UK service from Royal Mail for example, holds mail for up to 66 days for £4+ a month. Using the box service you can have in effect a new address for your post, which you have to pick up monthly (or as frequently as you like). This can create a professional image and let you decide when to handle the post rather than have it dumped on your doorstep at what may be an inconvenient time.

Other postal matters

If you do expect to have to handle a large volume of post these are some other matters to consider:

- Machine franking is a way to ensure you never run out of stamps and day or night have the right value of stamp for the size of letter and its destination. When postal tariffs change these systems automatically update (**www.royalmail.com/business/**

services/sending/pay-for-mail/franking). Machine providers claim to save up to 20 per cent on postage costs.

- Automated letter opening or folding may be useful if you are mailing or receiving a large volume of post. These machines cost upwards of £250.

- Shredding confidential papers may become important once you start your business. Any document with information on your bank account, supplier discounts or customer addresses or any document you would prefer competitors not to see should be shredded. Office shredders cost upwards of £40.

The Royal Mail (**www.royalmail.com/business**) has a guide to its services and a directory of approved franking and mailroom equipment providers. UK Office Direct (**www.ukofficedirect.co.uk**) has a comprehensive range of mailroom machines and guides to choosing which is right for your needs.

Computers: the vital tool

Computers and their software are the single most important tool for almost any type of business. These have in effect levelled the playing field between big established businesses and new entrants. In fact, as prices have dropped steeply and specifications risen anyone buying now will have a significant advantage over those buying a year or two back.

The general specification

To handle general business needs, run a basic website and design and print a newsletter you need an entry-level computer with this specification:

- For PCs look for one that has or can use the Windows 10 operating system. For Apple computers look for macOS Sierra. The operating system is the intelligent link between the computer's hardware and software: the language used, in effect, to 'speak' to the computer. These two are the latest.

- Look for at least a 500 GB hard drive, enough to hold 1.2 million pages of text at any one time. Capacity of 1 TB or more will be necessary if you are working with multimedia applications.

- Random access memory (RAM) is the memory available to work the programs as opposed to storing data. You need at least 4 GB of RAM and double that if you will be editing high-end graphics.

- Opt for a 19-inch flat-screen monitor, which will allow for preparing and editing price lists, news sheets and leaflets.

- Most information and computer programs are downloaded directly from the internet so DVD/CD drives are rarely used for business proposes. Backups are now done to the Cloud and external hard drives. Cloud storage services like Dropbox and Google Drive are inexpensive ways to continuously back up your data whilst having remote access.

- You will need at least three USB ports.

- Look for Core Duo architecture, which in essence squeezes two independent computer drives on to a single CPU (central processing unit). This means it handles doing two tasks at the same time a whole lot better than with single architecture.

To keep on top of what the latest specs and offers are, read *PC World* for Apple, see the MacReview (**http://macreview.com**).

Laptops vs desktops

Buying a laptop rather than a desktop means electing for portability over price and performance. There is virtually nothing that you are likely to want a computer for as a business owner that can't be done on a laptop, but as a rough rule of thumb the latter will cost 20 per cent more and be 20 per cent less powerful. If you will be travelling a lot then it may just be worth the additional cost, but with laptops selling in supermarkets for £299 you could consider having both.

There is a further consideration. Being portable, a laptop is more likely to get broken or stolen. So you will need to make sure your insurance will cover these eventualities.

You can keep abreast of developments in the laptop world at *What Laptop* (**www.whatlaptop.co.uk**).

Smart Phones and PDAs

'Personal digital assistant' was a rather pretentious name for what used to be little more than an electronic diary and address book. Today you can get Smart Phones/PDAs that: have sufficient memory to hold all the files you are working on, including PowerPoint presentations and spreadsheets; connect to the internet; send and receive e-mails; synchronize with your computer; work as a mobile phone; allow you to watch movies and listen to your music; operate as a digital camera; and act as a GPS navigation mapping system.

There are plenty of websites reviewing the latest offers in smart phones including Trusted Reviews (**www.trustedreviews.com**) and Techradar (**www.techradar.com**). Good-quality Chinese smart-phones are about a quarter of the price of a comparably specified Apple or Samsung.

Security and back-up systems

As everyone will confirm computers are wonderful until something goes wrong. You may not always be able to prevent problems but you can take some basic steps to limit the damage.

Keeping copies

The cardinal rule in working with computers is to do frequent back-ups and hold copies of your work somewhere other than on the drive of the machine you are working on at the time. There are a myriad of options, so there is no excuse other than absent-mindedness or laziness, neither of which is a behaviour that entrepreneurs should cultivate. Viruses, theft, computer crashes and physical damage are the most likely problems that cause data loss. Working at home only magnifies the opportunities for any of these problems to arise.

At the very least back-ups of the files you have been working with should be done at the end of every day and of your whole system once a week. These are the main options:

- Back up to a laptop, if you have one. This has the merit that you can work with the files if something has gone wrong with your main computer. If the computer is vital to your business, this is the favourite option, but will cost around £300 for a new laptop.

- Use an online back-up system; the provider's software is installed on your computer and it detects any changes or additions to your files and automatically makes copies in real time. Dropbox, Google Drive and SecuriData (**www.securidata.co.uk**) offer back-up services. Check if your internet service provider offers this service, which may come free.

- Use a separate hard drive, such as those provided by Iomega (**www.iomega.com**) or Western Digital (**www.wdc.com**). Prices start at £50, and expect to pay £70 for 1 TB.

- Use a USB pen drive. These have up to 64 GB of storage on a small cigarette lighter-sized implement that slots into a USB port. Sandisk has a 'Smart' flash drive, as these disks are usually referred to, that will automatically back up your e-mail, diary, My Documents folder, Internet Favourites and Skype phone system. This is priced from around £4, and £18 for the Sandisk Cruiser (**www.sandisk.com**), the system that automatically backs up data. Amazon (**www.amazon.co.uk**) offers one of the widest ranges of these products at very competitive prices.

Uninterruptible power systems

If you use a laptop then losing power at home won't be too big a problem – not for an hour or two at least, until the battery runs flat. But if you have an electric storm, or just one of those over-load problems when the dishwasher, washing machine, TV and a power drill push your domestic electric supply to its limit, your system could shut down by blowing a fuse. If that happens your desktop computer will shut instantly and you could lose everything you were working on. You will also have to wait until the power comes back.

You can get a basic back-up power system for between £40 and £200, which will kick in automatically when your power goes off and give you up to an hour's use of a computer, more than enough time to make a back-up, deal with vital e-mails and find the fuse box. Maplin (**www.maplin.co.uk**) and Adept Power Solutions (**www.adeptpower.co.uk**) have a range of products to handle power interruptions.

Surge protection

A rather different problem can occur both when you get a power cut and if you get a sudden spike in electric supply that increases the voltage sharply. When this happens your computer, and any other equipment connected to your supply, is at risk. A surge protector acts as a brake, making sure that whatever happens to the power source the actual power to your equipment stays within safe limits. If you use an uninterruptible power system for your computer system it will almost certainly have surge protection built in. For other equipment such as printers, fax machines, scanners, etc, you should consider getting a surge protector. A protector that will cope with up to six pieces of equipment will cost around £15. Belkin (**www.belkin.com**) and both the companies listed above that provide uninterruptible power systems offer surge protectors.

Other hardware needs

Your computer won't be much use on its own without other pieces of equipment to connect to. These are the most common elements to make a complete home office system:

- *Wireless networks.* This is a wireless way to connect your computers to the internet and to each other and can be a useful way to share a printer, scanner or any other device between several users.

You will need an ISP (Internet Service Provider) to connect you to the internet. Use a service such as Broadband Choices (**www.broadbandchoices.co.uk**) and Broadband Speed Checker (**www.broadbandspeedchecker.co.uk**) to find out what services are available in your area.

- *Powerline networks.* This is a system that uses your electricity power circuit to transmit data. You connect one plug to a router and other plugs can be used to link computers to the internet wherever they are on that electric circuit. This could be useful if there are areas you want internet reception, but can't get it via the router alone. Homeplugs (**www.homeplugs.co.uk**) and Maplin (**www.maplin.co.uk**) provide these systems.

- *Printers and copiers.* Printers and copiers do much the same task but for printers the input comes directly from a computer. You have two main options: inkjet (sometimes known as bubble jet) and laser. With inkjet, the ink is squirted in thousands of minute dots on to paper to form text or pictures. The advantages of inkjet are that the printers are inexpensive and they can print in colour. The drawbacks are that replacement ink cartridges are expensive, print speeds are slow and the print quality may not be that great. Laser printers use a drum and toner and produce crisper copies, faster and at a much lower cost per copy. The machines cost more than inkjets and if you want colour the machine will be more expensive still. If what you print or copy is for in-house consumption only an inkjet printer will meet all your needs. If you are sending documents to customers and quality is vital or you are making thousands of copies then consider going for a laser printer. *TrustedReviews* (**www.trustedreviews.com**) and *PC Advisor* (**www.pcadvisor.co.uk**) produce regular evaluations of printers so that you can evaluate both specifications and prices.

- *Scanners.* Normally you will input data into your computer using a keyboard. There may be occasions when you want to transfer something from paper on to your computer, a picture or image, for example. Scanners are usually incorporated into a printer's capability. A competent basic printer/scanner will cost under £50.

The vital software

This is the minimum software that you are likely to require. (Accounting software and business planning software are covered in Chapters 9 and 11 respectively.)

Office program suites

Microsoft provides the most universal business software program, the latest version of which is Office 365 Business (https://products.office.com/en-gb/sbusiness/office). This comprises fully installed Office applications Word, Excel, PowerPoint, Outlook, Publisher, OneNote and for a small additional payment HD video conferencing on up to five PCs or Macs per user. E-mail with 50 GB mailbox and 1 TB cloud file storage and sharing is included as are apps for your phone and tablet. Prices start from around £8 per user per month.

There are a few free suites of programs that will do much if not all of what a small business might require. There are a number of alternative software packages that claim compatibility with Microsoft, a factor that is important if you are sharing or exchanging documents or collaborating with people using Microsoft. They are invariably cheaper and mostly free. Google Docs (**www.google.com/docs**) has a word processor, spreadsheet and presentation program similar to PowerPoint. WPS Office Free (**www.wps.com**) has the three main tools for words, presentations and spreadsheets as well as being able to convert from PDF to Word. Apache Open Office (**https://openoffice.apache.org**) and SSuite Office Premium HD+ (**www.ssuitesoft.com**) are also workmanlike free software packages.

Antivirus

2017 will go down as the year that cyber attacks became mainstream and 'ransomware' entered the vocabulary. There are nearly as many programs to protect your computer against viruses as there are viruses. A good free system that seems to work well is that from Grisoft (**http://free.grisoft.com**). Their AVG Anti-Virus Free edition provides basic protection, but without any technical support. To get that you will have to pay £27. Norton (**www.symantec.com**) and McAfee (**www. mcafee.com**) are the market leaders in this sector, but keep an eye on The Top Ten Anti Virus (**www.thetop10antivirus.com**).

Key jobs to do

- Determine your telephone needs and make a list of key equipment required.
- Consider your postal needs and make a plan for inbound and outbound post.
- Decide your computer hardware and software needs and make a specification for the necessary purchases.
- Assess the communication risks to data, documents, software (viruses), power interruptions etc and determine the resources needed to mitigate such risks.

Bringing your product and service to market

Marketing mix refers to the mix of ingredients with which marketing strategy can be developed and implemented. The ingredients, originally referred to as the 4 Ps, are price, product (or/and service), promotion and place. This is now extended to 7 Ps – people, process and physical evidence – to accommodate the increasing emphasis on customer focus in business. Just as with cooking, taking the same or similar ingredients in different proportions can result in very different 'products'. The ingredients in the marketing mix represent only the elements that are largely, though not entirely, within a firm's control. Uncontrollable ingredients include the state of the economy, changes in legislation, new and powerful market entrants and rapid changes in technology.

A change in the way these elements are put together can produce an offering tailored to meet the needs of a specific market *segment*.

Deciding on your product or service range

The Blooming Marvellous (see page 26) product was described when the business started out as 'clothes for the mother-to-be that will allow them to still feel fashionably dressed'. That is specific in one sense but still leaves a question mark over exactly what clothes they will be: dresses, sweatshirts, coats, skirts, jeans? Johnnie Boden (see Chapter 11, page 204) started out with a hand-drawn catalogue with just eight items.

Is one product enough?

One-product businesses are the natural route for home-based businesses, particularly those with a streak of innovation, but they are extremely vulnerable to competition, changes in fashion and technological obsolescence. Having only one product can also limit the growth potential of the enterprise. A question mark must inevitably hang over such ventures until they can broaden out their product base into, preferably, a 'family' of related products or services.

CASE STUDY

Cambridge-educated and recently qualified accountant Karan Bilimoria started importing and distributing standard-size 660-millilitre bottles of Cobra beer, specifically brewed to complement Indian restaurant food in the UK. Soon it became 'the beer from Bangalore, brewed in Bedford'; it became available in 330-millilitre bottles and subsequently on draught. A low-alcohol version was then introduced, followed by the addition of 'General Billy's Wine' as Karan widened the product range to meet Indian restaurant demand. Sales had grown to over £200 million a year by December 2016.

Setting quality standards

One of the biggest problems for a new business is creating in the customer's mind an image of product quality. There was once an almost faddish belief in 'dynamic obsolescence', implying that low quality would mean frequent and additional replacement sales. The inroads that the Japanese car makers have made on Western car manufacturers through improving quality, reliability and value for money have clearly demonstrated the fallacy of this proposition.

You cannot sell a product you do not believe in and, as the founder of a farm-based cider business explained, 'in cold calling the only thing standing between you and the customers' scorn is the integrity of your product'.

Quality is not just what you do, but also how you do it; each contact point between the customer and company is vital, be it on the telephone, at the counter or at the till. The customer who complains could be your best friend compared to the one you never see again! Getting your customers to help you maintain your quality and standards is perhaps one of the keys to business success. The quality obsession is clear; if you do not catch it, you will not survive.

Assessing critical success factors

Whilst you may believe your product or service has dozens of great attributes, at the end of the day your customers will choose you over competitors for a handful of reasons only. These critical success factors (CSFs) are in effect the four or five things (aside from price, as you always have to offer value for money) that you have to get right with your product offer to succeed.

You should identify these CSFs for your product/service, rank their importance say by allocating them a share of 100 per cent and then score yourself and your competitors. In the example in

Table 7.1 Assessing competitive advantage for a bookshop

CSF	Importance %	Competitor score 0–5	Weighted score	Your score 0–5	Weighted score
Location	40	4	1.6	3	1.2
Range of books	20	4	0.8	4	0.8
Knowledgeable staff	20	1	0.2	5	1.0
Opening hours	10	1	0.1	5	0.5
Pleasant environment	10	1	0.1	5	0.5
Total	100		2.8		4.0

Table 7.1 you can see that location is considered the most important factor, and it accounts for 40 per cent of the reason to buy this type of product. Your competitor scores well on location, getting 4 out of a possible 5. By multiplying the score by the importance, we arrive at the weighted score, 1.6. Continuing in the same way we can see that our total weighted score is 4.0 and our competitor's is 2.8, giving us a distinct superiority in terms of our product/service offer.

Of course there is no easy way to arrive at exact figures for this table. Initially you will have to rely on your own judgement and the opinions of family and friends. Later, however, you can ask your customers, using market research.

Promotion and advertising

The answers to these five questions should underpin the advertising and promotional aspects of your strategy:

- What do you want to happen?
- If that happens how much is it worth?
- What message will make it happen?

- What media will work best?
- How will you measure the effectiveness of your effort and expense?

What do you want to happen?

Do you want prospective customers to visit your website, phone, write to or e-mail you, return a card or send an order in the post? Do you expect them to have an immediate need to which you want them to respond now, or is it that you want them to remember you at some future date when they have a need for whatever it is you are selling?

The more you are able to identify a specific response in terms of orders, visits, phone calls or requests for literature, the better your promotional effort will be tailored to achieving your objective and the more clearly you will be able to assess the effectiveness of your promotion and its cost versus its yield.

How much is that worth to you?

Once you know what you want a particular promotional activity to achieve, it becomes a little easier to estimate its cost. Suppose a £1,000 advertisement is expected to generate 100 enquiries for your product. If experience tells you that on average 10 per cent of enquiries result in orders, and your profit margin is £200 per product, then you can expect an extra £2,000 profit. That 'benefit' is much greater than the £1,000 cost of the advertisement, so it seems a worthwhile investment. Then with your target in mind decide how much to spend on advertising each month, revising that figure in the light of experience.

Deciding the message

Your promotional message must be built around facts about the company and about the product. The stress here is on the word 'fact' and, while there may be many types of fact surrounding you and your products, your customers are only interested in two: the facts that influence their buying decisions and the ways in which your business and its products stand out from the competition.

These facts must be translated into benefits (see also Chapter 3, 'Features, benefits and proofs'). There is an assumption sometimes that everyone buys for obvious, logical reasons only, when we all know of innumerable examples showing this is not so. Do people only buy new clothes when the old ones are worn out? Do bosses have desks that are bigger than their subordinates' because they have more papers to put on them?

Choosing the media

Your market research should produce a clear understanding of who your potential customer group are, which in turn will provide pointers as to how to reach them. But even when you know who you want to reach with your advertising message it's not always plain sailing. The *Fishing Times*, for example, will be effective at reaching people who fish, but less so at reaching their partners who might be persuaded to buy them fishing tackle for Christmas or birthdays. The *Fishing Times* will also be jam-packed with competitors. It might just conceivably be worth considering a web ad on a page giving tide tables to avoid going head to head with competitors or getting into a gift catalogue to grab that market's attention.

Another factor to consider in making your choice of media is the 'ascending scale of power of influence', as marketers call it. This is a method to rank media in the order in which it is most likely to influence your customers favourably. At the top of the scale is the personal recommendation of someone whose opinion is trusted and who is known to be unbiased. An example here is the endorsement of an industry expert who is not on the payroll, such as an existing user of the goods or services who is in the same line of business as the prospective customer. Whilst highly effective, this method is hard to achieve and can be expensive and time-consuming. Further down the scale is an approach by you in your role as a salesperson.

Table 7.2 Measuring advertising effectiveness

Media used	Cost per advert £/$/€	Number of enquiries	Cost per enquiry £/$/€	Number of customers	Advertising cost per customer £/$/€
Sunday paper	3,400	75	45	10	340
Daily paper	2,340	55	43	17	138
Posters	1,250	30	42	10	125
Local weekly paper	1,400	10	40	4	100

Whilst you may be seen to be knowledgeable, you clearly stand to gain if a sale is made, so you can hardly be unbiased. Sales calls, however they are made, are an expensive way to reach customers, especially if their orders are likely to be small and infrequent.

Further down still comes advertising in the general media: websites, blogs, social media, press, radio, TV and so forth. However, whilst these methods may be lower down the scale, they can reach much more of the market, and if done well can be effective.

Measuring results

A glance at the advertising analysis in Table 7.2 will show how to tackle the problem. It shows the advertising results for a small business course run in London. At first glance the Sunday paper produced the most enquiries. Although it cost the most, £3,400, the cost per enquiry was only slightly more than for the other media used. But the objective of this advertising was not simply to create interest; it was intended to sell places on the course. In fact, only 10 of the 75 enquiries were converted into orders – an advertising cost of £340 per head. On this basis the Sunday paper was between 2.5 and 3.5 times more expensive than any other medium.

Judy Lever, co-founder of Blooming Marvellous, the upmarket maternity-wear company, believes strongly not only in evaluating the results of advertising but in monitoring a particular media capacity to reach her customers. 'We start off with one-sixteenth-of-a-page ads in the specialist press', says Judy. 'Then once the medium has proved itself we progress gradually to half a page, which experience shows to be our optimum size. On average there are 700,000 pregnancies a year, but the circulation of specialist magazines is only around the 300,000 mark. We have yet to discover a way of reaching all our potential customers at the right time – in other words, early on in their pregnancies.'

Advertising options

In practice most home-based businesses will have little to spend on advertising. And there are an awful lot of options.

After a period of relative stability UK advertising expenditure is now growing at its highest rate since 2010, increasing by around 8% annually, according to the UK's definitive advertising statistics, the Advertising Association/Warc Expenditure Report. Internet ad

Table 7.3 UK advertising spend

Media	Spend £ Million	% of spend
Internet	8,606	42
TV	5,270	25
Direct Mail	1,871	9
National News	1,220	6
Regional News	1,176	6
Posters, digital panels etc	1,059	5
Magazines	942	5
Radio	592	3
Cinema	238	1
Total	20,087	100

SOURCE: Advertising Association/Warc Expenditure Report: April 2016

spending is the fastest-growing media channel with mobile accounting for nearly 80% of growth. The UK is by far the largest internet
advertising market in Europe and ranks third globally, behind the
US and China.

For a new small business the media used is likely to be confined
to direct mail both on and off line, some local advertising and leaf-
letting. But it all depends on your business sector and your appetite
for incurring upfront costs.

The power of print

The printed word, on-or offline, is probably still the way in which
most small businesses communicate with their public. The rules for
writing apply to advertising copy too. The content needs to be:

- Clear, using straightforward English, with short words, up to
  three syllables, and short sentences, no more than 25–30 words.
  The text should be simply laid out and easy to read.

- Concise, using as few words as possible and free from jargon or
  obscure technical terms.

- Correct, as spelling mistakes or incorrect information will
  destroy confidence in you and your product or service.

- Complete, providing all the information needed for the reader to
  do all that is required to meet *your* advertising objective.

Business cards and stationery   Everything you send out from
home needs to be accompanied by something with all your contact
details and a message or slogan explaining what you do. That
includes invoices, bills, price lists and technical specifications. This
may be all that anyone ever sees of you and your business. If it is
effective people will remember you by it and, better still, they will
remember to pass the information on to anyone else they know
who could be a customer.

Direct mail (emails, leaflets, flyers, brochures and letters)   These
are the most practical ways for a new business to communicate
with its potential customers. These forms of communication have
the merits of being relatively inexpensive, simple and quick to put

into operation, they can be concentrated into any geographic area, and they can be mailed or distributed by hand. Finally, it is easy to monitor results.

CASE STUDY

In April 2015 Cranfield MBA Nick Jenkins had reason to be excited about a new stage in his life. He was joining Dragon's Den, the long-running Bafta-nominated BBC show that sees novice entrepreneurs pitch for start-up funds. When Nick, 46, launched Moonpig, his online personalized greetings card business, in 1999, though quietly confident of success, he had no idea just how big his idea would become.

In July 2011, barely 12 years after launching, he sold his business to Photobox – the French-owned company who offer online photo albums – for £120 million. At that point the business had annual turnover in excess £32 million whilst netting £11 million in profits. Moonpig itself offers a range of over 10,000 customizable cards to which users can add photographs, names and their own personal message.

Nick's first marketing campaign was in his own words a pretty hit and miss affair. He tried a number of affiliate deals, some PR and invested in search engine optimisation. But none of these were as effective as the power of viral marketing – online word of mouth. The second leg of the promotional strategy came when they launched what is now recognized as one of the most annoyingly memorable jingles on TV. Over half of the UK population now recognise the brand, but this Nick asserts is down to more than just a catchy tune. According to Nick, 'Critical to our success is that it is a product that people like, and like to share. The TV ad would not have worked if it had not been backed up by a product worth talking about.'

Another key driver to the success of Moonpig has been its customer service. Moonpig has its own customer service team in its London Bridge head office all trained to talk to customers in a way that, according to Nick, 'reflects our brand'.

These organizations can provide information that will help you with leaflets, brochures and all other forms of direct mail:

- The British Council (https://eal.britishcouncil.org/resources/persuasive-writing-adverts-and-leaflets) has ''a pack of resources to support the teaching of writing in the advertisement writing genre', but useful for a home-based business on a tight budget.

- Direct Marketing Association (**www.dma.org**) is the trade association for all direct marketing activities. Their directory catalogue of lists (**www.dma.org.uk** > DMA List Manager) allows you to search their two list databases, Consumer and Business. From each of these you can search for a list by country around the world, by business sector, or for consumers by age, gender, income, interest, home ownership, etc.

- Edraw (www.edrawsoft.com) has a number of useful free built-in flyer templates to create and present your flyers, brochures and leaflets 'in minutes'.

- Experian (www.experian.co.uk/business-express) offers a List Builder service that gives you instant access to 5.2 million records to help you find new clients. You can filter by geographical region, business type, turnover, number of employees and much more. The choice is yours. They state that 'there are no upfront or hidden costs and a single lead costs only ten pence'.

Newspapers, magazines and classified ads   You can get readership and circulation numbers and the reader profile directly from the journal or paper or from BRAD (British Rate and Data) (**www.brad.co.uk**), which has a monthly classified directory of all UK and Republic of Ireland media. You should be able to access this through your local business library. The National Readership Survey (**www.nrs.co.uk** > Top Line Readership) produces average readership data on around 260 UK titles and a host of other data, much of which is free and available online to non-subscribers.

However, national newspapers, except for the classified ads sections, are likely to be outside the budget of most new businesses. If that is the case, don't despair, as local papers have a substantial readership, around 40 million adults a week, and the cost to advertise in them is significantly less and they have a much more focused readership. Hold the Front Page (**www.holdthefrontpage.co.uk** > Newspaper websites) has links to the 200 or so local daily and weekly papers. In the directory section you will find all the information you need about UK regional and local newspapers, newspaper websites, newspaper publishing companies and the people who work for them.

Posters, billboards and signs If you know where your audience are likely to pass you could put a poster or billboard somewhere in their line of sight. This could be something as simple and inexpensive as an A4 sheet in the local newsagent window, bus shelter or supermarket message board, or a more costly and elaborate structure such as those seen by the roadside.

There are rules governing positioning billboards, as one young business starter learnt to his cost. Steve Sayer, a 13-year-old from Cheddar, hit upon the idea of selling manure from his father's stables over the internet. Priced at £2.50 a bag his product was a hit with local gardeners. Rather than spend heavily on getting his website to the top of the search page he put a large board up in a field on their land adjoining a road. His business was flying and he had banked over £2,000 before the district council made him take the sign down.

Most businesses have a sign outside their door telling passers-by what they do. If the premises have a high footfall with lots of people passing this can get a lot of visibility for very little money. Obviously you don't have a free hand to put up any size or colour of sign you like; it needs to be in keeping with the local environment. Your local council's planning department will be able to advise you as to the rules and regulations prevailing in your area.

You could also consider advertising on taxis and buses, where costs are well within a small firm's budget. For information and advice on all outdoor advertising matters visit the Outdoor Advertising Association of Great Britain's website (**www.oaa. org.uk**).

Using other media

Increasingly, media such as television and radio, once the preroga-tive of big business, have filtered down the price band as they have further segmented their own markets with the introduction of digi-tal technology.

CASE STUDY

Barking a Lot, a home-based pet-boarding service, used Spot Runner (**www.spotrunner.com**), an internet-based ad agency franchised in the UK since 2006 that has revolutionised access to TV advertising. For around £300 to create the ad from Spot Runner's ad database and £1,500 in ad time, Barking a Lot ran its ads 144 times over two weekend periods on local cable TV. The quality is achieved by custom-izing from one of the several thousand Spot Runner has created for specific industry segments. Customer calls to Barking a Lot shot up by 20 per cent, and the company has earmarked £20,000 for future TV advertising.

Local radio, TV and cinema   These media are priced out on a cost per listener/viewer basis and you will need to be certain that the audience profile matches that of the market segment you are aiming at. As these media, unlike the written word, are not retained after the event, you will also need to support these media with something like local press advertising or an entry in a directory that you can signpost people to. 'See our entry in *Yellow Pages* and our advertisement in this week's *Cornishman*' is a message that radio, TV and cinema audiences can retain and act on.

The Radio Advertising Bureau (**www.rab.com**) and the Advertising Association (**www.adassoc.org.uk**) give further infor-mation on these media and contact details for professional firms operating in the sector. Rajar (Radio Joint Audience Research Ltd) publishes radio audience statistics quarterly (**www.rajar.co.uk**).

Internet and blogs   Your website (see Chapter 8) is an obvious place to advertise, but the millions of other websites and search engines provide plenty of opportunities to get your message in front of your market. The normal rules of advertising (see 'Promotion and advertising', page 109) apply in cyberspace as in any other medium. These are the main options:

- Search engine advertising comes in two main forms. Pay per click (PPC) is where you buy options on certain keywords so that someone searching for a product will see your 'advertisement' to the side of the natural search results. Google, for example, offers a deal where you only pay when someone clicks on your ad and you can set a daily budget stating how much you are prepared to spend, with $5 a day as the starting price.

- E-mail marketing is just like conventional direct mail sent by post, except this way e-mail is the medium and you buy targeted e-mail databases.

- Display advertising, like advertising in newsprint, takes the form of words and images of varying sizes on websites that people looking for your product are likely to come across. The Audit Bureau of Circulations Electronic (**www.abce.org.uk**) audits website traffic.

- Viral marketing is the process of creating something so hot the recipients will pass it on to friends and colleagues, creating extra demand as it rolls out, for example jokes, games, pictures, quizzes and surveys.

- Blogs are online spaces where the opinions and experiences of particular groups of people are shared. Online communities, MySpace for example, are an extension of this idea. The Community Roundtable (**www.communityroundtable. com**), which has tracked such communities since 2010, said in 2017 that it expected to become a $23 billion industry in its own right by 2019. Wikis, sites such as Wikipedia, are special types of blogs that allow users to contribute and edit content. It's space where you can make sure your product or service gets some visibility. Blogcatalog (**www.blogcatalog. com**) and UK Blog Directory (**www.ukblogdirectory.co.uk**) have blog indexing services to help you search out those appropriate to your business sector.

- Podcasts, where internet users can download sound and video free, are now an important part of the e-advertising armoury.

The Internet Advertising Bureau (**www.iabuk.net**) has a wealth of further information on internet advertising strategies, as well as a directory of agencies that can help with some or all of these methods of promoting your business.

Attending trade shows and exhibitions   Exhibitions are a way to get your product or business idea in front of potential customers face to face. That gives you first-hand knowledge of what people really want, as well as providing a means of gathering market research data on competitors.

UK Trade & Investment (**www.exhibitions.co.uk**) is the UK government organization responsible for all trade promotion and development work. It provides a comprehensive listing of all the consumer, public, industrial and trade exhibitions to be held in major venues around the UK. You can search the list by exhibition type, exhibition date, exhibition organizer or exhibition venue. There is also a complete list of main subject categories and subject headings, the main UK exhibition venues, and exhibition organizers.

The site covers all exhibitions being held in the UK for two or more years ahead. The data is updated regularly twice a month. (See also Appendix 3.)

Creating favourable publicity

This is about presenting yourself and your business in a favourable light to your various 'publics' – at little or no cost. It is also a more influential method of communication than general advertising – people believe editorials.

CASE STUDY

Chantal Coady, the Harrods-trained chocolatier who founded Rococo, was 22 when she wrote the business plan that secured her £25,000 start-up capital. The cornerstone of her strategy to reach an early break-even point lay in a carefully developed public relations campaign. By injecting fashion into chocolates and their packaging, she opened up the avenue to press coverage in such magazines as *Vogue, Harpers & Queen* and the colour supplements. She managed to get over £40,000 worth of column inches of space for the cost of a few postage stamps. This not only ensured a sound launch for her venture but eventually led to a contract from Jasper Conran to provide boxes of chocolates to coordinate with his spring collection. Today Rococo has outlets in Belgravia, Chelsea, Chester, Covent Garden, Marylebone and several hundred stockists around the country. In 2014 Chantal Coady was awarded an OBE in the Queen's Birthday Honours 'for services to chocolate'.

Writing a press release

To be successful, a press release needs to get attention immediately and be quick and easy to digest. Studying and copying the style of the particular paper, magazine or website you want your press release to appear in can make publication more likely:

- *Layout.* The press release should be typed on a single sheet of A4. Use double spacing and wide margins to make the text both more readable and easy to edit. Head it boldly 'Press Release' or 'News Release' and date it.

- *Headline.* This must persuade the editor to read on. If it doesn't attract interest, it will be quickly 'spiked'. Editors are looking for topicality, originality, personality and, sometimes, humour.

- *Introductory paragraph.* This should be interesting and succinct and should summarize the whole story; it could be in the form of a quote and it might be the only piece published. Don't include sales-orientated blurb, as this will offend the journalist's sense of integrity.

- *Subsequent paragraphs.* These should expand and colour the details in the opening paragraph. Most stories can be told in a maximum of three or four paragraphs. Editors are always looking for fillers, so short releases have the best chance of getting published.

- *Contact.* List at the end of the release your name, mobile and other telephone numbers and e-mail address as the contact for further information.

- *Style.* Use simple language and short sentences and avoid technical jargon (except for very specialized technical magazines).

- *Photographs.* Whilst you can send a standard photograph of yourself, your product or anything else relevant to the story being pitched you should also give the journalist concerned the option of having a digital version e-mailed.

- *Follow-up.* Sometimes a follow-up phone call or e-mail to see if editors intend to use the release can be useful, but you must use your judgement on how often to do so.

Find out the name of the editor or relevant writer or reporter and address the envelope to him or her personally. Remember that the target audience for your press release is the professional editor; it is he or she who decides what to print. So the press release is not a 'sales message' but a factual account designed to attract the editor's attention. The following can help you research for appropriate media for your press release:

- BRAD Group (tel: 020 8102 0904; website: **www.brad.co.uk**);

- the Chartered Institute of Public Relations (tel: 020 7631 6900; **www.cipr.org.uk**), which has a free search facility to find a PR consultant either in your area or with expertise in your business sector;

- Marketing Donut (www.marketingdonut.co.uk) provides a complete guide to writing press releases as well as useful ideas on how to handle complaints and bad publicity.

Pricing

Deciding what is a fair price is a problem, especially as value, like beauty, is in the eye of the beholder. This degree of subjectivity means that companies have a great deal of discretion in the area of pricing.

A good-quality product, priced too low, often does not have its quality recognized by the public. There is a strong belief that you get what you pay for.

Competitors: their prices vs value

While it is important to know your costs, this is only one element in the pricing decision. In addition you have to take account of the marketplace, your competition and the way you position the product (eg luxury item).

It is important to make detailed price comparisons with your competitors, using a scoring system such as the one in Table 7.3. You should also experiment with different prices in different market segments to get a feel for what the market will bear.

The higher your score the higher your price could be relative to the competition.

Formulating a pricing strategy

The price you set will directly influence your ability to find a market willing to buy your product or service, and you may have less flexibility in setting that price than you think. These are the factors to keep in mind in arriving at a pricing strategy:

- *Skim vs penetrate.* Two generic pricing strategies need to be decided between before you can fine-tune your plans. Skimming involves setting a price at the high end of what you believe the market will bear. This is a strategy to pursue if you have a very limited amount of product available for sale and would rather 'ration' than disappoint customers. To be successful with this strategy you need to be sure competitors can't just step in and soak up the demand that you have created. Penetration pricing is

Table 7.4 Pricing – how do you compare with the competition?

	Worse			Same	Better		
Product/service attribute	−3	−2	−1	0	+1	+2	+3
Design							
Performance							
Packaging							
Presentation and appearance							
After-sales service							
Availability							
Delivery							
Colour/flavour/odour/touch							
Image							
Specification							
Payment terms							
Others							

the mirror image; prices are set at the low end, whilst being above your costs. The aim here is to grab as much of the market as you can before competitors arrive on the scene and you hopefully lock them out. Dragon Lock, a firm making executive puzzles, who were Cranfield enterprise programme participants, adopted a penetration strategy when they launched their new product. Their product was easy to copy and impossible to patent, so they chose a low price as a strategy to discourage competitors and to swallow up the market quickly. In practice few new businesses will find this a safe strategy to pursue.

- *The danger of setting a low price.* The misconception that new and small firms can undercut established competitors is usually based on a misunderstanding of the meaning and characteristics of overheads, and a failure to appreciate that unit costs fall in proportion to experience. This last point is easy to appreciate if you compare the time needed to perform a task for the first time with the time needed when you are much more experienced (eg changing a fuse, replacing a vacuum cleaner bag, etc). Clearly, you have to take account of what your competitors charge, but remember that price is the easiest element of the marketing mix for an established company to vary. They could follow you down the price curve, forcing you into bankruptcy, far more easily than you could capture their customers with a lower price. And raising prices if you get it wrong is much harder than lowering them.

- *Real-time pricing.* The stock market works by gathering information on supply and demand. If more people want to buy a share than sell it, the price goes up until supply and demand are matched. If the information is perfect (that is, every buyer and seller knows what is going on), the price is optimized. For most businesses this is not a practical proposition. Their customers expect the same price every time for the same product or service – they have no accurate idea what the demand is at any given moment. However, for businesses selling on the internet, computer networks have made it possible to see how much consumer demand exists for a given product at any time. Anyone with a point-of-sale till could do the same, but the reports might come in weeks later. This means online companies could change their prices hundreds of times each day, tailoring them to certain circumstances or certain markets, and so improve profits dramatically. EasyJet, a budget airline, does just this. It prices to fill its planes, and you could pay anything from £30 to £200 (including airport taxes) for the same trip, depending on the demand for that flight. Ryanair and Eurotunnel have similar price ranges based on the basic rule – discounted low fares for early reservations and full fares for desperate late callers!

Distribution and selling

Product, promotion and price though vital elements in the marketing mix are rarely sufficient on their own to conclude a sale. The final steps in the marketing process is to secure a sale, get the product into your customers' hands or have the service fulfilled and get paid.

Selling

Marketing is the thinking process behind selling: in other words finding the right people to buy your product or service and making them aware that you are able to meet their needs at a competitive price. But just having customers knowing you are in the market is not in itself sufficient to make them buy from you. Even if you have a superior product at a competitive price they can escape your net.

The penultimate step in the process of bringing your product to market is getting customers to sign on the dotted line, and that involves selling. This is a process that businesspeople have to use in many situations other than in persuading customers to buy. They have to 'sell' their bank manager the idea that lending them money is worthwhile, their partner the idea of giving up part of the home to the business and eventually employees the idea that working for them is a good career move.

How selling works

There is an erroneous view that salespeople, like artists and musicians, are born not made. Selling can be learnt, improved and enhanced just like any other business activity. First, you need to understand selling's three elements:

- Selling is a *process* moving through certain stages if the best results are to be achieved. First, you need to listen to the customers to learn what they want to achieve from buying your product or service, and then you should demonstrate how you can meet their needs. The next stage is handling questions and objections, which are a good sign, as they show that the customer is sufficiently interested to engage. Finally comes 'closing the sale'. This is little more than asking for the order with a degree of subtlety.

- Selling requires *planning* in that you need to keep records and information on customers and potential customers so you know when they might be ready to buy or reorder.

- Selling is a *skill* that can be learnt and enhanced by training and practice, as shown in the case study below. Chambers of Commerce provide information on sales and other business courses, for members and non-members alike. Coventry Chamber has this online database of courses: www.cwtcov. co.uk/businesscourses/sales-marketing.

CASE STUDY

When Sumir Karayi started up in business in the spare room of his flat in West Ealing, London, he wanted his business to be distinctive. He was a technical expert at Microsoft, and with two colleagues he set up 1E (**www.1e.com**) as a commune aiming to be the top technical experts in their field. The business name comes from the message that appears on your screen when your computer has crashed. Within a year of starting up the team had learnt two important lessons: businesses need leaders not communes if they are to grow fast and prosper; and they need someone to sell.

On the recommendation of an adviser, Karayi went on a selling course and within months had won the first of what became a string of blue-chip clients. The company is now one of the 10 fastest-growing companies in the Thames Valley, with annual turnover approaching £15 million, profits of 30 per cent and partners and reseller partners worldwide.

Using agents

If you are not going to be your business's main salesperson you need to brace yourself for costs of around £50,000 a year to keep a good salesperson on the road, taking salary, commission and expenses into account.

A less risky sales route is to outsource your selling to freelance salespeople. Here you have two options: 1) employ a sales outsourcing company such as Freelancer (freelancer.co.uk) or People per Hour (**www.peopleperhour.com**) that can find and manage a salesperson for you on a short-term basis; or 2) find an agent yourself, ideally with existing contacts in your field, who knows buyers personally and can get off to a flying start from day one. The Manufacturers' Agents' Association (MAA) (**www.themaa.co.uk**) have a directory of commission agents selling in all fields of business. You have to pay £240 for contacting up to 20 agents in one search.

The International Union of Commercial Agents and Brokers (**www.iucab.com**) claim to have 470,000 commercial agents in Europe and North and South America, on their books.

Telesales

Telephone selling is an art in itself. Without the opportunity to see a customer's reaction, demonstrate your product or exhibit your personal abilities you need other techniques. These are the five tips the professionals recommend to succeed:

- Stand or sit up straight, as lounging can make you feel and sound casual.

- Psych yourself up before making calls so you feel alert and positive.

- Smile, as it relaxes the throat muscles and makes your voice sound friendly and unthreatening.

- Speak clearly, using positive language and not words like 'possibly' or 'perhaps'.

- Form a picture of the person you are speaking to in your mind and use the sort of gestures you would if you were in the room with the person. This helps you to get in the mood and your enthusiasm will show through.

If you want to get help with developing your telephone selling skills or find an organization to do the work for you, contact the Call Centre Association (**www.cca.org.uk**).

Getting your product to market

This step in the marketing process is known as distribution. This has become something of a science, as businesses now compete as much on their ability to get products and services to their customers as they do with any other aspect of the marketing process. For example, the miles travelled and consequent carbon footprint in bringing food and clothing products to a customer's door have become the front line in the green consumers battlefield.

If you are selling a service then chances are you deliver it yourself, as you do if you are running a hotel, guest house or restaurant. Otherwise you need to figure out the most cost-effective and reliable way to get your product to your customers. You should also have a back-up; for example, being completely reliant on the Royal Mail came close to bankrupting some small businesses during a recent series of stoppages.

Getting paid

The sale process is not complete until, as one particularly cautious sales director put it, 'the customer has paid, used your product and not died as a consequence'. Although there are theoretically regulations to ensure that big firms pay small businesses promptly there is little evidence they do. Visit the Forum of Private Business (www.fpb.org/your-voice/hall-of-shame) where you can see who are the biggest names for poor payment practices. One of the top three reasons that new businesses fail is because a customer fails to pay up in full or on time. You can take some steps to make sure this doesn't happen to you by setting prudent terms of trade and making sure the customers are creditworthy before you sell to them.

Checking creditworthiness

There is a wealth of information on credit status for both individuals and businesses of varying complexity at prices from £5 for basic information through to £200 for a very comprehensive picture of credit status. So there is no need to trade unknowingly with individuals or businesses that pose a credit risk.

The major agencies that compile and sell personal credit histories and small business information are Experian (**www.experian.co.uk**) or Creditsafe who offer a free one-off trial (**www.creditsafetrial.com/uk**). Between them they offer a comprehensive range of credit reports instantly online, including advice on credit limits and county court judgments (CCJs).

Most of these organizations offer international services covering overseas markets. Experian, for example, provides credit referencing in over 200 countries.

Setting your terms of trade

You need to decide on your terms and conditions of sale and ensure they are printed on your order acceptance stationery. Terms should include when and how you require to be paid and under what conditions you will accept cancellations or offer refunds. How to Law (**www.howtolaw.co/draft-terms-oftrade-392065**) contains information on most aspects of trading relationships.

Cash or cheque   Cash has the attraction in that if you collect as you deliver your product or service you are sure of getting paid and you will have no administrative work in keeping tabs on what is owed you. However, in many business transactions this is not a practical option, unless as in retailing, for example, you are present when the customer buys. A cheque underwritten with a bank guarantee card is as secure as cash, assuming the guarantee is valid. But the cheque will take time to process. In practice you would be wise, until you have checked out the creditworthiness of the customer in question, to await clearance of the cheque before parting with the goods.

You need to be careful in interpreting banking terminology here. Your bank may state that the cheque is 'cleared' when in fact it is only in transit through the system. The only term in bank parlance that means your money is really there is 'given value'. If you have any concerns, ring your bank and ask specifically if you can withdraw funds safely on the cheque in question.

Credit cards Getting paid by credit card makes it easier for customers to buy and certain that you will get your money almost immediately. With a merchant account, as the process of accepting cards is known, as long as you follow the rules and get authorization, the cash less the card company's 1.5 to 3 per cent gets to your bank account the day you charge.

You can get a merchant account without a trading history and if you are operating from home, dependent of course on your credit record. Streamline (www.streamline.com), part of worldpay(uk), or any of the big banks offer services in the field, with set-up costs for a small business from around £150. They claim you can be up and running in a fortnight.

Dealing with delinquents

However prudent your terms of trade and rigorous your credit checks, you will end up with late payers and at worst non-payers. There are ways to deal with them, but it must be said that experience shows that once something starts to go wrong it usually gets worse. There is an old investment saying, 'The first loss is the best loss', that applies here.

Chasing debtors The most cost-effective and successful method of keeping late payers in line is to let them know you know. Nine out of 10 small businesses do not routinely send out reminder letters advising customers that they have missed the payment date. Send out a polite reminder to arrive the day after payment is due, addressed to the person responsible for payments, almost invariably someone in the accounts department if you are dealing with a big organization. Follow this up within five days with a phone call, keeping the pressure up steadily until you are paid.

If you are polite and professional, consistently reminding them of your terms of trade, there is no reason your relationship will be impaired. In any event, the person you sell to may not be the person you chase for payment.

Your starting point is either to make a claim through the courts or to find someone to mediate and help settle your claim. The

Government claim service (www.gov.uk/make-court-claim-for-money) provides information on both these processes.

If you still have difficulty, consider using a debt collection agency. You can find a directory of registered agents on the Credit Service Agency website (**www.csa-uk.com/csa** > Members list).

People, Physical Evidence and Process

The originators of the extra 3Ps (which I introduced at the beginning of this chapter) had in mind the unique problems of marketing intangible services. But as almost every 'product' has a major service element, the 7Ps have been adopted into the mainstream marketing mix analysis.

Understanding the role of People in marketing

Marketing managers often believe that the most important aspects of marketing lie in areas such as creating sensational advertising campaigns, launching innovative and well-designed products or creating brand identity. Not to denigrate these factors in any way, but the single most prevalent reason for a marketing strategy failing lies in its implementation and, by extension, the people who carry out marketing tasks. The selection of people – often known as the fifth 'P' of the marketing mix – to implement strategy and the way in which they are organized contributes the most to your business's success. Unfortunately, people – both individually and collectively – are infinitely variable in their likely responses to situations, making their behaviour hard to predict.

The famous German military strategist Moltke originated a useful statement that applies here: 'No campaign plan survives first contact with the enemy.' This applies here if the word 'enemy' is replaced by 'organization'. However, by understanding and applying the some basic principles and concepts in the areas of leadership, motivation and team-building you can improve an organization's chances of achieving its objectives.

Sometimes something as basic as getting your employees to more properly reflect your customer base can change your business proposition as dramatically as a shift in price, promotion, product or place. In 1989, B&Q, the largest home improvement and garden centre retailer in the UK and Europe and the third largest in the world, made a major change to the profile of its workforce. In response to customer comments that they wanted to be served by someone who had lived in their own home and knew something about home improvements, B&Q set each of its 330 UK stores an objective to employ a workforce that reflects the make-up of the local community, but with an emphasis on employing people over 50. This initiative delivered 18 per cent higher profits, with one sixth of the previous level of staff turnover. Not only are the shareholders happy, the employees are too. The company is one of only eight organizations globally to have won Gallup's Great Workplace Award for three years in a row, scoring 4.24 out of 5, a near 'world class' achievement.

Physical evidence

The physical environment needs to be attractive and appropriate, particularly for retail businesses. So for McDonald's, a play area is a plus, but this would perhaps be inappropriate for a bank. Services as we know are largely intangible when you think about marketing them. However, customers tend to rely on physical cues to help them evaluate a product before they buy it.

To make a service tangible to the customer, marketers develop what is called physical evidence to replace these physical cues in a service. The role of the marketer is to design and implement such tangible evidence, varying it as appropriate in the marketing mix process.

For example ambience can be used to help customers experience the service on offer. In a club loud music and flashing lighting will be the order of the day, whilst in a spa candles and the smell of scent can be used to deliver a calm therapeutic environment. The marketer's task is to make ambience support and enhance the service being sold.

Process

How you deliver your product or service (the process) is another element in the marketing mix that you can vary or improve so as to give your business a competitive edge. Complicated ordering systems, confusing websites and unhelpful returns policies can work against your business. For example customers going on a package holiday will expect a streamlined process to ensure a satisfactory trip – they'll expect to find and book the holiday on a website, get their e-tickets by e-mail, check in and retrieve their baggage without lengthy queues, experience a smooth transit from the airport to the hotel, and receive a swift resolution to any problems.

Process is now such a critical element in the marketing mix that it has attracted a whole new business discipline, business process reengineering (BPR). This reengineering process involves a fundamental rethinking and radical redesign of business processes to achieve dramatic improvements in critical, contemporary measures of performance such as cost, quality, service and speed.

The term 'reengineering' was first introduced in July/August 1990 in the *Harvard Business Review* article 'Reengineering work: Don't automate, obliterate'. The article's author was Michael Hammer, a former computer science professor at the Massachusetts Institute of Technology. Hammer then went on to develop the concept further in a book, *Reengineering the Corporation* written jointly with James Champy.

IBM, for example, embarked on reengineering in 1992. Their goal was to become more customer-centred. At the time, the company had twelve customer relationship processes, including 'solutions delivery', a fully priced contract between IBM and the customer for a complete IT system, covering hardware, software, technical support and consulting services, as well as outsourced products. The redesigned process moved the responsibility for pricing to the frontline sales team, using specially developed pricing software. This removed the two-month delay that formerly occurred when pricing was referred to IBM's headquarters, during which time IBM was in danger of losing customers (especially where time was a critical buying benefit).

Organizations including the Small Business Administration (the US government's body for helping new and small businesses), Walmart, Ford and the city of San Diego have used BPR with success.

Marketing legals

From the claims being made by some businesses and the shoddy treatment handed out to customers you might be forgiven for believing that 'caveat emptor' (let the buyer beware) was the rule of the marketing road: far from it. You can see from Chapter 4 on the laws governing business structure and intellectual property, Chapter 5 on what you can and can't do when it comes to using your property for business purposes and Chapter 12 on employment law that businesses are heavily regulated. The UK government has explicitly recognized the burden of regulations and red tape when it renamed the Department of Trade and Industry the Department for Business, Enterprise and Regulatory Reform.

The following sections deal with the main marketing regulations that you will need to take account of in running a business from home.

Getting a licence or permit

Some businesses, such as those working with food or alcohol, employment agencies, mini-cabs and hairdressers, need a licence or permit before they can set up in business at all. Your local authority planning department can advise you what rules will apply to your business. You can also use the link to government licences and licence applications at www.gov.uk/browse/business/licences. (**www.businesslink.gov.uk** > Your type of business), from which you can use their interactive tool to find out which permits, licences and registrations will apply and where to get more information.

Complying with advertising and descriptive standards

You can't make just any advertising claims you believe to be appropriate for your business. Such claims must be decent, honest and truthful and take into account your wider responsibilities to consumers and anyone else likely to be affected; if you say anything that is misleading or fails to meet any of these tests then you could leave yourself open to being sued.

The government website page on 'Marketing and advertising: the law' (www.gov.uk/marketing-advertising-law) provides details on the current regulations that affect advertising and advertising codes of practice.

Dealing with returns and refunds

Customers buying products are entitled to expect that the goods are 'fit for purpose' in that they can do what they claim and, if the customer has informed you of a particular need, they are suitable for that purpose. The goods also have to be of 'satisfactory quality', that is durable and without defects that would affect performance or prevent enjoyment of the goods. For services you must carry the work out with reasonable skill and care and provide it within a reasonable amount of time. The word 'reasonable' is not defined and is applied in relation to each type of service. So, for example, repairing a shoe might reasonably be expected to take a week, whilst three months would be unreasonable.

If goods or services don't meet these conditions, customers can claim a refund. If customers have altered the goods or services or waited an excessive amount of time before complaining or have indicated in any other way that they have 'accepted', they may not be entitled to a refund but may still be able to claim some money back for a period of up to six years. The government web link at www.gov.uk/accepting-returns-and-giving-refunds provides a summarized guide to the relevant laws in clear plain English.

Distance selling and online trading

Selling by mail order via the internet, television, radio, telephone, fax or catalogue requires that you comply with some additional rules to those concerning the sale of goods and services described above. In summary you have to provide written information, an order confirmation and the chance to cancel the contract. During the cooling-off period, customers have the unconditional right to cancel within seven working days, provided they have informed you in writing by letter, fax or e-mail.

There is, however, a wide range of exemptions to the right to cancel, including accommodation, transport, food, newspapers, audio or video recordings and goods made to a customer's specification. Business Companion, a free service provided by the Chartered Trading Standards Institute, provides an impartial guide to sales contracts, service contracts and digital content (www.businesscompanion.info/en/quick-guides/distance-sales/consumer-contracts-distance-sales).

Protecting customer data

If you hold personal information on a computer on any living person, a customer or employee for example, then there is a good chance you need to register under the Data Protection Act. The rules state that the information held must have been obtained fairly, be accurate, be held only for as long as necessary and be held only for a lawful purpose.

You can check if you are likely to need to register at www.gov.uk/ data-protection/the-data-protection-act.

Getting a consumer credit licence

If you plan to let your customers buy on credit or you hire out or lease products to private individuals or to businesses then you will in all probability have to apply to be licensed to provide credit. If you think you may need to be licensed read the regulations at www. gov.uk/ offering-credit-consumers-law.

International marketing legal issues

For information on marketing legal issues around the world contact:

- The US: Lawyers.com (**www.lawyers.com**)
- The world: Worldwide-tax (see Appendix 3)
- Europe: European Commission (**http://ec.europa.eu/index_en.htm** > Judicial atlas).

Key jobs to do

- Using Table 7.1 assess your position relative to your competitors.
- What do you want to achieve from advertising and promotion and how much do you plan to invest to achieve that?
- Review the media options that could allow you to achieve your goals.
- Prepare a press release for your start-up and assemble a list of media to send it to.
- How will you sell and get your product/service into customers hands?
- Outline the steps you will take to ensure prompt and reliable payment by customers.
- Check out the legal implications of selling and distributing your product or service.
- Review your plans with regard to 'People, physical evidence and process'.

Building and using your website

According to the Centre for Retail Research (www.retailresearch. org) e-commerce is the fastest-growing retail market in Europe. Sales in the UK reached £60 billion in 2016 and are growing at a rate of 17% each year. By the time you read this book online sales will account for over one in five of all retail sales, up from just over one in ten five years ago. The Centre's research shows that many retailers already report that around two-thirds of website browsing takes place on smartphones and tablets, though relatively few browsers conclude their purchase in this way.

The range of products sold online is extending considerably, and with it the way business does business is changing. For example, car buyers used to make five or more visits to a dealer while making up their mind, but now, according to research by the University of Buckingham, 86 per cent do most of their tyre-kicking online, barely making one showroom visit before making their choice. So showrooms have been supplanted by websites and social media work on platforms like Facebook and Twitter.

Making your online presence effective, then, is vitally important. This chapter gives you a good grounding in what you need to know to harness the power of the internet.

Many small businesses start with a presence on the web and quickly become disillusioned with it. This is partly due to reasons explained by the MD of Microsoft UK: 'So many websites are just online brochures – a real e-commerce solution allows customers to buy and sell products and services just as they would in a traditional supply chain.' Moving away from a static, rarely updated website is clearly advisable, yet changing to a regularly updated shopping website such as that maintained by Gap can cost seven figures in Year 1 – Amazon's 'virtual shopping world' came with an eight-figure price tab from the outset!

Website basics

But the web world has come a long way since Amazon and a handful of other brave souls blazed the way. For a home-based business a visible place in cyberspace is all but essential if you want to make any impact on the wider business world. Alongside the greater use of the internet, just as with computers, the price of getting on is dropping sharply and the power and quality of what that lower price will buy are immeasurably improved.

Selling on the internet

Everything from books and DVDs, through computers, medicines and financial services, to vehicles and property is being sold or having a major part of the selling process transacted online. Holidays, airline tickets, software, training and even university degrees are bundled in with the mass of conventional retailers such as Walmart,

Carrefour, Metro and Tesco that fight for a share of the ever-growing online market.

Not all business sectors are penetrated to the same extent by the internet; according to Forrester (**www.forrester.com**), the internet research company, although the sale of clothing and footwear online is a multibillion-dollar business it accounts for only 8 per cent of total sales. Contrast that with computers, where 41 per cent of sales occur online.

According to eMarketer (**www.emarketer.com**), 88 per cent of shoppers prefer online to conventional shopping because they can shop at any time; 66 per cent like being able to shop for more than one product and in many outlets at the same time; 54 per cent claim to be able to find products they can only find online; 53 per cent like not having to deal with salespeople; 44 per cent reckon product information is better online; and, perhaps the most revealing statistic of all, only 40 per cent preferred online to offline because they expected to find lower prices.

Doing it yourself

Whilst selling online may be a sound way into market you still have a choice. Tag along with someone else, much as you would if you were selling a product into a shop; or you could set up shop yourself. The procedures of selling on the internet, aside from having your own website, require systems for showing and describing the goods and services on offer, as well as ordering, payment and fulfilment facilities. These topics are the subject of the other sections in this chapter.

The main advantages to setting up your own selling procedures are that you have greater control over where your products appear, which can be important to people passionate about their venture, and you get to keep the whole profit margin rather than sharing it with others in the channels of distribution. In varying ways you could end up passing on up to a quarter of your margin in this way. Against that, setting up your own online sales operation will require several thousand pounds of investment up front and a continuing stream of investment to keep your systems up to date, much as a retailer would need new shop fittings.

Piggybacking on other websites

There is, however, another way of getting your goods and services to internet markets: piggybacking on established, ready-built e-tail platforms. The best known of these is eBay, which is covered in Appendix 2. There are, however, dozens of other sites that you can sell on, with or without going through the auction process. Between them the UK sales generated through sales on other providers' websites are estimated to be around £2 billion, up from £600 million in 2004.

The other way of getting your goods and services to internet markets is to piggyback on established, ready-built e-tail platforms. These are some of the most popular sites:

- Amazon (www.amazon.co.uk/gp/seller/sell-your-stuff.html) will list, take payment, insure and, if required, pick, pack and deliver your products through its distribution system. Amazon provides tools to make it easy for you to upload inventory onto the website and you can have an unlimited number of listings to sell to its millions of customers. No fixed-term contract exists and charges depend on the type of products sold.

- eBay (http://pages.ebay.co.uk/businesscentre) isn't just a place to pick up a bargain and sell last year's ski gear when you move on to a snowboard. Sure, that's one side of the businesses. The other is the 160,000 or so people in the UK, Power Sellers as they're known, who make anything from a few hundred to tens or even hundreds of thousands of pounds. You can become a Bronze-level Power Seller when your minimum value of sales reaches £750.

- IBidFree.com (www.ibidfree.com) was set up by Shane McCormack, a former eBay seller, with the proposition that you can have all the features of eBay but for free. IBidFree.com was created as a perfect opportunity for the person working from home trying to market their products without all their profits being swallowed up by charges and fees. The rules are few and, unlike eBay sellers, sellers are encouraged to place a link in their auctions back to their own websites. They're also allowed to directly e-mail each other to allow for better communication.

Other reasons why you need a website

You might be forgiven for thinking that a website is just for those selling on the internet; that, however, is just one of the many uses a website can be put to. These are some other valuable uses you can put your website to:

- *Generating advertising revenue.* Once you have a website you have 'readers' whom other people will pay to reach, just as they would if you had a hard-copy magazine. You can sell space on your website yourself, but you should be too busy running your business to get diverted with this type of distraction. The easiest way to get advertising revenue is to get someone else to do the hard work. Google Adsense (**www.google.com/adsense**), for example, matches advertisements to your site's content and you earn money every time someone clicks one. You can check out the dozens of other affiliate advertising schemes such as FastClick Ad Network, Click Bank and Revenue Pilot at Internet Ad Sales (**www.internetadsales.com**), a site that reviews all online advertising products and trends.

- *Recruitment.* When you start to grow your business you can advertise for staff on your own website. In that way you can be sure applicants will know something of your business and you could cut out most of the costs of recruitment.

- *Market research.* By running surveys (see Chapter 3, 'Carrying out DIY research', page 45) you can find out more about your customers' needs, check out if new products or services would appeal to them and monitor complaints and so prevent them becoming problems.

- *FAQ.* Businesses get dozens of phone calls and letters asking essentially the same questions. By having an FAQ (frequently asked questions) section on your website you can head off most of those enquiries and save time and money.

CSG Network (www.csgnetwork.com/csgfaqsgen.html) has a free FAQ generator. Just enter the questions you receive frequently and their respective answers, click the generate button and the script outputs a complete FAQ page for you.

- *Selling online 24/7 and 365 without being there.* Once you have set up your shop front, got your shopping cart, arranged a payment system and organized fulfilment all you have to do is 'stack the shelves'.

Choosing an internet service provider (ISP)

An internet service provider keeps you connected to the internet. Without a fast, reliable, cost-effective and well-supported service your website may not realize its full potential. Speeds of 20 Mbps are about the minimum to work effectively online. Ideally superfast broadband – 50 Mbps and upwards – is desirable with unlimited usage. Set-up costs, monthly charges, length of contract and support are also factors to look out for.

Broadband Finder (**www.broadband-finder.co.uk**) and Broadband Checker (**www.broadbandchecker.co.uk**) provide information and rate ISPs according to your criteria.

Checking out your competitors' online presence

To get some idea of what to include on and exclude from your website check out your competitors' websites and those of any other small businesses that you rate highly. You can also get some pointers from the Web Marketing Association's WebAwards (**www. webaward.org** > Winners > Search Winners Database), where you can see the best websites in each business sector, and the Good Web Guide (**www.thegoodwebguide.co.uk**), whose site contains thousands of detailed website reviews.

Getting a storefront, shopping cart and fulfilment system

If you were selling from a shop you would set out your window display and have a basket for customers to drop their shopping into prior to checking out and paying. Your online store has much the same features, with buttons and boxes around your order page allowing customers to select colours, sizes and quantities, place their order, pay and track the progress of their delivery. You need to decide what you want your online store to do, as with linkages to other services you can arrange payment, delivery and even stock reordering, all of which come at an increasing price, eating into your profit margin.

You can choose between dozens of companies in the field such as Altcom (http://altcom.co.uk) and ekmpowershop (www.ekmpowershop.com) which offer turnkey online shop fronts from £19.99 a month. GoECart (www.goecart.com), founded in 2000, doesn't charge any listing or transaction fees and a merchant can open a store for around £600 a month. That fee includes all you need: a shop front, trolley buying system, payment acceptance, fraud protection, compete order and stock management and Web traffic statistics. This fee covers up to five admin users. GoECart also claims to have the most search-engine-friendly architecture.

Getting paid online: PayPal et al

If you are going to trade on the internet then some form of online payment such as a credit card merchant account is essential. An alternative is one of a new breed of businesses tailored expressly for the internet. The leader of the pack is PayPal (**www.paypal.com**). They claim to have over 100 million accounts around the world, and firms using their services get an average of 14 per cent uplift in sales.

Using PayPal you can in effect get a merchant account with all major credit and debit cards in one bundle without set-up fees or a lengthy application process and start accepting payments within minutes. PayPal isn't free; you pay 20p per transaction and a sliding charge ranging from 3.4 per cent if your transactions amount to £1,500 in any month down to 1.4 per cent if sales are above £55,000 a month.

Other similar services are offered by WorldPay (**www.worldpay.com**) and Durango (www.durango-direct.com) offer similar services. You can keep up with all the various services by reading the *Merchant*

Account Forum (**www.merchantaccountforum.com**), a free newsletter set up by Richard Adams, who was so frustrated in his efforts to set up a merchant account for his first online business he decided to set up a site to review merchant accounts.

Getting seen

Nine out of 10 visitors reach internet sites via a search engine or equivalent so you need to fill the first page with 'key terms' that search engines can latch on to.

This process is known as search engine optimisation (SEO), where your website is 'optimised' so that it improves its position in search engine rankings. It also helps if you know a little about how search engines work.

Finding a search engine

Whilst Google is one of the best-known search engines it is certainly not the only one, nor is it necessarily the best for every type of business. The Search Engine Guide (**www.searchengineguide.com** has a directory that) lists search engines by business sector; some of them may be better for your products and services than the market leaders. Search Engine Watch (**www.searchenginewatch.com**) provides tips and information that can help website owners to improve their likelihood of being found in search engines.

You can track user satisfaction with search engines, a good indication of whether or not it's worth investing effort in getting on to their site, at the American Customer Satisfaction Index (**www.theacsi.org**), established by the University of Michigan. The latest survey ranks Google top at 84% satisfaction, up 8% from 2015 and 9% ahead of Bing, its nearest competitor.

Getting listed

If you want to be sure of getting listed appropriately in a search engine, first make a list of the words that you think a searcher is most likely to use when looking for your products or services.

For example, a repair garage in Penzance could include keywords such as 'car', 'repair', 'cheap', 'quick', 'reliable', 'insurance', 'crash' and 'Penzance' in the home page to pull in searchers looking for a competitive price and a quick repair. As a rule of thumb, for every 300 words you need a keyword or phrase to appear between 10 and 15 times. Search engines thrive on content, so the more relevant content the better. You can use products such as that provided by Good Keyword (**www.goodkeyword.com**), which has a free Windows software program to help you find words and phrases relevant to your business and provides statistics as to how frequently those are used. Keywords Strategy Studio is their paid-for product, priced at £38, which has several additional filters and tools to help you refine your keyword lists. There is a try before you buy option on site.

Search engine algorithms also like important, authoritative and prestigious terms. So whilst you may not be able to boast 'by Royal Appointment', if you can get your press releases quoted in the *Financial Times*, your comments included in postings on popular blogs or your membership of professional institutes and associations into your home page your chances of being seen will rise accordingly.

Next on the list of strategies is to get your website linked to other sites with related but not competing information. So if you are selling garden pots, websites selling plants, gardening tools, fencing or compost are likely to have people hitting their sites who are of value to you. Being linked to dozens of other sites improves your chances of being spotted by a search engine. You can offer the sites in question a link to your site as a quid pro quo and you could both benefit from the relationship.

Using a submissions service

You can build words into your website to help search engines find you. You can also go to a professional. Submission services such as Submit Express (www.submitexpress.co.uk), Rank4u (www.rank4u.co.uk) and Wordtracker (www.wordtracker.com) have optimization processes that aim to move you into the top ten ranking in key search engines. 'Aim' is the important word here. These services don't guarantee anything, so the proof of the pudding is in the eating. If it works, you can always go back for a second helping.

Payment methods vary. For example, Rank4u has a no-placement, no-fee deal where you pay only after it's achieved the positioning you want. This service isn't on offer to every business all the time, so you need to check it out yourself. 123 Ranking (www.123ranking.co.uk) has optimization packages aimed at small and new businesses from £344 per annum. Search Engine Guide (www.searchengineguide. com; go to Search Engine Marketing) has a guide to all aspects of search engine marketing.

Paying for placement

If you don't want to wait for search engines to find your website, you can pay to have your Web pages included in a search engine's directory. That won't guarantee you a position; so, for example, if your page comes up at 9,870 in Google's list then the chance of a customer slogging his way to your page is zero. The only way to be sure you appear early in the first page or two of a search is to advertise in a paid placement listing. Major search engines such as Google AdWords (www.google.co.uk/adwords) and Microsoft's Bing (https://secure.bingads.microsoft.com) invite you to bid on the terms you want to appear for, by way of a set sum per click.

If you have a compelling proposition, you may persuade a search engine to offer you a pay-for-performance deal, where it takes a share of the profits you make from having extra visibility. You can check out companies working this way at http://pay-for-performance-seo.topseosratings.com.

Tracking traffic

A wealth of information is available on who visits your website: where they come from in terms of geography, search engine and search term used; where they enter your website (homepage, FAQs, product specifications, price list, order page) and how long they spend in various parts of your website. That information is aside from the basic information you automatically receive from orders placed, enquiries made or e-mail contacts.

You can use visitor data to tweak your website and content to improve the user experience and so achieve your goals for the website. For example, you may find that lots of visitors are entering your website via a link found on a search engine that takes them to an inappropriate section of your site, say the price list, when you want them to start with the benefits of your product or success stories. By changing the key words on which your website is optimized, or by putting more visible links through the site, you can drive traffic along your chosen path.

Check that your website is accessible and user-friendly at all times. Many people are impatient when it comes to web usage, and if a website doesn't work immediately, go elsewhere!

A good way to measure the success of your website is to make use of the free Google Analytics package available from the Google website (https://analytics.google.com). Google Analytics tracks the traffic that comes to your website from all referrers – e-mail marketing, search engines, pay-per-click downloads, display advertising and links from PDF documents. In doing so, Google Analytics gathers and reports data that shows how well your website is doing and enables you to make sense of all this information. The package also serves up statistics that provide details about the people who visit your website and allows you to track your landing page quality, and to see the specific pages that your visitors are viewing.

Going mobile

The Internet Society Global Report (2015) lists the following as the compelling reasons for paying attention to mobiles in your marketing and the main reason that the world online population will grow from 3 bn to 4 bn before 2020.

- 192 countries have active 3G mobile networks, which cover almost 50% of the global population and 4G and 5G are already in much of the developed world.

- Smartphone sales are the majority of mobile handsets sold worldwide; tablet sales will soon exceed total PC sales.

- There are well over a million apps available, which have been downloaded more than 100 billion times.

- Time spent using apps exceeds time spent on mobile browsers, and in the US, at least, exceeds time spent on desktop and mobile browsers combined.

- Mobile internet has already leapfrogged fixed access in many countries because of limitations in the coverage of the fixed network. In Kenya and other parts of Africa the farming and fishing sectors have been given a significant boost from access to pricing intelligence and market presence delivered on mobile networks.

Google's Webmaster site has the lowdown on how to make the move to mobile and the mistakes to avoid (https://developers.google.com/webmasters/mobile-sites/get-started).

Designing your website

Good website design is essential, with short loading time (use graphics, not photographs), short-and-sweet legible text and an attractive layout. Research indicates that, within three clicks, visitors must be captivated or they will leave, so clear signposting is necessary, including a menu on every page so that visitors can return to the home page or move to other sections in just one click.

Promote your website by acquiring links on other commercial websites, using keywords to ensure you can be found, and by promoting outside the internet – feature your website address on all products and publications. Fill your home page with regularly updated 'success stories', give discounts to first-time buyers and ask customers to 'bookmark' your site or add it to their list of 'favourites' on their browser. You could also try partnering with manufacturers and distributors in related business fields.

Dos and don'ts in website design

Dos

- *Think about design.* Create a consistent visual theme, grouping elements together so that your readers can follow the information you are presenting easily.

- *Prepare your content.* It should be focused on the needs of your target audience and be credible, original, current and varied.

- *Plan your site navigation.* Your pages need to be organized intuitively so they are easy to navigate.

- *Consider usability and accessibility.* Use graphics sparingly as not everyone has super access speeds. Optimize your HTML, especially on your home page, to minimize file size and download time by removing excess spaces, comments, tags and commentary.

- *Optimize for searching.* Build in keywords, tags and markers so your site will be found easily.

Don'ts

- *Have long pages.* Content beyond the first 1.5 to 2 page lengths is typically ignored.

- *Have pointless animations.* Many are distracting and poorly designed in terms of colour and fonts, and add unnecessarily to file size, slowing down your readers' searches.

- *Use the wrong colours.* Colour choice is crucial; black text on a white background is the easiest to read whilst other colours such as reds and greens are harder to read. Check out Visibone's website (**www.visibone.com/colorblind**) for a simulation of the web designer's colour palette of browser-safe colours.

- *Have stale information anywhere, especially on your home page.* Nothing turns readers off so much as seeing information that relates to events long gone, recipes for Christmas pudding at Easter, for example.

- *Waste your readers' time.* Making readers register on your site may be useful to you, but unless you have some compelling value to offer don't. If you absolutely must, keep registration details to a couple of lines of information.

Doing it yourself

You probably already have a basic website writing tool with your office software. If you use Microsoft Office, you can find free web design tools in the Publisher section of your software. Basic stuff, but it gets you up and running.

You can also find hundreds of packages from £50 to around £500 that, with varying amounts of support, help you create your own website. Also take a look at these sites:

- BT Business (http://business.bt.com) has dozens of articles on how to improve your website design.

- Top Ten Reviews (www.top10bestwebsitebuilders.co.uk) provides a regular report on the best website creation templates rated by ease of use, help and support, value for money and a score of other factors. The best buy as I write this edition is available on an indefinite free trial, albeit on a slightly cut-down basis. You won't get an e-commerce facility unless you upgrade to a plan costing £6.39 a month.

- Web Wiz Guide (www.webwiz.co.uk/kb/website-design) has a tutorial covering the basics of Web page design and layout.

More expensive options come with access to an editor, hours of webmaster assistance per month, a domain name, hosting, e-mail and more.

Getting outside help

There are literally thousands of consultants who claim to be able to create a website for you. Prices start from £300, where an off-the-peg website package will be tweaked slightly to meet your needs, to around £5,000 to get something closer to tailor-made for you. The Directory of Design Consultants (**www.designdirectory. co.uk** and Web Design Directory (**www.web-design-directory-uk. co.uk**) list hundreds of consultants, some one-person operations and others somewhat larger. You can look at their websites to see if you like what they do. Web Design Directory has some useful pointers on choosing a designer. If you are working within a set budget you could consider auctioning off your web design project. With sites such as Get a Freelancer (**www.getafreelancer.com**), you state how much you are prepared to pay, with a description of the project, and freelancers around the world bid under your price, with the lowest bidder winning.

Key jobs to do

- Check out which of your competitors sells online and how important that route to market is for them.

- Look in detail at other websites in your market sector and identify what you like and don't like about them. Build those findings into your own website design.

- Determine your SEO (Search Engine Optimisation) strategy to maximize your website's visibility.

- Decide what you want your website to do – inform – communicate or fulfil orders and accept payment.

- With that in mind review the options for getting your website designed.

- Review the best options for using social media, starting by checking out your competitors' websites.

Doing the numbers

Business is not just about numbers, much as say football is not only about goals. But as with football anyone watching or playing will want to know the score, periodically at least; and at the end of the day winners have higher scores than losers.

Throughout this chapter a simplified version of the layout of accounting reports and their underlying rules and principles has been used for ease of explaining them. The latest rules, Financial Reporting Standards for Smaller Entities, can be downloaded from the Financial Reporting Council's website (www.frc.org.uk).

Keeping the books

While bad luck plays a part in some business failures, a lack of reliable financial information plays a part in most. All that needs to be done is for the information on income and expenditure to be recorded and organized so that the financial picture becomes clear. The way financial information is recorded is known as 'bookkeeping'.

But it is not just the owner of a company who needs these financial facts. Bankers, shareholders and tax inspectors will be unsympathetic audiences to anyone without well-documented facts to back them up. Keeping even the simplest of records – perhaps as little as writing down the source of a deposit on a slip or in your cheque book – and recording the event in a book or ledger will make your relations with tax inspectors and bankers go much more smoothly.

If you just pile your bills, receipts and cheque stubs into an old shoebox and take it to an accountant at the end of the year (or when you run out of cash), it will cost a lot more to get your accounts done than if you had kept good records in the first place. In addition, you will have had a stressful period of being unsure of how well or badly you are doing.

The accounts you have to keep

There are no rules about the format to be used for a bookkeeping system. Records can be on paper, in ledgers or on a computer. You must, however, be able to account for where all your business income came from and who you have paid and for what services. If you are registered for VAT (see page 177) you will also need to keep a record of the VAT element of each invoice and bill and produce a summary for each accounting period covered by your VAT returns.

Starting simple

If you are doing books by hand and don't have a lot of transactions, the single-entry method is the easiest acceptable way to go. This involves writing down each transaction in your records once, preferably on a ledger sheet. Receipts and payments should be kept and summarized daily, weekly or monthly, in accordance with the needs of the business. At the end of the year, the 12 monthly summaries are totalled up – you are ready for tax time.

This simple record system is known as a 'cash book' – an example is given in Table 9.1.

In the left-hand four columns, the month's receipts are entered as they occur, together with some basic details and the amount. At the head of the first column is the amount of cash brought forward from the preceding month.

On the right, expenses are listed in the same way. The total of receipts for the month is £ ($/€) 1,480.15 and that for expenses is £ ($/€) 672.01. The difference between these two figures is the amount of cash now in the business. As the business shown in Table 9.1 has brought in more cash than it has spent, the figure is higher than the amount brought forward at the beginning of the month. The figure of £808.14 is the amount that is 'brought down' to be 'brought forward' to the next month. The total of the month's payments and the amount 'carried down' are equal to the sum of all the receipts in the left-hand columns.

If there are a reasonably large number of transactions, it would be sensible to extend this simple cash book to include a basic analysis of the figures – this variation is called an 'analysed cash book'. An example of the payments side of an analysed cash book is shown in Table 9.2 (the receipts side is similar, but with different categories). You can see at a glance the receipts and payments, both in total and by main category. This breakdown lets you see, for example, how much is being spent on each major area of your business or who your most important customers are. The payments are the same as in Table 9.1, but now we can see how much we have spent on stock, vehicles and telephone expenses. The sums total both down the amount columns and across the analysis section to arrive at the same amount: £/$/€672.01. This is both a useful bit of management information and essential for your tax return.

If you are taking or giving credit, you will need to keep more information than the cash book – whether it is analysed or not. You will need to keep copies of paid and unpaid sales invoices and

Table 9.1 A simple cash-book system

		Receipts					Payments	
Date	Name	Details	Amount £/$/€		Date	Name	Details	Amount £/$/€
1 June	Balance	Brought forward	450.55		4 June	Gibbs	Stock purchase	310.00
4 June	Anderson	Sales	175.00		8 June	Gibbs	Stock purchase	130.00
6 June	Brown	Sales	45.00		12 June	ABC Telecoms	Telephone charges	55.23
14 June	Smith & Co	Refund on returned	137.34		18 June	Colt Rentals	Vehicle hire	87.26
17 June	Jenkins	Sales	190.25		22 June	VV Mobiles	Mobile phone	53.24
20 June	Hollis	Sales	425.12		27 June	Gibbs	Stock purchase	36.28
23 June	Jenkins	Sales	56.89					672.01
					30 June	Balance	Carried down	808.14
			1,480.15					1,480.15
1 July	Balance	Brought foward	808.14					

Table 9.2 Example of an analysed cash book

| | Payments | | Amount | | Analysis | | |
Date	Name	Details	£/$/€	Stocks	Vehicles	Telephone	Other
4 June	Gibbs	Stock purchase	310.00	310.00			
8 June	Gibbs	Stock purchase	130.00	130.00			
12 June	ABC Telecoms	Telephone charges	55.23			55.23	
18 June	Colt Rentals	Vehicle hire	87.26		87.26		
22 June	VV Mobiles	Mobile phone	53.24			53.24	
27 June	Gibbs	Stock purchase	36.28	36.28			
Totals			672.01	476.28	87.26	108.47	

the same for purchases, as well as your bank statements. The bank statements should then be 'reconciled' to your cash book to tie everything together. For example, the bank statement for the example given in Table 9.1 should show £/$/€808.14 in the account at the end of June. Figure 9.1 outlines how this works.

Building a system

If you operate a partnership, trade as a company or plan to get big, then you will need a double-entry bookkeeping system. This calls for a series of day books, ledgers, a journal, a petty cash book and a wages book, as well as a number of files for copies of invoices and receipts.

The double-entry system requires two entries for each transaction – this provides built-in checks and balances to ensure accuracy. Each transaction requires an entry as a debit and as a credit. This may sound a little complicated, but you only need to get a general idea.

A double-entry system is more complicated and time-consuming if done by hand, since everything is recorded twice. If done manually,

Figure 9.1 A simple system of business records

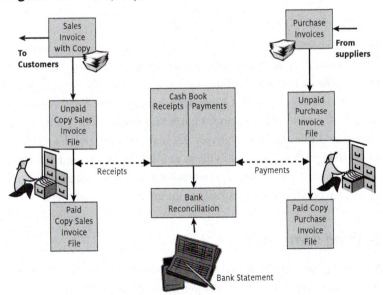

Table 9.3   An example of a double-entry ledger

General Journal of Andrew's Bookshop			
Date	Description of entry	Debit (£/$/€)	Credit (£/$/€)
10th July	Rent expense	250	
	Cash		250

the method requires a formal set of books – journals and ledgers. All transactions are first entered into a journal and then 'posted' (written) on a ledger sheet – the same amount is written down in two different places. Typical ledger accounts include those for titled income, expenses, assets and liabilities (debts).

To give an example, a payment of rent in a double-entry system might result in two separate journal entries – a debit for an expense of, say, £/$/€250 and a corresponding credit of £/$/€250 – a double entry (see Table 9.3). The debits in a double-entry system must always equal the credits. If they don't, you know there is an error somewhere. So double entry allows you to balance your books, which you can't do with the single-entry method.

Paper-based bookkeeping systems

If you expect to have fewer than 50 transactions each month, either buying or selling, then you can simply use analysis paper, either loose or in books that are available from any larger stationer. These are sheets of paper A3 size, with a dozen or so lined columns already drawn so you can enter figures and extend your analysis, as shown in Table 9.2. Alternatively you can buy a manual accounting system with a full set of ledgers and books for around £/$/€20 from Hingston Publishing Co (**www.hingston-publishing.co.uk**) or Collins Account Books, available from most larger stationers.

Getting some help

You don't have to do the bookkeeping yourself, though if you do for the first year or so you will get a good insight into how your business works from a financial perspective. There are a number of ways in which you can reduce or even eliminate the more tedious aspects of the task.

Bookkeeping and accounting software

With the cost of a basic computerized bookkeeping and accounting system starting at barely £50, and a reasonable package costing between £200 and £500, it makes good sense to plan to use such a system from the outset. Key advantages include having no more arithmetical errors and speedy preparation of VAT returns, and preparing your accounts at the year end will be a whole lot simpler.

Sourcing accounting and bookkeeping software There are dozens of perfectly satisfactory basic accounting and bookkeeping software packages on the market. The leading providers are:

- Mamut (www.visma.co.uk/mamutone), a product from Visma, offers a range of accounting package systems, starting with its Mamut One Office Accounting costing £407 including VAT and a year's support.

- QuickBooks (www.intuit.co.uk/quickbooks) offers a range of products from around £8 a month up to £30 a month for a system that can automate the VAT return as well as help with budgeting, purchase orders and stock-holding. The software is cloud-based.

- SageOne (http://shop.sage.co.uk) is Sage's entry-level product. It costs £5 a month plus VAT, with more sophisticated desktop-based products available for a one-off purchase price of up to £619 plus VAT.

Using a bookkeeping service

Professional associations such as the International Association of Bookkeepers (IAB) (tel: 01732 897750; website: **www.iab.org.uk**), the Institute of Certified Bookkeepers (tel: 0845 060 2345; website: **www.book-keepers.org**), offer free matching services to help small businesses find a bookkeeper to suit their particular needs. Expect to pay upwards of £20 an hour for services that can be as basic as simply recording the transactions in your books, through to producing accounts, preparing the VAT return or doing the payroll.

Hiring an accountant

If you plan to trade as a partnership or limited company or look as though you will be making over £30,000 net profit before tax you may be ready to hire an accountant to look after your books.

Finding an accountant Personal recommendation from someone in your business network is the best starting point to finding an accountant. Meet the person and if you think you could work with him or her take up references, as you would with anyone you employ, and make sure he or she is a qualified member of one of the professional bodies. The Association of Chartered Certified Accountants (**www.accaglobal.com**) the Institute of Chartered Accountants (**www.icaew.com**) or the American Institute of CPAS (**www.aicpa.org**) have online directories of qualified accountants, which you can search by name, location, the business sector you are in or any specific accountancy skills you are looking for.

The business accounting reports

Accounting is not exactly a new subject. Luca Pacioli wrote what was in essence the world's first accounting book over 500 years ago.

As a business owner you need to keep a handle on these important financial aspects of your business: cash flow, profitability, and assets and liabilities. With that information you can steer any venture safely to your chosen destination.

Measuring cash flow

There is a saying in business that profit is vanity and cash flow is sanity. Both are necessary, but in the short term, and often that is all that matters to a new business as it struggles to get a foothold in the shifting sands of trading, cash flow is life or death.

Making assumptions

The future is impossible to predict with great accuracy but it is possible to anticipate likely outcomes and be prepared to deal with events by building in a margin of safety. The starting point for making a projection is to make some assumptions about what you want to achieve and testing those for reasonableness.

Take the situation of High Note, a home-based business being established to sell sheet music, small instruments and CDs to schools and colleges, which will expect trade credit and members of the public who will pay cash. The owner plans to invest £/$/€ 10,000 and to borrow £/$/€10,000 from a bank on a long-term basis. The business will be run out of a double garage adjoining the home and will require £/$/€11,500 to install windows, heat, light, power, storage shelving and a desk and chairs. A further £/$/€ 1,000 will be needed for a computer, software and printer. That should leave around £/$/€7,500 to meet immediate trading expenses such as buying in stock and spending £/$/€1,500 on initial advertising. It is hoped that customers' payments will start to come in quickly to cover other expenses such as some wages for bookkeeping, administration and fulfilling orders. Sales in the first six months are expected to be £/$/€60,000 based on negotiations already in hand, plus some cash sales that always seem to turn up. The rule of thumb in the industry seems to be that stock is marked up by 100 per cent, so £/$/€30,000 of bought-in goods sell on for £/$/€60,000.

Forecasting cash needs

On the basis of the above assumptions it is possible to make the cash flow forecast set out in Table 9.4. It has been simplified, and some elements such as VAT and tax have been omitted for ease of understanding.

The maths in Table 9.4 is straightforward; the cash receipts from various sources are totalled, as are the payments. Taking one from the other leaves a cash surplus or deficit for the month in question. The bottom row shows the cumulative position. So, for example, whilst the business had £/$/€2,450 cash left at the end of April, taking the cash deficit of £/$/€1,500 in May into account by the end of May only £/$/€950 (£/$/€2,450 – £/$/€1,500) cash remains.

Table 9.4 High Note six-month cash flow forecast (£/$/€)

Month	Apr	May	June	July	Aug	Sept	Total
Receipts:							
Sales	4,000	5,000	5,000	7,000	12,000	15,000	48,000
Owner's cash	10,000						
Bank loan	10,000						
Total cash in	24,000	5,000	5,000	7,000	12,000	15,000	
Payments:							
Purchases	5,500	2,950	4,220	7,416	9,332	9,690	39,108
Rates, electricity, heat, telephone, internet, etc	1,000	1,000	1,000	1,000	1,000	1,000	
Wages	1,000	1,000	1,000	1,000	1,000	1,000	
Advertising	1,550	1,550	1,550	1,550	1,550	1,550	
Fixtures/fittings	11,500						
Computer, etc	1,000						
Total cash out	21,550	6,500	7,770	10,966	12,882	13,240	
Monthly cash surplus/(deficit)	2,450	(1,500)	(2,770)	(3,966)	(882)	1,760	
Cumulative cash balance	**2,450**	**950**	**(1,820)**	**(5,786)**	**(6,668)**	**(4,908)**	

Avoiding overtrading

In the example in Table 9.4 the business has insufficient cash, based on the assumptions made. An outsider, a banker perhaps, would look at the figures in August and see that the faster sales grew the greater the cash flow deficit became. We know, using our crystal ball, that the position will improve from September and that if we can only hang on in there for a few more months we should eliminate our cash deficit and perhaps even have a surplus. Had we made the cash flow projection at the outset and raised more money, perhaps by way of an overdraft, spent less on refurbishing the garage or set a more modest sales goal, hence needing less stock and advertising, we would have had a sound business. The figures indicate a business that is trading beyond its financial resources, a condition known as overtrading, anathema to bankers the world over.

You can do a number of 'what if' projections to fine-tune your cash flow projections using a spreadsheet. SME Toolkit has a free Excel spreadsheet at www.smetoolkit.org.

Estimating start-up cash requirements

The example in Table 9.4 takes the cash flow projection out six months. You should project your cash needs forward for between 12 and 18 months. Make a number of projections using differing assumptions, for example seeing what will happen if you get fewer orders or people take longer to buy or adapting your office costs more. Finally, when you arrive at a projection you have confidence in and you believe you can justify the cash needed, build that figure into the financing needs section of your business plan.

If that projection calls for more money than you are prepared to invest or raise from outside don't just steam ahead and hope for the best. The result could well mean that the bank pulls the plug on you when you are within sight of the winning post. There is a useful spreadsheet that will prompt you through the most common costs on the BusPlans website (www.bplans.co.uk).

Calculating profit

You may by now be concerned about the financial situation at High Note. After all, the business has sold £/$/€60,000 worth of goods that it only paid £/$/€30,000 for, so it has a substantial profit margin to play with. Whilst £/$/€39,108 has been paid to suppliers, only £/$/€30,000 of goods at cost have been sold, meaning that £/$/€9,108 worth of instruments, sheet music and CDs are still in our stock. A similar situation exists with sales. We have billed for £/$/€60,000 but only been paid for £/$/€48,000; the balance is owed by debtors. The bald figure at the end of the cash flow projection showing High Note to be in the red to the tune of £/$/€4,908 seems to be missing some important facts.

The difference between profit and cash

Cash is immediate and takes account of nothing else. Profit, however, is a measurement of economic activity that considers other factors that can be assigned a value or cost. The accounting principle that governs profit is known as the 'matching principle', which means that income and expenditure are matched to the time period in which they occur.

So for High Note the profit and loss account for the first six months will be as shown in Table 9.5.

Structuring the profit and loss account

This account is set out in more detail for a business in order to make it more useful when it comes to understanding how a business is performing. For example, though the profit shown in our worked example is £/$/€8,700, in fact it would be rather lower. As money has been borrowed to finance cash flow there would be interest due, as there would be on the longer-term loan of £/$/€10,000.

In practice we have four levels of profit:

- Gross profit is the profit left after all costs related to making what you sell are deducted from income.

Table 9.5 Profit and loss account for High Note for the six months April–September

	£/$/€	£/$/€
Sales		60,000
Less cost of goods to be sold		30,000
Gross profit		30,000
Less expenses:		
Heat, electricity, telephone, internet, etc	6,000	
Wages	6,000	
Advertising	9,300	
Total expenses		21,300
Profit before tax, interest and depreciation charges		8,700

- Operating profit is what's left after you take away the operating expenses from the gross profit.
- Profit before tax is what is left after deducting any financing costs.
- Profit after tax is what is left for the owners to spend or reinvest in the business.

For High Note this could look much as set out in Table 9.6.

You can find a spreadsheet to help you construct your own profit and loss account at SME Toolkit (www.smetoolkit.org – search for Income Statement Template).

Balancing assets and liabilities

So far in our example the money spent on 'capital' items such as the £/$/€12,500 spent on a computer and on converting the garage to suit business purposes have been ignored, as has the £/$/€9,108 worth of sheet music, etc remaining in stock waiting to be sold and the £/$/€12,000 of money owed by customers who have yet to pay up. An assumption has to be made about where the cash deficit will

Table 9.6 High Note extended profit and loss account

	£/$/€
Sales	60,000
Less the cost of goods to be sold	30,000
Gross profit	30,000
Less operating expenses	21,300
Operating profit	8,700
Less interest on bank loan and overdraft	600
Profit before tax	8,100
Less tax	1,377
Profit after tax	6,723

be made up, and the most logical short-term source is a bank overdraft. The balance sheet is the accounting report that shows at any moment of time the financial position, taking all these longer-term factors into account: Pacioli's account that would 'give the trader without delay information as to his assets and liabilities'.

For High Note at the end of September the balance sheet is set out in Table 9.7.

You will find a spreadsheet template to help you construct your own balance sheets at www.smetoolkit.org – search for Balance Sheet (Projected).

Balance sheet conventions

The terms used in financial statements often seem familiar but they are often used in a very particular and potentially confusing way. For example, look up at the balance sheet in Table 9.7 and you will see the terms 'Assets' and 'Liabilities'. You may think that the money put in by the owner and the profit retained from the year's trading are anything but liabilities, but in accounting 'liability' is the term used to show where money has come from. Correspondingly, 'asset' means, in the language of accounting, what has been done with that money.

Table 9.7 High Note balance sheet at 30 September

	£/$/€	£/$/€
Assets		
Fixed assets:		
Garage conversion, etc	11,500	
Computer	1,000	
Total fixed assets		12,500
Working capital:		
Current assets:		
Stock	9,108	
Debtors	12,000	
Cash	0	
	21,108	
Less: Current liabilities:		
Overdraft	4,908	
Creditors	0	
	4,908	
Working capital (CA–CL)		16,200
Total assets		28,700
Liabilities		
Owner's capital introduced	10,000	
Long-term loan	10,000	
Profit retained (from P&L account)	8,700	
Total liabilities		28,700

You will also have noticed that the assets and liabilities have been jumbled together in the middle to net off the current assets and current liabilities and so end up with a figure for the working capital. 'Current' in accounting means within the trading cycle, usually taken to be one year. Stock will be used up and debtors will pay up within the year, and the overdraft, being repayable on demand, also appears as a short-term liability.

There are a number of other items not shown in this balance sheet that should appear, such as the liabilities for tax and VAT that have not yet been paid, which should appear as current liabilities.

Depreciation matters

A further important figure not shown in our simplified balance sheet is how to treat capital expenditure on fixed assets over time. Such fixed assets are usually depreciated over their working life rather than taken as one hit on the profit and loss account. There are accounting rules on the appropriate period to depreciate different assets over, usually somewhere between 3 and 20 years.

If we believe the computer has a useful life of four years and the rules allow it, we take £/$/€250 a year of cost, by way of depreciation, as an expense item in the profit and loss account for the year in question. Depreciation, though vital for your management accounts, is not an allowable expense for tax purposes. The tax authorities allow a 'writing down' allowance say of 25 per cent of the cost of an asset each year, which can be set as an expense for tax purposes. There are periods when the government of the day wants to stimulate businesses to invest, say in computers, and they will boost the writing down allowance accordingly. This figure will almost certainly not correspond to your estimate of depreciation so you need a profit for tax purposes and a profit for management purposes. You can see the effect of depreciation on the accounts in Table 9.8. Fixed assets reduce by £/$/€125 of depreciation, and there is a corresponding reduction in profit retained for the year, thus ensuring the balance sheet balances.

One of the books you will keep will be a capital register keeping track of the cost and depreciation of all fixed assets. Another accounting rule, that of 'materiality', comes into force here. Technically, a pocket calculator costing £/$/€5 is a fixed asset in that it has been bought to use rather than sell and it has a life of over one year. But it is treated as an expense as the sum involved is too small to be material.

Table 9.8 The changes to High Note's balance sheet to account for depreciation

Balance sheet	£/$/€
Asset changes:	
Fixed assets at cost	12,500
Less: Depreciation for six months	125
Net book assets	12,375
Liability changes:	
Profit from P&L account reduced by £125 to	8,575

There are no clear rules on the point at which a cost becomes material. For a big organization it may be for items costing a few thousand pounds. For a small business a hundred pounds may be the appropriate level.

Understanding the numbers

Just having the accounts of a business is not of much use in itself if you can't analyse and interpret them. There are two sets of tools for carrying out these tasks: using basic ratios and working out break-even. Both concern measuring the relationship between various elements of performance to see whether things are getting better or worse.

Using basic ratios

A ratio is simply something expressed as a proportion of something else, and it is intended to give an appreciation of what has happened.

Ratios are used to compare performance in one period, say last month or year, with another – this month or year. They can also be used to see how well your business is performing compared with another, say that of a competitor. You can also use ratios to compare how well you have done against your target or budget. In the financial field the opportunity for calculating ratios is great, for computing useful ratios not quite so great. Here we will concentrate on explaining the key ratios for a home-based business.

Levels of profit

Look back to Table 9.6, where you can see High Note's profit performance in some detail. Using those figures the following ratios are calculated:

- *Gross profit*. This is calculated by dividing the gross profit by sales and multiplying by 100. In this example the sum is $30,000/60,000 \times 100 = 50$ per cent. This is a measure of the value we are adding to the bought-in materials and services we need to 'make' our product or service: the higher the figure the better.

- *Operating profit*. This is calculated by dividing the operating profit by sales and multiplying by 100. In this example the sum is $8,700/60,000 \times 100 = 14.5$ per cent. This is a measure of how efficiently we are running the business, before taking account of financing costs and tax. These are excluded, as interest and tax rates change periodically and are outside our direct control. Excluding them makes it easier to compare one period with another or to compare our business with another business. Once again the rule here is the higher the figure the better.

- *Net profit before and after tax*. This is calculated by dividing the net profit before and after tax by the sales and multiplying by 100. In this example the sums are $8,100/60,000 \times 100 = 13.5$ per cent and $6,723/60,000 \times 100 = 11.21$ per cent. This is a measure of how efficiently we are running the business, after taking account of financing costs and tax. The last figure shows how successful we are at creating additional money either to invest back in the business or to distribute to the owner(s) as either drawings or dividends. Once again the rule here is the higher the figure the better.

Working capital relationships

The money tied up in day-to-day activities is known as working capital, the sum of which is arrived at by subtracting the current liabilities from the current assets. In the case of High Note we have £/$/€21,108 in current assets and £/$/€4,908 in current liabilities, so the working capital is £/$/€16,200.

Current ratio As a figure the working capital doesn't tell us much. It is rather as if you knew your car had used 20 gallons of petrol but had no idea how far you had travelled. It would be more helpful to know how much larger the current assets are than the current liabilities. That would give us some idea if the funds would be available to pay bills for stock, the tax liability and any other short-term liabilities that may arise. The current ratio, which is arrived at by dividing the current assets by the current liabilities, is the measure used. For High Note this is 21,108/4,908 = 4.30. The convention is to express this as 4.30:1, and the aim here is to have a ratio of between 1.5:1 and 2:1. Any lower and bills can't be met easily, and much higher and money is being tied up unnecessarily.

Average collection period We can see that High Note's current ratio is high, which is an indication that some elements of working capital are being used inefficiently. The business has £/$/€12,000 owed by customers on sales of £/$/€60,000 over a six-month period. The average period it takes High Note to collect money owed is calculated by dividing the sales made on credit by the money owed and multiplying it by the time period, in days; in this case the sum is as follows: 12,000/60,000 × 182.5 = 36.5 days.

If the credit terms are cash with order or seven days, then something is going seriously wrong. If it is net 30 days then it is probably about right. In this example it has been assumed that all the sales were made on credit.

Days' stock held High Note is carrying £9,108 stock of sheet music, CDs, etc, and over the period it sold £/$/€30,000 of stock at cost (the cost of sales is £/$/€30,000 to support £/$/€60,000 of invoiced sales, as the mark-up in this case is 100 per cent). Using a similar sum as with the average collection period we can calculate that the stock being held is sufficient to support 55.41 days' sales (9,108/30,000 × 182.5). If High Note's suppliers can make weekly deliveries then this is almost certainly too high a stock figure to hold. Cutting stock back from nearly eight weeks (55.41 days) to one week (7 days) would trim 48.41 days or £/$/€7,957.38 worth of stock out of working capital. This in turn would bring the current ratio down to 2.68:1.

Return on investment

The fundamental financial purpose in business is to make a satisfactory return on the funds invested. Return on investment is calculated as a percentage in the same way as is the interest you get on any money on deposit in a bank. In High Note £/$/€28,700 has been put into the business from various sources including the bank, to generate an operating profit of £/$/€8,700, that is profit before we pay the bank interest on money owed or tax. The return is calculated as 8,700/28,700 × 100 = 30.31 per cent.

Appreciating gearing   The return on investment ratio is arrived at taking into account all the sources of money used. However, High Note's owner has only £/$/€10,000 of own money invested, and the profit after paying bank interest of £/$/€600 is £/$/€8,100. So the return on the owner's investment is 8,100/10,000 × 100 = 81 per cent, which by any standards is acceptable.

If the owner had been able to get an overdraft of £/$/€15,000 rather than the £/$/€10,000 secured and so had put in only £/$/€5,000 of own cash, the return on the investment would have been better still. Interest cost would increase to £/$/€900, so profit after interest would drop to £/$/€7,800, but the owner's investment being just £/$/€5,000 means that the return on the investment would rise to 156 per cent (7,800/5,000 × 100).

There is a limit to the amount of money a bank will put up compared to the amount an owner puts in. Typically, banks will look to no more than match pound for pound the owner's funding and in any event they will want to secure their loan against some tangible asset such as a property.

Ratio analysis spreadsheets

Bookkeeping and accounting software often have 'report generator' programs that crunch out ratios for you, sometimes with helpful suggestions on areas to be probed further. Excellence in Financial Management (www.exinfm.com) has this and a large number of other useful financial spreadsheet templates.

Working out break-even

Whilst you usually have to invest some money up front to get a business off the ground, it's essential to know when you will start to make money. The break-even analysis, as this process is known, is an important tool to be used both in preparing a business plan and in the day-to-day running of a business.

Categorizing costs

Difficulties usually begin when people become confused by the different characteristics of costs. Some costs, for instance, do not change, however much you sell. For example, when working from home, any business rates, internet connection charges, cleaning and say the rent of a Portakabin if space is scarce are relatively constant figures, quite independent of the volume of sales. On the other hand, the cost of the products you are selling, such as, in the case of High Note, sheet music, DVDs and instruments, is completely dependent on volume. The more you sell, the more it 'costs' to buy stock. The former of these costs are called 'fixed' and the latter 'variable', and you cannot add them together to arrive at total costs until you have made some assumptions about sales.

Calculating break-even

Let's take an elementary example: a business plans to sell only one product and has only one fixed cost: the annual rent and business rates associated with a Portakabin established in the garden and

Figure 9.2   Graph showing break-even point

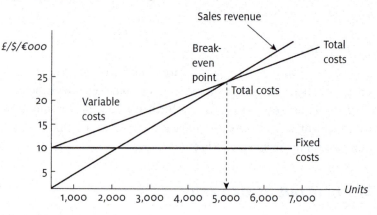

adjoining the owner's home. In Figure 9.2 the vertical axis shows the value of sales and costs in pounds/dollars/euros and the horizontal axis the number of 'units' sold. The second horizontal line represents the fixed costs, those that do not change as volume increases. In this case it is the rent of £/$/€10,000. The angled line running from the top of the fixed costs line is the variable costs. In this example we plan to buy in at £/$/€3 per unit, so every unit we sell adds that much to our fixed costs.

Only one element is needed to calculate the break-even point – the sales line. That is the line moving up at an angle from the bottom left-hand corner of the chart. We plan to sell out at £/$/€5 per unit, so this line is calculated by multiplying the units sold by that price.

The break-even point is the stage at which a business starts to make a profit, that is when the sales revenue begins to exceed both the fixed and the variable costs. Figure 9.2 shows our example break-even point as 5,000 units.

A formula, deduced from the figure, will save time for your own calculations:

$$\text{Break-even point} = \frac{\text{Fixed costs}}{\text{Selling price} - \text{Unit variable cost}}$$

$$\frac{10,000}{5 - 3} = 5,000 \text{ units}$$

Setting a profit goal

To complete the break-even picture we need to add one further dimension – profit. It is a mistake to think that profit is an accident of arithmetic calculated only at the end of the year. It is a specific and quantifiable target that you need at the outset.

Let's go back to our previous example. You plan to invest £/$/€10,000 in fixed assets in a business, and you will need to hold another £/$/€5,000 worth of stock too – in all say £/$/€15,000. You could get £/$/€1,500 profit just leaving that money in a bank or building society, so you will expect a return of say £/$/€4,000 (equal to an ambitious 27 per cent) for taking the risks of setting up on your own. Now let's see when you will break even.

The new equation must include your 'desired' profit, so it will look like this:

$$\text{Break-even profit point (BEPP)} = \frac{\text{Fixed costs + Profit objective}}{\text{Selling price – Unit variable cost}}$$

$$= \frac{10{,}000 + 4{,}000}{5 - 3} = 7{,}000$$

We know that to reach our target we must sell 7,000 units at £/$/€5 each and have no more than £/$/€10,000 tied up in fixed costs.

Allowing a margin of safety

The great strength of this equation is that each element can be changed in turn on an experimental basis to leave a margin of safety if events don't turn out as planned. For instance, suppose you decide that, whilst it is probable you can sell 7,000 units, it is possible sales could be as low as 6,500. What would your selling price have to be to make the same profit?

Using the BEPP equation and inserting x (the unknown) for the selling price, you can calculate the answer:

$$\text{BEPP} = \frac{\text{Fixed costs + Profit objective}}{\text{Selling price – Unit variable costs}}$$

$$6{,}500 = \frac{14{,}000}{x - 3}$$

You will need a little knowledge of algebra now, as the x has to be separated out by moving it back across the = sign, exchanging places with the 6,500 as follows:

$$x - 3 = \frac{14,000}{6,500} = 2.15$$

$$£x = £2.15 + 3 = £5.15$$

If your market will bear a selling price of £/$/€5.15 as opposed to £/$/€5, all is well; if it won't, then the ball is back in your court. You have to find ways of decreasing the fixed and/or variable costs, or of selling more, rather than just accepting that a lower profit is inevitable.

Dealing with multiple products

The example used to illustrate the break-even profit point model was of necessity simple. Few if any businesses sell only one or two products, so a more general equation may be more useful if your business sells hundreds of products, as, for example, a real shop does.

In such a business, to calculate your break-even point you must first establish your gross profit. If you are already trading, this is calculated by deducting the money paid out to suppliers from the money received from customers. If you are not yet trading, then researching your competitors will give you some indication of the sort of margins you should aim for.

For example, if you are aiming for a 40 per cent gross profit, expressed in decimals as 0.4, your fixed costs are £/$/€10,000 and your overall profit objective is £/$/€4,000, then the sum will be as follows:

$$BEPP = \frac{10,000 + 4,000}{0.4} = \frac{14,000}{0.4} = £35,000$$

So, to reach your target you must achieve a £/$/€35,000 turnover. (You can check this out for yourself: look back to the previous example where the BEPP was 7,000 units and the selling price was £/$/€5 each. Multiplying those figures out gives a turnover of £/$/€35,000. The gross profit in that example was 2/5, or 40 per cent, also.)

Getting help with break-even

You have a few options in getting help with making break-even calculations. Your accountant can show you, or alternatively there are a number of online spreadsheets such as Excellence in Financial Management (www.exinfm.com – for instance Breakeven Analysis) and BizPep (**www.bizpeponline.com/PricingBreakeven. html**), which sells a software program that calculates your break-even for prices plus or minus 50 per cent of your proposed selling price. You can tweak costs to see how to optimize your selling price and so hit your profit goal.

Computing taxes

As a business you are responsible for paying a number of taxes and other dues to the government of the day, both on your own behalf and for any employees you may have, as well as being an unpaid tax collector required to account for end consumers' expenditure.

There are penalties for misdemeanours and you are required to keep your accounts for six years, so at any point should the tax authorities become suspicious they can dig into the past even after they have agreed your figures. In the case of suspected fraud there is no limit to how far back the digging can go.

Value added tax (VAT)

VAT, a tax common throughout Europe though charged at different rates, is a tax on consumer spending, collected by businesses. Basically it is a game of pass the parcel, with businesses that are registered for VAT (see 'Starting thresholds' below) charging each other VAT and deducting VAT charged. At the end of each accounting period the amount of VAT you have paid out is deducted from the amount you have charged out and the balance is paid over to HM Revenue & Customs.

In the UK the standard rate is 20 per cent, whilst some types of business charge lower rates and some are exempt altogether. The way VAT is handled on goods and services sold to and bought from other European countries is subject to another set of rules and proce-dures. HM Revenue & Customs (**www.gov.uk/topic/Business-tax/ vat** has a comperehensive guide to current VAT regulations).

Starting thresholds

You should register for VAT if your sales are expected to reach the threshold, which at April 2017 was £83,000. This level rises by £1,000 or so each year. You can register for VAT below that figure, as you could benefit from being able to recover VAT on your busi-ness expenses, such as purchasing equipment or paying for petrol.

You will be given a VAT number when you register, which should be stated on all your invoices.

Payment methods

Normally VAT is paid each quarter, but small businesses can take advantage of a number of schemes to simplify procedures or aid their cash flow. The annual accounting scheme lets you pay monthly or quarterly estimated figures, submitting a single annual return at the end of the year with any balancing payment. The cash account-ing scheme allows you to delay paying over any VAT until you have actually collected it from your customers. The flat rate scheme allows you to calculate your VAT as a flat percentage of your total sales, rather than having to record the VAT charged on individual purchases and sales.

Accounting for profit

You will pay tax on any profit made in your business. The rate at which you will pay depends on the legal structure chosen. In the UK, if you are a sole trader or in a partnership you will pay tax at your personal marginal rate. Limited companies pay tax of 20 percent, a rate that is reviewed annually. You can find out the current tax rate in all major countries at the Worldwide-Tax website (see Appendix 3).

The financial year and payment dates

The financial year for tax purposes is usually 6 April to 5 April though some businesses use a different date such as the calendar year if it is more appropriate for their type of business. You need to get your tax return back to HMRC by 30 September if you want them to calculate the tax due, or by 31 January if you are happy for you or your accountant to do the sums. The tax itself is paid in two stages, at the end of July and the end of January. Companies have to calculate their own tax due and pay it nine months after their year-end. You will be fined and charged interest on any late tax payments.

Filing accounts for a company

A company's financial affairs are in the public domain. As well as keeping HMRC informed, companies have to file their accounts with Companies House. Accounts should be filed within 10 months of the company's financial year-end. Small businesses (turnover below £5.6 million) can file abbreviated accounts that include only very limited balance sheet and profit and loss account information, and these do not need to be audited. You can be fined up to £1,000 for filing accounts late. In the United States, only quoted public companies are required to file accounts.

Estimating tax due

Tax is due on the profits of your business, which may not be the same as the figure arrived at in your profit and loss account (see below). For example, you will include depreciation, entertainment and perhaps other expenses that, though it's important for you to know how much and on what they were incurred, are not allowable expenses for tax purposes. Your accountant will be able to give you a good steer in this area. HMRC provides specific guidance on home-based businesses.

PAYE (Pay As You Earn)

Employers are responsible for deducting income tax from employees' accounts and making the relevant payment to HMRC. If you trade as a limited company then as a director any salary you receive will be subject to PAYE. You will need to work out the tax due. HM Revenue & Customs give details on PAYE (www.gov.uk – search for 'employing people – payroll').

Dealing with National Insurance (NI)

Almost everyone who works has to pay a separate tax, National Insurance, collected by HMRC, which, in theory at least, goes towards the state pension and other benefits. NI is paid at different rates, and self-employed people pay Class 4 contributions calculated each year on the self-assessment tax form.

The amount of National Insurance paid depends on a mass of different factors, covering married women, volunteer development workers, share fishermen, the self-employed and those with small earnings. These factors attract NI rates of between 1 per cent and 12 per cent. HMRC the government website at www.gov.uk covers everything you need to konow about NI.

Help and advice with tax

HMRC (www.gov.uk/topic/business-tax/self-employed) has some pointers and Taxcafe (www.taxcafe.co.uk/business-tax. html) publish a series of helpful guides including Small Business Tax Saving Tactics – 284 pages of tax-saving ideas and their VAT Question and Answer Service.

Key jobs to do

- Review your bookkeeping needs and decide on a system.
- Make your initial sales projections and the ensuing cash flow, profit and loss account and balance sheet.
- Calculate and interpret the key ratios using the financial statements produced earlier.
- Work out your break-even volume and assess when that point will be reached.
- Assess the tax liability that will ensue from your financial projections.
- Check out your competitors and customers accounts at HMRC (www.gov.uk/get-information-about-a-company).

Raising the money

It is a fact of business life that all business ventures need some cash to get going, even if it is just to get some inexpensive software to keep the books, a bigger desk or some racking to keep stock in the garage. The more successful you are the more money you will need to finance and store stock if you are selling products or to pay wages if you are in a service business. To remain competitive and visible, your products and services will need to be kept bang up to date, as will your website, all of which will call for some additional investment.

There are many sources of funds available to independent businesses. However, not all of them are equally appropriate to all businesses at all times. These different sources of finance carry very different obligations, responsibilities and opportunities for profitable businesses. Having some appreciation of these differences will enable you to make an informed choice.

Most businesses starting from home confine their financial strategy to bank loans, either long-term or short-term, viewing the other financing methods as either too complex or too risky. In many respects the reverse is true. Almost every finance source other than banks will to a greater or lesser extent share some of the risks of doing business with the recipient of the funds.

Estimating financing needs

The starting point in raising money for your business is unsurprisingly to estimate how much you need and for how long you expect to need that money. This is not an exact science and no spreadsheet however complex will enable you to get the sum dead right. In the first place you need to decide your objectives in terms of the size of business you want to have. Then you can work out approximately what you need to spend to achieve those sales and when you will need the money.

The cash flow forecast (see Chapter 9) and your business plan (see Chapter 11) will help you to flesh out your funding requirements more fully.

Fixtures, fittings and other long-term costs

The most obvious items you may have to spend money up front on are office furniture, rearranging some areas of your home to store stock or to fit in office space away from general family traffic and almost certainly a website. These are all expenditures for items that will stay with your business for the long term. These fixed assets, as they are termed, need to be financed by way of a long-term loan from a bank, leasing finance or funds provided by an investor – all financing methods explained further in later sections in this chapter.

Working capital

If you are selling products then it is likely that you will either have to buy in materials and work on them to have finished goods to sell or buy in items ready to sell on. In either case you will need to buy in stock from suppliers that may well have minimum order levels or have prices that make it attractive to buy in bulk. Until your customers pay up you will have to bear the burden of this cost.

This short-term money that circulates in and out of a business as it trades is known as working capital. Money to finance working capital can come via bank overdraft or supplier credit or from an invoice discounter or factor – all financing methods explained further in later sections in this chapter.

Handling contingencies

Little in life goes exactly to plan, and in business there is considerable scope for the unexpected. It may be a pleasant surprise, such as an unexpectedly large order or a sudden influx of new customers, or something less pleasant, say a customer going bust and being unable to pay up, your website costing considerably more than you had budgeted for, or being ill and having to take time off work. In order to deal with these unforeseen events you should build in some extra money over and above that needed for items you have identified.

There are no hard-and-fast rules as to what is the right amount of money to have in reserve, but raising around 10 per cent more than is strictly called for in your cash flow forecast would be prudent.

Calculating start-up costs for different businesses

Santander has a neat tool (**www.santander.co.uk** > business guides). You choose the trade you are interested in starting a business in – several hundred are shown, from acupuncture to windscreen services – and the cost calculator will provide a list of the items you may have to buy and their current cost. Scrolling through eight screens of cost prompts you will arrive at the costs involved in starting that particular type of business. Every business guide also gives you links to other sources of information you might need.

Using your own resources

The first port of call when looking to finance your business should be your own resources. This is usually easier to arrange, cheaper, quicker and less time-consuming than any other source of money. There is of course another important advantage in that if you don't tap into bank borrowing and the like you may get a better reception later on once your business is up and running.

Going for redundancy

Redundancy is a continuing feature of the international industrial landscape as the pace of change continues to accelerate. If you are in employment and could be eligible for redundancy this could be a way of financing your business. In any event if your business takes off you are likely to have your hands full. These are the key factors to consider:

- Are you eligible for redundancy? This is a complex area, but the Citizens Advice Bureau (**www.citizensadvice.org.uk > redundancy**) has a summarized guide to the topic with useful links to other information.

- The first £30,000 of redundancy pay is free of tax. After that you pay tax at your highest marginal rate. Redundancy Help (www. redundancyhelp.co.uk) has a number of useful guides covering this area and a free advice service.

- Your pension entitlement may be adversely affected if you draw your pension earlier than your designated retirement age. The Association of British Insurers and the Financial Services Authority have a pension calculator (**www.pensioncalculator. org**), which you can use to see what will happen to a pension by paying in for fewer years and retiring early.

Dipping into savings

If you have any savings put aside for a rainy day then you could also consider dipping into them now. You will need to discuss this with your financial adviser, as there may be penalties associated with cashing in insurance policies early, for example. The Association of Investment and Financial Advisers (**www.apfa.net**) can help you to find an adviser in the UK or abroad.

Remortgaging

If you bought your present home five years or more ago the chances are that you are sitting on a large amount of equity – the difference between the current market value of your house and the amount you still owe the mortgagor. You can dip into this equity by remortgaging for a higher sum and taking out some cash. You should be able to take out between 80 and 90 per cent of the equity, though this may mean paying between 0.5 per cent and 1 per cent more for the whole mortgage, as well as an arrangement fee. If you need a relatively small amount of finance or only need the money for a short period to finance working capital this is probably not the best option.

You will find a guide to the whole subject at Mortgage Sorter (**www.mortgagesorter.co.uk** > Remortgages), where you will also find a remortgage quote service. The banks also offer advice on this subject (**www.barclays.co.uk** > Mortgages > Remortgage with us).

Using credit cards

Why would anyone pay 18 per cent interest when they could get a bank overdraft at a third of that cost? The simple answer is that banks put their borrowers through a fairly stringent credit check (see 'Using a bank', page 188), whilst credit card providers have built a large volume of defaulting customers into their margins. In other words, you are paying over the odds to get fairly easy money.

Use a credit card by all means for travel and the like. Keep one to hand as part of your contingency planning to handle financial emergencies. But this type of money should not become part of the core funding of any business. Moneysupermarket (**www. moneysupermarket.com** > Money > Credit Cards) has a comparison tool that lets you compare over 300 cards, and About Your Money (**www.aboutyourmoney.co.uk** > Credit Cards > Business Cards) has an A–Z listing of business credit card providers and a comparison of the interest rates and other charges.

Earning sweat equity

Just because you are starting a business doesn't mean that every other moneymaking option is closed off. The attraction to earning money rather than borrowing it is that it is interest free and never has to be paid back, as it would if it were borrowed from a bank. The harder you work the more you can earn and put into the business: hence the name 'sweat equity'.

Using a Local Exchange Trading Scheme

Local Exchange Trading allows anyone who joins a scheme to offer skills or services, such as plumbing, gardening or the use of a photocopier, to other members. A price is agreed in whatever notional currency has been adopted, but no money changes hands. The system is more ambitious than straight barter. The provider receives a credit on his or her account kept by a local organizer, and a debit is marked up against the user. The person in credit can then set this against other services.

The benefits of using LETS are that you can start trading and grow with virtually no start-up capital. All you need is time and saleable skills – once you have 'sold' your wares, payment is immediate by way of a LETS credit. Also, using LETS means that the wealth is kept in the local community, which means customers in your area may be able to spend more with you. One of the keys to success in using LETS is to have an enterprising organizer who can produce, maintain and circulate a wide-ranging directory of LETS services and outlets. Find out from Letslink UK (**www. letslinkuk.net**) more about the system and how to find your nearest organizer.

LETS-Linkup (**www.lets-linkup.com**) provides a guide to over 1,500 LETS groups from 39 countries.

Borrowing money

At one end of the financing spectrum are the various organizations that lend money to businesses. They all try hard to take little or no risk, but expect some reward irrespective of performance. They want interest payments on money lent, usually from day one. While they too hope the management is competent, they are more interested in securing a charge against any assets the business or its managers may own. At the end of the day (and that day can be sooner than the borrower expects), they want all their money back – no more and certainly no less. It would be more prudent to think of these organizations as people who will help you turn a proportion of an illiquid asset such as property, stock in trade or customers who have not yet paid up into a more liquid asset such as cash, but of course at some discount.

Using a bank

Banks are the principal, and frequently the only, source of finance for 9 out of every 10 new and small businesses. Small firms around the world rely on banks for their funding.

Bankers, and indeed any other sources of debt capital, are looking for asset security to back their loan and provide a near-certainty of getting their money back. They will also charge an interest rate that reflects current market conditions and their view of the risk level of the proposal.

Bankers like to speak of the 'five Cs' of credit analysis, factors they look at when they evaluate a loan request. When applying to a bank for a loan, be prepared to address the following points:

- *Character.* Bankers lend money to borrowers who appear honest and who have a good credit history. Before you apply for a loan, it makes sense to obtain a copy of your credit report and clean up any problems.
- *Capacity.* This is a prediction of the borrower's ability to repay the loan. For a new business, bankers look at the business plan.

For an existing business, bankers consider financial statements and industry trends.

- *Collateral.* Bankers generally want a borrower to pledge an asset that can be sold to pay off the loan if the borrower lacks funds.

- *Capital.* Bankers scrutinize a borrower's net worth, the amount by which assets exceed debts.

- *Conditions.* Whether bankers give a loan can be influenced by the current economic climate as well as by the amount.

Finding a business banker

Usage among small firms of telephone and internet banking has significantly increased over the past few years. According to the BBA (British Banking Association) banking by smartphone and tablet has become the leading way customers manage their finances, as mobile banking overtakes branches and the internet as the most popular way to bank. Branch location seems less likely to be a significant factor to bank customers in the future, so you no longer have to confine your search for a bank to those with a branch nearby. All the major clearing banks offer telephone banking and internet services to their small business customers, or are in the process of doing so.

The British Banking Association (**www.bba.org.uk/customers/ business-banking/business-accounts/business-account-finder-tool**) have a business bank account finder tool that also lets you compare your present bank against any others you may choose.

Giving bank guarantees

Where the assets of a business are small, anyone lending it money may seek the added protection of requiring the owner to guarantee the loan personally. In the case of limited companies, this is in effect stripping away some of the protection that companies are supposed to afford the risk-taking owner-manager. You should resist giving guarantees if at all possible. If you have to, then try to secure the guarantee against the specific asset concerned only and set clear conditions for the guarantee to come to an end, for example when your overdraft or borrowings go down to a certain level.

Remember, everything in business finance is negotiable, and your relationship with a bank is no exception. Banks are in competition too, so if yours is being unreasonably hard it may be time to move on. Obviously, to be able to move on, you need to have some advance notice of when the additional funds are needed. Rushing into a bank asking for extra finance from next week is hardly likely to inspire much confidence in your abilities as a strategic thinker. That is where your business plan will come into its own.

Overdrafts

The principal form of short-term bank funding is an overdraft, secured by a charge over the assets of the business. A little over a quarter of all bank finance for small firms is in the form of an overdraft. If you are starting out in a contract cleaning business, say, with a major contract, you need sufficient funds initially to buy the mop and bucket. Three months into the contract they will have been paid for, and so there is no point in getting a five-year bank loan to cover this, as within a year you will have cash in the bank and a loan with an early redemption penalty!

However, if your bank account does not get out of the red at any stage during the year, you will need to re-examine your financing. All too often companies utilize an overdraft to acquire long-term assets, and that overdraft never seems to disappear, eventually constraining the business.

The attraction of overdrafts is that they are very easy to arrange and take little time to set up. That is also their inherent weakness. The keywords in the arrangement document are 'repayable on demand', which leaves the bank free to make and change the rules as it sees fit. (This term is under constant review, and some banks may remove it from the arrangement.) With other forms of borrowing, as long as you stick to the terms and conditions the loan is yours for the duration. It is not so with overdrafts.

Term loans

Term loans, as long-term bank borrowings are generally known, are funds provided by a bank for a number of years.

The interest can either be variable, changing with general interest rates, or fixed for a number of years ahead. The proportion of fixed-rate loans has increased from a third of all term loans to around one in two. In some cases it may be possible to move between having a fixed interest rate and a variable one at certain intervals. It may even be possible to have a moratorium on interest payments for a short period, to give the business some breathing space. Provided the conditions of the loan are met in such matters as repayment, interest and security cover, the money is available for the period of the loan. Term loans are unlike overdrafts in that the bank cannot pull the rug from under you if circumstances (or the local manager) change.

Just over a third of all term loans are for periods greater than 10 years, and a quarter are for three years or less.

Government enterprise finance guarantee schemes

These are operated by banks at the instigation of governments in the UK, Australia, the United States and elsewhere. These schemes guarantee loans from banks and other financial institutions for small businesses with viable business proposals that have tried and failed to obtain a conventional loan because of a lack of security. The British Business Bank is a government-owned business development bank dedicated to making finance markets work better for smaller businesses. Since its launch in 2009, the Enterprise Finance Guarantee (EFG) has supported the provision of £2.7bn of finance to more than 26,000 smaller businesses. Typically EFG facilitates lending to smaller businesses that are viable but unable to obtain finance from their lender due to having insufficient security to meet the lender's normal security requirements.

EFG guarantees loans to fund the future growth or expansion of a business, from £1,000 to £1.2 million. Finance terms are from three months up to 10 years for term loans and asset finance and up to three years for revolving facilities and invoice finance. You can find out all about EFG, the associated costs, eligibility criteria and the 40 or so providers at http://british-business-bank.co.uk/ourpartners/enterprise-finance-guarantee.

Online peer-to-peer platforms

In the last few years, P2PL has become a fast-growing and vital source of finance for new and growing businesses. Many business owners, who had been turned down in the traditional funding markets, turned to their peers to raise funding. Lenders are primarily looking for a better return than they can get elsewhere, so it's a perfect synergy between the two sides of a very valuable coin for the continued growth of the UK economy as a whole.

P2PL portals:

- are intermediaries between lenders and borrowers;
- manage their transactions online;
- carry out credit checks and due diligence on applicants;
- enable lenders to choose from clients seeking loans;
- provide a wider range of cheap unsecured loans than banks.

More than £300 million is lent to businesses every 12 months through these lending platforms in the UK, and that figure has been doubling each year. In fact, the recent boom in online P2PL loans has been so successful that high street banks, corporate finance providers, pension funds and even government departments have also become lenders, getting on the platform bandwagon.

Some P2PL portals are well established, while others are new on the financial block. They tend to have lower overheads than traditional banking institutions, so they have fewer costs to pass on to customers. P2P Money (www.p2pmoney.co.uk/companies.htm) has a directory of lenders.

Money through credit unions

If you don't like the terms on offer from the high-street banks, as the major banks are often known, you could consider forming your own bank. This is not quite as crazy an idea as it sounds. Credit unions formed by groups of small businesspeople, both in business and aspiring to start up, have been around for decades in the United

States, the UK and elsewhere. They have been an attractive option for people on low incomes, providing a cheap and convenient alternative to banks. Some self-employed people such as taxi drivers have also formed credit unions. They can then apply for loans to meet unexpected capital expenditure for repairs, refurbishments or technical upgrading.

The popularity of credit unions varies from country to country. In the UK, for example, fewer than one in 300 people belong to one, compared with more than one in three in Canada, Ireland and Australia. Certainly, few could argue about the attractiveness of an annual interest rate 30 per cent below that of the high-street lenders, which is what credit unions aim for. Members have to save regularly to qualify for a loan, although there is no minimum deposit, and after 10 weeks members with a good track record can borrow up to five times their savings, although they must continue to save while repaying the loan. There is no set interest rate, but dividends are distributed to members from any surplus, usually about 5 per cent a year. This too compares favourably with bank interest on deposit accounts.

Finding a credit union

You can find more about credit unions and details of those operating in your area from the Association of British Credit Unions Limited (**www.abcul.coop**). For credit unions in the United States and in countries from Australia to the West Indies see Credit Unions Online (**www.creditunionsonline.com**).

World Council of Credit Unions (**www.woccu.org** > Member Services > Members) has a directory of more than 60,500 credit unions in 109 countries.

Leasing and hiring equipment

Physical assets such as cars, vans, computers, office equipment and the like can usually be financed by leasing them, rather as a house or flat may be rented. Alternatively, they can be bought on hire purchase. This leaves other funds free to cover the less tangible elements in your cash flow.

Leasing is a way of getting the use of vehicles, plant and equipment without paying the full cost all at once. Operating leases are taken out where you will use the equipment (for example a car, photocopier, vending machine or kitchen equipment) for less than its full economic life. The lessor takes the risk of the equipment becoming obsolete, and assumes responsibility for repairs, maintenance and insurance. As you, the lessee, are paying for this service, it is more expensive than a finance lease, where you lease the equipment for most of its economic life and maintain and insure it yourself. Leases can normally be extended, often for fairly nominal sums, in the latter years.

Hire purchase differs from leasing in that you have the option eventually to become the owner of the asset, after a series of payments.

Finding a leasing company

The Finance and Leasing Association (**www.fla.org.uk**) gives details of all UK-based businesses offering this type of finance. The website also has general information on terms of trade and a code of conduct.

Discounting and factoring

Customers often take time to pay up. In the meantime you have to pay those who work for you and your less patient suppliers. So, the more you grow, the more funds you need. It is often possible to 'factor' your creditworthy customers' bills to a financial institution, receiving some of the funds as your goods leave the door, hence speeding up cash flow.

Factoring is generally only available to a business that invoices other business customers, either in its home market or internationally, for its services. Factoring can be made available to new businesses, although its services are usually of most value during the early stages of growth. It is an arrangement that allows you to receive up to 80 per cent of the cash due from your customers more quickly than they would normally pay. The factoring company in effect buys your trade debts, and can also provide a debtor accounting and administration service. You will, of course, have to pay for factoring services. Having the cash before your customers pay will cost you a little more than normal overdraft rates. The factoring service will cost between 0.5 and 3.5 per cent of the turnover, depending on volume of work, the number of debtors, average invoice amount and other related factors. You can get up to 80 per cent of the value of your invoice in advance, with the remainder paid when your customer settles up, less the various charges just mentioned.

If you sell direct to the public, sell complex and expensive capital equipment, or expect progress payments on long-term projects, then factoring is not for you. If you are expanding more rapidly than other sources of finance will allow, this may be a useful service that is worth exploring.

Invoice discounting is a variation on the same theme, where you are responsible for collecting the money from debtors; this is not a service available to new or very small businesses.

Finding an invoice discounter or factor

The Asset Based Finance Association (**www.thefda.org.uk**) is the association representing the UK's 41 factoring and invoice discounting businesses. This link is to their directory of members.

Supplier credit

Once you have established creditworthiness, it may be possible to take advantage of trade credit extended by suppliers. This usually takes the form of allowing you anything from seven days to three months from receiving the goods before you have to pay for them. Even if you are allowed time to pay for goods and services, you will have to weigh carefully the benefit of taking this credit against the cost of losing any cash discounts offered. For example, if you are offered a 2.5 per cent discount for cash settlement, then this is a saving of £/$/€25 for every £/$/€1,000 of purchases. If the alternative is to take six weeks' credit, the saving is the cost of borrowing that sum from, say, your bank on overdraft. So, if your bank interest rate is 8 per cent per annum, that is equivalent to 0.15 per cent per week. Six weeks would save you

0.92 per cent. On £/$/€1,000 of purchases you would save only £/$/€9.20 of bank interest. This means that the cash discount is more attractive.

Checking your creditworthiness

However, your suppliers will probably run a credit check on you before extending payment terms. You should run a credit check on your own business from time to time, just to see how others see you. You can check out your own credit rating before trying to get credit from a supplier by using a credit reference agency such as Snoop4 Companies (**www.snoop4companies.co.uk**) for businesses or Experian (**www.experian.co.uk**) for sole traders. Basic credit reports cost between £3 ($4.3/€3.5) and £25 ($36/€29.5) and may save you time and money if you have any reservations about a potential customer's ability to pay.

Graydon (**www.graydon.co.uk**) provide credit reports on businesses in over 190 countries.

Family and friends

Those close to you might be willing to lend you money or invest in your business. This helps you avoid the problem of pleading your case to outsiders and enduring extra paperwork and bureaucratic delays. Help from friends, relatives and business associates can be especially valuable if you have been through bankruptcy or had other credit problems that would make borrowing from a commercial lender difficult or impossible.

Their involvement brings a range of extra potential benefits, costs and risks that are not a feature of most other types of finance. You need to decide which of these are acceptable.

Some advantages of borrowing money from people you know well are that you may be charged a lower interest rate, may be able to delay paying back money until you are more established, and may be given more flexibility if you get into a jam. But once the loan terms are agreed to, you have the same legal obligations as you would with a bank or any other source of finance.

In addition, borrowing money from relatives and friends can have a major disadvantage. If your business does poorly and those close to you end up losing money, you may well damage a good personal relationship. So, in dealing with friends, relatives and business associates, be extra careful not only to establish clearly the terms of the deal and put them in writing, but also to make an extra effort to explain the risks. In short, it is your job to make sure your helpful friend or relative will not suffer true hardship if you are unable to meet your financial commitments.

Getting an investor

If you are operating as a limited company or limited partnership you will have a potentially valuable opportunity to raise relatively risk-free money. It is risk-free to you, the business founder, that is, but risky, sometimes extremely so, to anyone advancing you money. Businesses such as these have shares that can be traded for money, so selling a share of your business is one way to raise capital to start up or grow your business. Shares also have the great additional attraction of having cost you nothing – nothing, that is, except blood, sweat, tears and inspiration.

Individual business angels, or corporates such as venture capital providers, share all the risks and vagaries of the business alongside you, the founder, and expect a proportionate share in the rewards if things go well. They are not especially concerned with a stream of dividends, which is just as well, as few small businesses ever pay them. Nor do they look for the security of buildings or other assets to underpin their investment. Instead they hope for a radical increase in the value of their investment. They expect to realize this value from other investors who want to take their place for the next stage in the firm's growth cycle, rather than from any repayment by the founder.

Business angels

One likely first source of equity or risk capital will be a private individual with his or her own funds and perhaps some knowledge of your type of business. In return for a share in the business, such investors will put in money at their own risk. They have been christened 'business angels', a term first coined to describe private wealthy individuals who back a play on Broadway or in London's West End.

Most angels are determined upon some involvement beyond merely signing a cheque and may hope to play a part in your business in some way. They are hoping for big rewards – one angel who backed Sage with £10,000 in its first round of £250,000 financing saw his stake rise to £40 million.

These angels frequently operate through managed networks, usually on the internet. In the UK and the United States there are hundreds of networks, with tens of thousands of business angels prepared to put up several billion pounds each year into new or small businesses.

Finding a business angel

The UK Angels Association (**www.ukbusinessangelsassociation.org. uk**) has an online directory of UK business angels. The European Business Angels Network (EBAN) has directories of national business angel associations both inside and outside Europe (**www.eban. org**) from which you can find individual business angels.

The World Business Angels Association (**www.wbaa.biz > Directory**) provides links to Angel networks worldwide, including China, India and Chile, for example.

CASE STUDY HIPPYCHICK

When new mother Julie Minchin discovered the Hipseat, she knew she'd found a helpful product. Anything that makes carrying a baby around all day without ending up with excruciating backache has got to be a benefit. It was only later that she realised that selling the product for the German company that made the Hipseat could launch her into business. At first, Julie acted as their UK distributor, but later she wanted to make major improvements to the product. That meant finding a manufacturer to make the product especially for her business. China was the logical place to find a company flexible enough to make small quantities as well as being able to help her keep the cost of the end product competitive. Julie funded the business, Hippychick, with a small family loan, an overdraft facility and a variety of government grants. By its tenth year, the company had a turnover of £3 million a year, selling 14 new and unique products aimed at the baby market. Hippychick supplies national chains such as Boots and Mothercare as well as independents. It also sells via a catalogue and website, and is in the process of building a network of distributors for its branded products.

www.hippychick.com

Venture capital/private equity

Venture capital providers (VCs) are investing other people's money, often from pension funds. They have a different agenda from that of business angels and are more likely to be interested in investing more money for a larger stake.

VCs go through a process known as 'due diligence' before investing. This process involves a thorough examination of both the business and its owners. Past financial performance, the directors' track record and the business plan are all subjected to detailed scrutiny, usually by accountants and lawyers. Directors are then required to 'warrant' that they have provided *all* relevant information, under pain of financial penalties. The cost of this process will have to be borne by the firm raising the money, but it will be paid out of the money raised, if that is any consolation.

In general, VCs expect their investment to have paid off within seven years, but they are hardened realists. Two in every 10 investments they make are total write-offs, and six perform averagely well at best. So, the one star in every 10 investments they make has to cover a lot of duds. VCs have a target rate of return of 30 per cent plus, to cover this poor hit rate.

Raising venture capital is not a cheap option, and deals are not quick to arrange either. Six months is not unusual, and over a year has been known. Every VC has a deal done in six weeks in its portfolio, but that truly is the exception.

Finding venture capital

The British Invest Europe (**www.investeurope.eu**) Venture Capital Association (**www.bvca.co.uk**) and Private Equity and both have online directories giving details of hundreds of venture capital providers. The National Venture Capital Association in the United States has directories of international venture capital associations both inside and outside the United States (**www.nvca.org > Resources**).

You can see how those negotiating with or receiving venture capital rate the firm in question at The Funded website (**www.thefunded.com**) in terms of the deal offered, the firm's apparent competence and how good it is at managing the relationship. There is also a link to the VC's website. The Funded is an online community of over 20,000 CEOs, founders and entrepreneurs who discuss fund raising, rate and review angel investors and venture capitalists, and discuss strategies to grow and start up a business.

Crowdfunding

Crowdfunding business finance is a new, game-changing concept that puts the power firmly into the hands of entrepreneurs looking to raise finance. Instead of one large investor putting money into a business, larger numbers of smaller investors contribute as little as £10 each to raise the required capital. They then review propositions put up by business owners for loans or investments and make individual decisions on whether and how much to invest. Crowdfunding lets you make your proposition directly to individual investors and lenders. The more of these people you convince with your business proposition, the more likely you are to secure the full amount of funding you require. The process is quick – think of it as speed dating for business. You can register and apply online in less than 30 minutes and have the money in your bank account in as little as three days. As investors and lenders have to bid for your business, you should get the best terms possible.

Crowdfunders don't just back equity investments, they lend money, fund property purchase and you can offer returns other than money to your backers. Gyms offer membership discounts, musicians raise cash for instruments offering free concert tickets and restaurants offer free meals.

A few organizations to check out are Crowdcube (www. crowdcube.com), Crowd Funder (www.crowdfunder.co.uk) and Funding Circle (www.fundingcircle.com/businesses). The UK Crowdfunding Association (www.ukcfa.org.uk) was formed in 2012 by 14 crowdfunding businesses in order to 'Promote crowdfunding as a valuable and viable way for UK businesses, projects or ventures to raise funds'. They estimate that over £2 billion a year is raised through crowdfunding with sums ranging from a few thousand to over £1.5 million.

Private capital preliminaries

Two important stages will be gone through before a private investor will put cash into a business. The emphasis put on these stages will vary according to the complexity of the deal, the amount of money and the legal ownership of the funds concerned. For example, a business angel investing on their own account can accept greater uncertainty on their own account than say a venture capital fund using pension funds money.

Due diligence

Usually, after a private equity firm signs a letter of intent to provide capital and you accept, they will conduct a due diligence investigation of both the management and the company. During this period the private equity firm will have access to all financial and other records, facilities, employees, etc., to investigate before finalizing the deal. The material to be examined will include copies of all leases, contracts, and loan agreements in addition to copious financial records and statements. He or she will want to see any management reports, such as sales reports, inventory records, detailed lists of assets, facility maintenance records, aged receivables and payables reports, employee organization charts, payroll and benefits records, customer records and marketing materials. They will want to know about any pending litigation, tax audits, or insurance disputes. Depending on the nature of the business, they might also consider getting an environmental audit and an insurance check-up. The sting in the due diligence tail is that the current owners of the business will be required to personally warrant that everything they have said or revealed is both true and complete. In the event that proves not to be so they will be personally liable to the extent of any loss incurred by those buying the shares.

Term sheet

A term sheet is a funding offer from a capital provider. It lays out the amount of an investment and the conditions under which the new investors expect the business owners to work using their money.

The first page of the term sheet states the amount offered and the form of the funds (a bond, common stock, preferred stock, a promissory note or a combination of these). A price, either per £/$/€1,000 unit of debt or per share of stock, is quoted to set the cost basis for investors 'getting in' on your company. Later that starting price will be very important in deciding capital gains and any taxes due.

The next section of the term sheet is typically a table that summarizes the capital structure of your company. Investors generally start with preferred stock in order to gain a priority of distribution, should the enterprise fail and the liquidation of assets occur. The typical way to handle this is to have the preferred stock be convertible into common stock on a 1:1 ratio at the investors' option, such that the preferred position is essentially a common stock position, but with priority of repayment over the founders' own common-stock position.

Other terms included on the sheet could cover rents, equipment, levels of debt vs equity, minimum and maximum time periods associated with the transfer of shares, vesting in additional shares, and option periods for making subsequent investments and having 'right of first refusal' when other rounds of funding are sought in the future.

Free money

Strangely enough there is such a thing as a free lunch in the money world. It may come in the form of a benevolent government whose agenda is either to get businesses to locate in an area more full of sheep than customers or to pioneer new technologies. In addition businesses, newspapers and magazines run competitions galore that offer prizes to the best-run, fastest-growing, biggest-exporting business and so forth. For the sponsor the reward is publicity and good stories, and for the business founders there is money.

Gaining grants

Grants are constantly being introduced (and withdrawn), but there is no system that lets you know automatically. You have to keep yourself informed.

The UK Business Funding Centre, a private sector research and advisory organization, has a grant finding search engine on its website (www.ukbusinessgrants.org). The UK Government also has a grant finding resource (www.gov.uk/business-finance-support-finder). Grants.Gov (www.grants.gov) is a guide to how to apply for over 1,000 federal government grants in the United States.

Winning competitions

There are thousands of annual awards around the world aimed at new or small businesses. Most are based around a business plan or other presentation of your business ideas. For the most part, these are sponsored by banks, the major accountancy bodies, chambers of commerce, local or national newspapers, business magazines and the trade press. Government departments may also have their own competitions as a means of promoting their initiatives for exporting, innovation, job creation and so forth. There is a Business

Plan Competition Directory on the Small Business Notes website run by Judith Kautz (**www.smallbusinessnotes.com/planning/ competitions.html**). Business link (**http://onlinebusinesslink.gov. uk/bdotg/action/batsearch**) has a business awards finder – just put in your postcode and business sector to identify the awards you could be eligible for.

CASE STUDY Innocent

In the summer of 1998, when Richard Reed, Adam Balon and Jon Wright had developed their first smoothie recipes but were still nervous about giving up their jobs, they bought £500-worth of fruit, turned it into smoothies and sold them from a stall at a London music festival. They put up a sign saying 'Do you think we should give up our jobs to make these smoothies?' next to bins labelled YES and NO, inviting people to put the empty bottle in the appropriate bin. At the end of the weekend the YES bin was full, so they went to work the next day and resigned. The rest, as they say, is history. Virtually a household name, Innocent Drinks has experienced a decade of rapid growth.

But the business stalled in 2008, with sales slipping back and European expansion soaking up cash at a rapid rate. The founders, who had an average age of 28, decided that they needed heavyweight advice and talked to Charles Dunstone, Carphone Warehouse founder, and Mervyn Davies, chairman of Standard Chartered. The strong advice was to get an investor with deep pockets and ideally something else by way of business experience to bring to the party to augment the youthful enthusiasm of the founders. They launched their search for an investor the day that Lehman Brothers filed for bankruptcy. In April 2009 the Innocent team accepted Coca-Cola as a minority investor in their business, paying £30 million for a stake of between 10–20 per cent. They chose Coca-Cola because, as well as providing the funds, the company could help get Innocent products out to more people in more places. They could also learn a lot from Coca-Cola, which has been in business for over 120 years.

Key jobs to do

- Assess how much money your business will need to finance it till you reach break-even.

- Calculate your gearing/leverage ratio for the coming year.

- To what extent are you planning to make use of the various sources of borrowed money and does your business have the capacity or need for more debt?

- To what extent are you planning to make use of the various sources of equity and does your business have the capacity or need for more equity?

- Check out crowdfunding and P2P lending options for the amount of money you need to raise.

- Review your options for getting free money from grants and competitions.

Preparing a business plan

As most businesses start without a business plan you could be forgiven for believing that preparing one is a luxury you can live without. Time is short and it is surely more important to find some customers and get selling. Beguiling though this may sound the statistics are against you. According to research carried out at Cranfield School of Management, over 70 per cent of the fastest-growing and most successful businesses started out with a written business plan. You might, as in the case study below, survive without a business plan, but as this founder discovered he needed one anyway and would have saved a lot of pain had he started out with one.

CASE STUDY

Johnnie Boden's first catalogue was hand drawn by a friend, with just eight items in it. That was back in 1991, and since then the business has come from bedroom to boardroom by way of a near-catastrophic lack of capital. The mail order company now competes with Gap, Marks & Spencer and John Lewis for a slice of the mainstream fashion market. ($244m/€198m) and one million customers in the UK, Germany and the United States, Boden (**www.boden.co.uk**) has reason to feel pleased, but it very nearly wasn't the success story it undoubtedly is. In an interview with *Real Business* (**www.realbusiness.co.uk** > Article) Boden explained why for the first three years the mail order clothes company was losing money hand over fist: 'We kept on running out of cash. Although the concept was strong, I had no decent business plan.'

Why you need a business plan

Every business could have a less rocky start than Boden if it starts out with a soundly based business plan rather than ending up with one to rescue it from the brink of catastrophe. Certainly, preparing a plan can take a couple of weeks' hard work, albeit spread over the months before you commit to the venture. There are at least four compelling reasons why every business founder should start out with a business plan:

- *It gives you confidence in the concept.* Carrying out the basic customer and competitor research that is the foundation of any business plan gives you a greater certainty that the business will actually work. All businesses have a number of wrinkles that can be smoothed out when preparing the business plan and at a much lower cost than by letting your customers tell you later.

- *It clarifies the scale of resources needed.* Although in his own words Boden did not have a 'swanky start-up' he did pump in £300,000 early on. With hindsight he felt the company really needed double that sum to have a decent chance of success, but as Boden started with money from a legacy left by an uncle he not unnaturally wanted to live within those means.

- *It improves your financing prospects.* As Johnnie Boden inherited a legacy he was able to sidestep some of the problems of raising money. But most start-ups need some money, even if it is only by way of a bank loan or an overdraft. And the more successful you are the more money you need. Typically a mail order business has £/$/€1 of capital invested to generate £/$/€2 of sales so, whilst Boden could squeak by with £300,000 when its turnover was less than £2 million ($2.9m/€2.35m), now it needs more like £50 million.

- *It rehearses you for the future.* When your business is successful, grows and takes on staff you will need to prepare and update business plans on a regular basis. This will be one of the primary ways of involving everyone in your business in shaping future plans and putting them into effect. No one expects every event as recorded on a business plan to occur as predicted, but the understanding and knowledge created by the process of business planning will prepare the business for any changes that it may face and so enable you to adjust quickly.

Contents of the plan

Whilst there is no such thing as a 'universal' business plan format, certain layouts and contents seem to have gone down better than others. The following sections offer some guidelines to producing an attractive business plan, from both an owner's and a financier's perspective.

Cover and table of contents

First, the cover should show the name of the business, the date on which the plan was prepared and your name, addresses (including e-mail), phone number and mobile number. Anyone reading the business plan may want to talk over some aspects of the proposal before arranging a meeting.

Having written the business plan you will know exactly where everything in it is, but any other readers need some pointers to guide them through the maze: that's what the table of contents does. Number each main section, marketing, finance, people and so forth, 1, 2, 3; important elements within a section can then be designated 1.1, 1.2 and so on.

Executive summary

This is the most important part of your plan and will form the heart of your 'elevator pitch' (see page 211). Written last, this should be punchy and short – ideally one page but never more than two – and should enthuse any reader. Its primary purpose is to get an outsider – bank manager, business angel or prospective partner – to want to read the rest of the business plan and to persuade your spouse or housemates that you have a better use for the spare room than them. It should include:

- what your product/service is, why it's better than or different from what is around now and why customers need what you plan to offer;

- how close you are to being ready to sell your product/service and whether anything remains to be done;

- why you have the skills and expertise to start up and run this business, who else you need to help in your business and how you will recruit them;

- financial projections showing how much money you need to start up and operate for the first year or so and, if you don't have sufficient money, how much you will need to raise and what security you can offer in the case of a lender or shareholding for an investor;

- how you will operate your business – sketch out the key steps from buying in any raw materials, through to selling, delivering and getting paid;

- why you want to start from home rather than elsewhere, how much space you will need and for how long you believe it will be possible to run the business from home.

The contents – putting flesh on the bones

Unlike the executive summary, which is structured to reveal the essence of your business proposition, the plan itself should follow a logical sequence such as this:

- *marketing:* with information on the product/service on offer, customers and the size of the market, competitors, proposed pricing, and promotion and selling method;

- *operations:* with information on any processes such as manufacture, assembly, purchasing, stock holding, delivery/fulfilment and the website;

- *financial projections:* with information on sales and cash flow for the next 12–18 months, showing how much money is needed, for what and by when;

- *premises:* what space and equipment will be needed and how your home will accommodate the business whilst staying within the law;

- *people:* what skills and experience you have that will help you run this business, what other people you will need and where you will find them;

- *administrative matters:* whether you have any IP (intellectual property) on your product or service, what insurance you will need, what bookkeeping and accounting system you will use, and how you will keep customer, supplier and employee records;

- *milestone timetable:* showing the key actions you have still to take to be ready to sell your product or service and the date these will be completed;

- *appendices:* for any bulky information such as market studies, competitors' leaflets, customer endorsements, technical data, patents, CVs and the like that you refer to in your business plan.

All these topics are covered in this book, and by using the index and table of contents you can find your way to them quickly.

Using business planning software

There are a number of free software packages that will help you through the process of writing your business plan. The ones listed below include some useful resources, spreadsheets and tips that may speed up the process, but are not substitutes for finding out the basic facts about your market, customers and competitors:

- Lloyd's bank offers Sage Business Planning free to anyone opening an account with them. See http://businesshelp.lloydstsb-business.com/starting/business-plan.

- NatWest bank's Business Planner is easy-to-use software that takes the hassle out of planning (it claims to offer a business plan in 60 seconds!). PC and Mac versions are available. On the website, you can also find tips on writing plans. Visit https://app.natwestplanner.co.uk/signup and http://support.natwest.com/business-tools-resources where you can find links to their business planning tools. You have to register to get access to them.

- Bradley University, Illinois, provides a range of business planning resources at www.bradley.edu/academic/colleges/fcba/centers/turner/business/planning.

Tips on communicating the plan

If you are going to show your business plan to people outside of your business, including family or friends, you need to take some steps to ensure that the way it's put together reflects the work that has been carried out and the value of your proposition. If you take it seriously you can expect others to do the same.

Packaging

Appropriate packaging enhances every product, and a business plan is no exception. A simple spiral binding with a plastic cover on the front and back makes it easy for the reader to move from section to section, and it ensures the plan will survive frequent handling.

Writing clearly

You and any partners should write the first draft of the business plan yourselves. The niceties of grammar and style can be resolved later. When your first draft has been revised, then comes the task of editing. Here the grammar, spelling and language must be carefully checked to ensure that your business plan is crisp, correct, clear and complete – and not too long: *circa* 10–15 pages will be more than sufficient in most cases.

A 'prospectus', such as a business plan seeking finance from investors, can have a legal status, turning any claims you may make for sales and profits (for example) into a 'contract'. Your accountant and legal adviser will be able to help you with the appropriate language that can convey your projections without giving them contractual status.

This would also be a good time to talk over the proposal with a 'friendly' financier. The financier can give an insider's view as to the strengths and weaknesses of your proposal.

Presentation techniques

If getting someone interested in your business plan is half the battle in raising funds, the other half is the oral presentation. Any organization financing a venture will insist on seeing the person or team involved presenting and defending their plans. They know that they are backing people every bit as much as the idea. You can be sure that any financier you are presenting to will be well prepared.

Keep these points in mind when preparing for the presentation of your business plan:

- Find out how much time you have; then rehearse your presentation beforehand. Allow at least as much time for questions as for your talk.

- Use visual aids and if possible bring and demonstrate your product or service. A video or computer-generated model is better than nothing.

- Explain your strategy in a businesslike manner, demonstrating your grasp of the competitive market forces at work. Listen to comments and criticisms carefully, avoiding a defensive attitude when you respond.

- Make your replies to questions brief and to the point. If they want more information, they can ask. This approach allows time for the many different questions that must be asked, either now or later, before an investment can proceed.

- Your goal is to create empathy between yourself and your listener(s). While you may not be able to change your personality, you could take a few tips on presentation skills. Eye contact, tone of speech, enthusiasm and body language all have a part to play in making a presentation successful.

- Wearing a suit is never likely to upset anyone. Shorts and sandals could just set the wrong tone! Serious money calls for serious people.

- Be prepared. You need to have every aspect of your business plan in your head and know your way around the plan forwards, backwards and sideways! You never know when the chance to present may occur. It's as well to have a 5-, 10- and 20-minute presentation ready to run at a moment's notice.

Making an elevator pitch

Often the person you are pitching your proposal to is short of time. As a rough rule of thumb, the closer you get to an individual with the power to make decisions the less time you will get to make your pitch. So you need to have a short presentation to hand that can be made in any circumstance – in a plane, at an airport or between floors in a lift, hence the name 'elevator pitch'.

CASE STUDY

Lara Morgan, founder of Pacific Direct, the hotel toiletries supplier, had come a long way from the garage in Bedford, England, where she started up her business, when she had the opportunity to pitch for a strategic alliance with one of the most influential players in her market. The scene was set for her to make a relaxed pitch over coffee at the Dorchester Hotel in Park Lane, when at a moment's notice the situation changed dramatically. Lara was told that owing to a diary change she had 15 minutes in a chauffeur-driven limousine en route to Harrods to make her proposition.

She was prepared, made her presentation and secured a deal that was instrumental in creating Pacific's unique five-star hotel strategy. Pacific now has Penhaligon's, Elemis, Ermenegildo Zegna, Nina Campbell, Floris, the White Company and Natural Products in their world-class product portfolio. Seventeen years later she sold her majority share for £20 million.

Using a non-disclosure agreement (NDA)

If you are going to show or discuss your business plan with business partners and it contains confidential information on your business or on the development of a unique idea you should consider getting them to sign an NDA. NDAs are confidentiality agreements that bind recipients to maintain your 'secrets' and not to take any action that could damage the value of those 'secrets'.

This means that they can't share the information with anyone else or act on the idea themselves, for a period of time at least. NDAs are a helpful way of getting advice and help whilst protecting you from someone using your information to compete against you.

The Intellectual Property Office provides a guide that can help you put together an NDA. See www.ipo.gov.uk/nda.pdf.

Key jobs to do

- Review your present business plan and compare to the structure recommended.

- Examine available software to see if anything available would make life easier.

- Check current methods of ensuring confidentiality of business plans.

- Prepare an elevator pitch.

- Check your executive summary to make sure it explains and excites.

Taking on employees

Taking on your first employee can be an unnerving task requiring that you take on board new skills. But unless you do your business will have limited growth prospects and may never realize its full potential or value.

Recruitment and selection

No aspect of dealing with employees is particularly easy, and it's an interesting indictment that few people starting a second business after successfully selling their first actively search for one with more employees than they had before.

The starting point in the process is to decide what employees you need (someone with selling skills or who can make deliveries, for example), set about finding them and then get them to work effectively in your business doing what you want them to do because they want to do it.

Who do you need?

Working out the sort of person you need means more than just looking at existing problems. Taking on an employee may take weeks, even months, and employment law means that, once you have taken someone on, shedding that person without good reason will be difficult. So you need to look a year or so ahead and decide on your growth objectives. Then it will be possible to determine the number of employees you are going to need, when you will need them and where the gaps in your organization are likely to appear.

Before rushing into looking for a full-time employee consider the possibility of using part-timers or job sharers. There are advantages going this route. In the first place you may tap into a better pool of job seekers. Those looking to work this way may well be recently retired, or returning to work after discharging family responsibilities; as such they may have valuable skills and knowledge. Secondly, you can put a toe into the world of becoming an employer and see if it's for you before getting in too deep.

Settling on the job description

Often employers draw up the job description after they have found the candidate. This is a mistake; having it from the outset narrows down your search for suitable candidates, focuses you on specific search methods and gives you a valid reason for declining unwelcome job requests from family and friends. In any event you have to give employees a contract of employment when you take them on, and the job description makes this task much easier.

Include the following in a job description:

- the title, such as telesales person, bookkeeper or delivery van driver;
- the knowledge, skills and experience you expect the person to have or acquire;
- the main duties and measurable outputs expected;

- the work location and general conditions such as hours to be worked, lunch breaks and paid holiday arrangements;
- the pay structure and rewards;
- who the employee will work for if not for you.

Where can you find great employees?

There are many ways to find employees; to find great employees the choices are more limited. Research at Cranfield revealed some alarming statistics. Firstly, nearly two-thirds of all first appointments failed and the employee left within a year having been unsatisfactory. Secondly, there were marked differences in the success rate that appear to be dependent on the way in which employees are looked for.

Tapping into the family

Employing family members has a number of key advantages. Firstly, they are a known quantity and you can usually vouch for their honesty and reliability. In the second place, you can ask them to work in conditions and for hours that would be neither acceptable nor legally allowed for any other employee. As against that you need to weigh up the difficulties you may have if they can't do the work to the standard or in the manner you like.

Employing an agency or consultant

This is the least popular, most expensive and most successful recruitment method. Only 1 in 15 small firms do so for their early appointments, but when they do they are three times more likely to get the right person. The reasons for success are in part the value added by the agency or consultant in helping get the job description and pay package right and that the agency or consultant has already pre-interviewed prospective employees before putting them forward. These organizations can help here:

- Universal Jobmatch is a service offered through Government Gateway, the centralized registration service for e-Government services in the UK. This service has been designed to help you find and employ the most suitable jobseekers for potential jobs. You can post jobs, review CVs and get updates on jobseekers who match your requirements (**www.gov.uk/advertise-job**).

- The Recruitment & Employment Confederation (**www.rec.uk.com/membership**) is the professional association that supports and represents over 8,000 recruitment agencies and 6,000 recruitment professionals. As well as advice on choosing an agent there is a mass of information on employment law and a directory of members listed by business sector and geographic area.

Advertising in the press

You have a large number of options when it comes to press advertising. Local papers are good for generally available skills and for jobs where the pay is such that people expect to live close to where they work. National papers are much more expensive but attract a wider pool of people with a cross-section of skills including those not necessarily available locally. Trade and specialist papers and magazines are useful if it is essential your applicant has a specific qualification, say in accountancy or computing.

The goal of a job advertisement is not just to generate responses from suitably qualified applicants, but also to screen out applicants who are clearly unqualified. If you make the job sound more attractive than it really is and are too vague about the sort of person you are looking for you could end up with hundreds of applicants.

You need to consider the following elements when writing the job advertisement:

- *Headline.* This is usually the job title, perhaps with some pertinent embellishment, for example 'Dynamic salesperson required'.

- *Job information.* This is a line or two about the general duties and responsibilities of the job.

- *Business information.* Always include something explaining what you do and where you do it.

- *Qualifications.* Specify any qualifications and experience that are required. You can qualify some aspects of this by saying a particular skill would be useful but is not essential.

- *Response method*. Tell applicants how to reply and what information to provide.

Try to include something about your business culture in the advertisement. One small firm puts its advertisements sideways on, so applicants have to turn the paper round to read them. They claim this lets people see they want people who look at things in unconventional ways to apply and that they are not a run-of-the-mill firm that works like any other firm. Using an active rather than a passive voice will give your advertisement a sense of buzz and enthusiasm.

Using the internet

The fastest-growing route to finding new job applicants is via the internet. The number of websites offering employment opportunities has exploded in recent years. The advantages of Internet recruitment to both candidates and clients are obvious. Internet recruitment offers a fast, immediate and cheap service compared to more traditional methods of recruitment. A number of recruitment sites have established formidable reputations in Europe and the US. These include:

- Futurestep (**www.futurestep.comwww.futurestep.com**), which is now part of Korn Ferry, a conventional recruitment agency. It covers all job functions and industry sectors.

- Monster (**www.monster.co.uk**) has a Power CV Search for employers that quickly sifts its database for the most suitable candidates. The site attracts approximately 100,000 visits per month and contains over a million CVs. Its vacancies cover every industry sector and regional area.

- Web Recruit (**www.webrecruit.co.uk**) has successfully recruited for over 65,000 roles in 10 years.

Another option is to have a job-listing section on your own website. This is absolutely free, although you're certain to be trawling in a very small pool. This may not matter if the right sort of people are already visiting your site. At least they know something about your products and services before they apply that lets you look for the job boards by country, region and those most suited to the job on offer and the industry you are in.

Using your network

Nearly two out of every three very small businesses use business contacts and networks when they are recruiting. This route is favoured because it is cheap and informal and can be pursued without the bother of writing a job description, which can in effect be infinitely varied to suit the candidates that may surface.

Unfortunately the statistics indicate that two out of five appointments made through personal contacts fail within six months and the business is back in the recruiting game again. The reasons for this being an unsatisfactory route lie somewhere in the absence of rigour that the approach encourages; only if you can take a thorough approach and be sure of a genuine reason why someone would want to recommend someone to you should you recruit in this way.

Hiring people

Once you have candidates for your vacancy the next task is to interview, select and appoint. If you have done your homework the chances are that you will have a dozen or more applicants, too many to interview, so this process is somewhat like a funnel, narrowing down until you have your ideal candidate appointed.

Selecting a candidate

You need to find at least two and ideally three people who could fill your vacancy to a standard that you would be happy with. This gives you contrast, which is always helpful in clarifying your ideas on the job, and a reserve in case the first candidate drops by the wayside or turns you down. The stages in making your selection are as follows:

- Make a shortlist of the three or four candidates that best suit the criteria set out in your job definition.
- Interview each candidate, ideally on the same day, so all the information is fresh in your mind. Plan your questions in advance but

be sure to let the candidate do most of the talking. Use your questions to plug any gaps in your knowledge about the candidate. Monster (**www.monster.co.uk** > Resource Centre) has a number of guides to recruitment and hiring practices. as well as plenty of other aspects of employment.

- Use tests to assess aptitude and knowledge if the job is a senior one such as accountant or sales manager. You can find a test to measure almost any aspect of a candidate's skills, attitude, aptitude and almost anything else you care to name. Thousands of the most successful companies use them and claim to get better candidates and higher staff retention than they would otherwise achieve. Tests cost from £10 a candidate. The British Psychological Society (**www.bps.org.uk**) Psychological Testing Centre and the Chartered Institute of Personnel and Development (**www.cipd. co.uk**) list various types of test, their purpose and how to use them and interpret results.

Making job offers

Having found the ideal candidate, you next need to get him or her hired and happy to work for you. However well the interview may have gone, resist making a job offer on the spot. Both you and the candidate need to sleep on it, giving you both the chance to discuss with your partners and consider what has come out of the interviews.

Take up references   Always take up references before offering the job. Use both the telephone and a written reference and check that any necessary qualifications are valid. This may take a little time and effort, but is essential as a protection against unsuitable or dishonest applicants.

Put the offer in writing   Whilst you may make the job offer on the telephone, face to face or in an e-mail, always follow up with a written offer. The offer should contain all the important conditions of the job, salary, location, hours, holiday, work, responsibilities, targets and the all-important start date. This in effect will be the backbone of the contract of employment you will have to provide shortly after the person starts working for you.

Make the new employee welcome　When new employees join you, be on hand to meet them, show them the ropes and introduce them to anyone else they are likely to come into contact with. This is crucial if they are going to work in your home alongside you, and these introductions should extend to your spouse, even if he or she doesn't work in the business, your children, your pets, the postman and the neighbours.

They also need to know about the practical aspects of working for you: where they can eat inside and out, coffee making and any equipment they will be working with. If they will be in your home when it is otherwise empty then they need to know where the fuses are and whom to contact if say the internet or telephone goes down.

Dealing with unsuccessful candidates　By the very nature of the recruitment task the person appointed is just the tip of a big iceberg of applicants and interviewees. These people have to be responded to, advising them that they do not have the job. For your first reserve list, those whom you may call on if the appointment goes wrong for any reason, it is worth taking particular care with your reply. Here you can emphasize the strength of their application but that the background of another candidate was closer to your needs. You don't have to go into details as to specifically why a particular candidate got the job and they did not.

Managing employees

Bringing a new employee into your home business is a bit like carrying out a heart transplant. Even if the surgeon finds a compatible organ and the operation goes to plan, the new heart can be rejected because it doesn't quite fit in the surrounding parts. Even in the smallest of firms the 'rejection' rate of new employees is very high. One study of key staff appointments in small firms showed that over 50 per cent of first appointments failed in the first six months. The cost of failure in this area can be very high, setting back your plans by months or even years.

Aside from making a new employee welcome and to feel comfortable in what after all is your home environment, you need to become a manager, a skill often alien to entrepreneurial types. The central elements that between them add up to successful management are discussed in the following sections.

Delegate

At first when you start to delegate you may well feel you could do the job better and more quickly yourself. You may even resent the time you have to invest to get a new employee up and running in the way you would like. But having appointed someone and given him or her a specific set of tasks, clear goals and a timetable you need to step back and let the person get on with it.

Discreetly offer help and advice and set times aside, daily or weekly dependent on the nature of the work, to review achievements and progress. But don't lean over the employee's shoulder all day scrutinizing every move. This is demotivating and counterproductive, as you are depriving yourself of the main reason you took the employee on in the first place – to free you up to do even more important work.

Motivate

Very often the problem is not so much that of motivating people, but of avoiding demotivating them! If you can keep off the backs of employees, it is quite possible that they will motivate themselves. After all, most of us want the same things: a sense of achievement or challenge, recognition of our efforts, an interesting and varied job, and opportunities for responsibility, advancement and job growth. But in a small firm the potential for demotivation is high. Workloads invariably peak and there is never any slack in the systems of a small firm. Inevitably an employee will feel overloaded, neglected or just plain hard done by on occasions.

You can motivate employees with some fairly basic techniques, such as:

- Give praise as often as you can and minimize your reaction to bad results. You can always leaven out criticism with some favourable comment.

- Show an interest in what employees do, as everyone likes attention.

- Train, coach and add to employees' skills. Employees rate this area as the greatest motivator, as it is a sign of commitment on the part of an employer and it will improve the value to you of the work they do. You can find a course on more or less anything on one of the MOOC (Massive Open Online Course) platforms. These courses are free for everyone, but some courses charge a fee for a verified certificate (you can still participate for free, however).

The two main MOOCs are:

- Coursera (**www.coursera.org**). Founded at Stanford in 2012, Coursera's mission is to 'provide universal access to the world's best education'. It is 'an education platform that partners with top universities and organisations worldwide, to offer courses online for anyone to take, for free'. Over a hundred universities offer lecture courses through Coursera, including Stanford, IE Business School, Yale, Princeton, Northwestern, Rutgers, Duke, Copenhagen, Tokyo, HEC Paris, Columbia and Ludwig-Maximilians-Universität München.

- edX (www.edx.org). Founded by the Massachusetts Institute of Technology (MIT) and Harvard University in May 2012, edX provides over 400 courses from universities including MIT, Harvard, Berkeley, Caltech, Georgetown, Paris-Sorbonne, Peking, IIT Bombay, Rice, Kyoto, Columbia, Australian National and Cornell. edX's goal is to 'offer the highest quality courses from institutions who share our commitment to excellence in teaching and learning'. Many other MOOC course providers (often universities) that participate in Coursera or edX programmes also run their own MOOCs through their websites. However, such offerings aren't easy to find. A better route to supplement MOOC lectures and courses is to use the Multimedia Educational Resource for Learning and Online Teaching (MERLOT, **www. merlot.org** – click on the 'Search Merlot' tab). The MERLOT project began in 1997 at the California State University Center for Distributed Learning. For budding students, the search facility is all you really need to know about.

- Improve working conditions. You probably started up on a shoe-string, and money rarely gets much easier in the early stages of growth. One area where corners are frequently cut is working conditions. There is an obligation on an employer to provide healthy and safe working conditions, but it also makes good business sense to provide pleasant working conditions that can favourably affect motivation.

- Make the job more fun. Dull, repetitive and boring jobs lead to demotivation and loss of performance. Often jobs can be made more interesting by rethinking the way they are done. This can be achieved by giving people whole tasks to perform rather than small parts, by empowering people to make decisions themselves on such matters as refunds or by letting them see more of the world in which your business works, say by attending exhibitions or visiting customers.

Reward

People come to work to get paid, and if they achieve great results they expect great rewards. There is no single aspect of an employee's life more susceptible to gripes and complaints than pay. So how can you make sure that doesn't happen in your business?

- Firstly, make sure you are paying at least the going rate for the job in the area. Don't think you are getting a bargain if you get employees to work for less than that figure; if they do either they are not good at their job, are poor timekeepers or have some other shortcoming that you will find out about later, or they are good and when they find out will feel cheated and leave. The easiest way to find the going rate is to look at advertisements for similar jobs in your area or visit PayScale (**www.payscale.com/hr**), where you can get accurate real-time information on pay scales.

- Include an element of incentive for achieving measurable goals. This could be commission, perhaps the easiest reward system, but it really only works for those directly involved in selling. Or it could be a bonus for successful performance, usually paid in a lump sum related as closely as possible to the results obtained. The Chartered Institute of Personnel and Development (**www.cipd.co.uk/knowledge**) gives further guidance on a comprehensive range of reward options.

- Benefits in kind are any form of compensation that is not part of basic pay and isn't tied directly to employees' performance in their job. Pension, working conditions, being allowed to wear casual dress, on-site childcare, personal development training, company product discounts, flexible hours, telecommuting and fitness facilities are all on the list of benefits that are on offer in certain jobs today. There may be tax implications on benefits in kind, and the Digita 'Use of employer's assets: benefits in kind calculator' (**www.digita.com/tiscali/home/calculators/employersassetscalculator/default.asp**) will help work out if tax is due and if so how much.

Legal issues in employing people

Employing people full or part time is something of a legal minefield, starting with the job advert and culminating with the point at which you decide to part company. Three comprehensive sources of information on the legal aspects of employment are:

- Acas (**www.acas.org.uk** > Tools and Resources) where you can find the latest updates on employment law and most other areas relating to employing people.

- The government website (https://www.gov.uk/employing-staff) has a useful guide to 'Employing staff for the first time'.

- The Mix (www.themix.org.uk/work-and-study/workers-rights-and-pay) is a site that helps young people have access to high-quality, impartial information as an aid to making decisions. It covers everything to do with work, including drug testing at work. Whilst the site's centre of gravity is young people, the law as described applies to employers.

Advertising the job

As with any advertising you are governed by the laws on discrimination and equal opportunities. That means any reference to gender, age, nationality, sexual orientation or religion is not permitted. You can still describe the job and the ideal candidate in terms of the candidate's experience, knowledge, attitude and qualifications. For tips on how to advertise without discriminating visit this link on the government website: **www.gov.uk/**employer-preventing-discrimination/recruitment.

Contracts of employment

You are required to give employees a contract of employment within two months of their starting work. The contract has to contain all the obvious things such as where the job is to be, what the responsibilities are, pay and holiday entitlement, as well as details on sick pay, pension, period of notice and the grievance and disciplinary procedure.

This government web page www.gov.uk/employment-contracts-and-conditions has everything you are required by law to give a new employee. The law requires: that all workers have a statutory right to at least four weeks' paid annual leave, pro rata for part-timers; that you pay the statutory minimum wage, dependent on the age of the employee; that employees work within the working time limits (48 hours a week); and that parents are entitled to periods of paid leave when they have children (up to 52 weeks for women and one or two weeks for men).

Employment records

You need to maintain records on your employees, keeping note of absences, sickness, disputes, disciplinary matters, accidents, training, holidays and any appraisals or performance reviews. If you have an unsatisfactory employee and want to dismiss him or her, this information will be vital. The government web page www.gov.uk/personal-data-my-employer-can-keep-about-me provides details of all details you are allowed to keep about an employee.

Safety at work

You have a 'duty of care' to ensure anyone working for you is working in a safe environment and is not exposed to possible health and safety hazards. You need to make an assessment of risk and working conditions covering everything from fire exits to ensuring that ventilation, temperature, lighting and toilet facilities meet health and safety requirements. The Health and Safety Executive (**www.hse.gov.uk/guidance**) have ready-made risk assessment forms and a basic guide to health and safety at work.

Unfair dismissal

Although it's the handful of cases usually brought by City workers that grab the headlines, in the year to 31 March 2016 a total of 83,031 tribunal applications were made, up from 61,308 the previous year. The highest award for an unfair dismissal claim was £470,865 whilst the average award was £13,851, up by some £1,500 on 2015. Employers who have been through the process say that it's the stress and administrative burden rather than the settlement itself that are of greatest concern. Iambeingfired (**www.iambeingfired.co.uk** > Claim Evaluator) is worth examining, as it gives the employee's side of the argument. The Claim Evaluator tool takes an employee through a series of questions to see if he or she has a case for unfair dismissal. The site also has comprehensive information on all aspects of employment law that impinge on the likelihood of being dismissed.

Employment law in other jurisdictions

Employment legislation varies greatly between countries. In Appendix 3, the Human Development Index provides useful information on employment issues. Also, Chapter 14 provides links to an international network of lawyers (Martindale-Hubbell Lawyer Locator) and **PayScale.com** that provide salary comparisons for thousands of jobs in countries ranging from Afghanistan to Zimbabwe.

Key jobs to do

- Assess the numbers and type of employees you might need in the first six months of operating.
- Review your possible options for finding those staff.
- Prepare recruitment and selection interview questions and criteria.
- Determine pay and reward systems.
- Plan methods to motivate and manage staff.
- Examine any legal issues that might arise in connection with employment.

Growing profitably

The most successful businesses, when it comes to growing, concentrate their efforts in three areas: optimizing resources, maintaining or improving profit margins and of course building up sales revenue. It is this last strategy alone that draws the most attention, but without pursuing the other two it may lead only to unprofitable growth, so leaving a business more vulnerable as it gets bigger. All three of these generic growth strategies are to a greater or lesser extent intertwined so you should look on this categorization process more as an *aide-mémoire* rather than a rigid structure.

Put simply, you can see that any action that tends to increase profits whilst either not increasing or actually reducing the resources employed to generate those profits produces healthy growth. Using the summarized financial statements for High Note shown in Table 13.1, the example used in Chapter 9, we can see the effect of various growth strategies. If we can increase sales say by £/$/€10,000, whilst maintaining the profit margin at 11.21 per cent, we will have

Table 13.1 High Note's profit and loss account and balance sheet

Profit and loss account	£/$/€	Balance sheet	£/$/€	£/$/€
Sales	60,000	Fixed assets		
Less the cost of goods to be sold (materials, labour, etc)	30,000	Garage conversion, etc		11,500
		Computer		1,000
Gross profit	30,000	Total fixed assets		12,500
Less operating expenses (rent, utilities, admin, etc)	21,300			
Operating profit	8,700	Working capital		
Less interest due to bank	600	Current assets		
Profit before tax	8,100	Stock	9,108	
Less tax	1,377	Debtors	12,000	
Profit after tax (11.21%)	6,723	Cash	0	
			21,108	
		Less		
		Current liabilities		
		Overdraft	4,908	
		Creditors	0	
			4,908	
		Working capital (CA–CL)		16,200
		Total assets		28,700

grown profits by £/$/€1,121. So both sales and profits will have grown by 17 per cent. If that can also be done without needing any more working space or money tied up in stocks, so much the better. Our return on capital will also improve. Contrast that say with a strategy that grows sales, whilst costs rise disproportionately and more assets are employed to achieve that growth, and an unhealthy growth pattern will emerge.

Optimizing resources

The first and in some ways the simplest way to grow profits is to get more of what you sell ready for market using fewer resources. This strategy improves profit margins, whilst either reducing the actual amount of money needed to run the business or allowing you to grow without recourse to additional financing. Both are desirable outcomes, as they leave you with a more secure venture as well as a bigger one.

Review working methods

The richest source of opportunities to optimize comes from finding ways to work smarter rather than harder. Finding out about better ways to work can be difficult for a small firm where the founder has few senior employees to learn from, one of the benefits big businesses get by virtue of continuously recruiting new people. Owner-managers can compensate for that by getting out themselves and seeing what is going on in their industry. These are some ways you can keep abreast of the latest developments in your field:

- Read widely both the magazines that relate to your industry and those of neighbouring topics. You don't have to rush out and buy hundreds of magazines and learned journals. Use Find Articles (**www.findarticles.com**), which has a database of over 10 million articles on a range of topics, many of which are free and online.

- See if your competitors are doing much better than you and then try to find out why. Get their catalogues, leaflets and price lists and examine their websites. Get their accounts from **www.gov. uk**/get-information-about-a-company and calculate some key ratios to compare performance, such as those shown in chapter 9. Use Google News to read stories about them in the press (announcing new products, recruiting more staff, etc).

- Attend exhibitions, conferences and seminars where you are likely to meet and hear movers and shakers in your industry. AllConferences.com (**www.allconferences.com**) is a directory focusing on conferences, conventions, trade shows, exhibitions and workshops, which can be searched by category, keyword, date and venue as well as by title.

CASE STUDY

Tim Roupell started his business, Daily Bread, at the age of thirty-one by making fifty sandwiches in the basement of a friend's deli. Twenty-three years later, Tim sold the business, having built it up to making 50,000 sandwiches a day, employing 230 people and turning over £14million a year.

Initially he invested £800 in a meat-slicing machine and a couple of baskets, made up his fifty delicious sandwiches and walked around local offices trying to sell them. His day started at 4.30 am, literally making sandwiches, and finished after dark when he placed orders for ingredients and did the books.

As with other companies that supplied sandwiches to Marks and Spencer, Daily Bread was required to discard four slices from each loaf, the crusts and the first slice in. As well as being a sheer waste of food, the company was paying around £65,000 a year to send this food to be turned into gas for power generation.

As a result of advice from a UK government-sponsored body Environwise, the company started to sell its unwanted bread to a local farmer for use as animal feed. Benefits to the company include turning a cost into a revenue stream as they get £25 a tonne from the farmer. Also the process emits no carbon dioxide and contributed to their green strategy culminating in them being named the tenth greenest company in the UK, and *the* greenest company in the food and drink sector in the Sunday Times Best Green Companies Awards.

The business is now part of the Hain Celestial Group, a leading natural and organic food and personal care products company. The groups other brands include Linda McCartney and they have operations in North America and Europe. The company still makes delicious sandwiches and has earned a royal warrant to prove it, but more conventional routes to market have supplanted basket deliveries.

Control working capital

If you are working from home the biggest element of cost, your property and land, will be substantially fixed, at least until you make a major strategic decision to move into dedicated business premises. During your early growth period the main levers in your hands for ensuring healthy growth will be in the working capital area. If sales and profit growth can be achieved using the same proportion of working capital or less then healthy growth is being achieved.

Debtor control

If you are selling on credit and take 90 days to collect your money in from customers, which is by no means uncommon, then you are tying up an extra £/$/€150,000 cash for every £/$/€1 million of sales, compared to a firm getting its money in 35 days. For a small firm that could amount to the whole value of its overdraft. Or, looking at it another way, getting paid a week earlier would free up nearly tens of thousands in life-saving cash.

A very small amount of extra effort put in here can pay great dividends, and it's important to remember the less cash needed to finance the business the more profitable that business will be. Here are some things you can do to get paid faster:

- If you sell on credit set out your terms of trade clearly on your invoices. Unless customers know when you expect to be paid, they will pay when it suits them.

- Find out when your biggest customers have their monthly cheque run and make sure your bills reach them in time.

- Send out statements promptly to chase up late payers, and always follow up with a phone call.

Always take trade references when giving credit and look at their accounts to see how sound they are.

Control stocks

Just-in-time production methods mean that most big businesses hold barely a few days of essential supplies. In turn the people they buy from hold light stock levels too, which goes some way to explaining why motorways and shipping lanes are busier than ever: most materials are on the move.

Small businesses tend to hold too high a level of stocks as they grow, for the simple reason that they have not yet developed a control system. You can control stock levels using a manual system of record cards with details of quantities held, who supplies you, what their delivery lead time is and what your reorder stock level is. As you enter information on the cards you can see when it's time to take action. When you get to the point of having too many items of stock to manage manually, move up to a software solution. The more sophisticated accounting packages listed in Chapter 9 will include stock management.

Improving profit margins

Over time, costs tend to creep ahead of the value you are getting for the money spent. The rises happen steadily, often nearly invisibly and in increments sometimes apparently insignificant in themselves. There are a number of courses of action you can take to improve margins, which are discussed in the following sections.

Charge more

It is never easy raising prices but it can, if done selectively, be a path to healthy growth. First, let's examine the potential rewards and risks. Using High Note as our working model, assume its £/$/€60,000 of sales come from 60 customers all buying £/$/€1,000 worth of goods and services from us, at 50 per cent gross profit margin. If by raising our prices by 10 per cent we lost no customers then our profit would rise by £/$/€6,000, all of which would drop to the bottom line, before tax, as there are no additional costs involved, almost doubling our profit before tax. But what would happen if we lost six customers (10 per cent) as a result of the price rise? Now we would have only 54 customers paying £/$/€1,100 each, or £/$/€59,400. That's only £/$/€600 less than before, and there are other benefits that have not been shown.

Putting the pressure on price rather than volume means carrying less stock, having fewer bills to chase, using less capital and wearing out equipment less quickly. That is not to imply that putting up prices is an easy task, but it may not be much harder than finding new customers, and it is nearly always more profitable. When raising prices, try to offer some extra value in return in terms of improved service or extra features.

The above sums depend on your level of gross profit. The lower your gross profit the less business you can afford to lose for any given price rise. Download a spreadsheet that does all the arithmetic of changing prices for you from Harvard and Business School (**http://hbswk.hbs.edu**)

Retain more customers

Acquiring customers is an expensive process; they have to be found, wooed and won. Once you have them onside they cost less to keep, spend more money with you and are less price-sensitive than new customers. Retaining them will do more than almost any other marketing strategy to grow your profit margin. According to research carried out by Bain (**www.bain.com**), a 5 per cent increase in customer retention can improve profitability by 75 per cent. The Harvard Business Review article 'The value of keeping The right customers (**http://hbr.org**). To retain customers:

- Listen to them, actively. Follow-up phone calls, short question-naires on reply-paid cards, blogs and mystery shopping are all successful listening strategies. Ninety-six per cent of complaints never get made; dissatisfied customers just go elsewhere.

- Act on complaints. Ninety-four per cent of customers who complain will give their supplier another chance if they are dealt with quickly and fairly.

- Build loyalty by giving customers a reason to stay with you, such as discounts or VIP treatment, or give them something more than they expect to show that you appreciate them and their business.

- Understand your customer's goals and make sure your products and services are closely aligned to them.

- Demonstrate your commitment by getting to know their business thoroughly and adding products to your range unique to their needs.

Change the product/service mix

If you sell more than one product or service, or are planning to introduce new ones as part of your growth strategy, analyse costs so that energies are focused on those with the highest profit margin. Very few owner-managers have any true idea as to which products or services generate the most profit, so collecting the data has to be the first step.

Buy less

The challenge here is to strip out waste or find ways to step up yield. When you are working on your own this will probably not be a fertile field, but once you have employees, however dedicated, the problems start. The classic question when people want to buy something is to ask 'If it were your money would you spend it this way?' One entrepreneur who had built his company to a £3 million business from a standing start five years earlier formed his 20 employees into what he called Smart Circles. He challenged them to find ways the firm could do things faster, better and at a lower cost. In the following year he doubled profits, and five years later his business was valued at £10 million.

Pay less

However smart you are and however efficiently you operate there are plenty of costs you can't eliminate. There is the rather telling story told of the man who cuts his donkey's feed back a few grains a day and didn't notice a thing until it died. So once unnecessary costs are eliminated look for ways to pay out less of your hard-won profits to other people. Go down your biggest areas of expense and start looking for savings.

Improve your buying

There are three ways in which you can get more for less, when it comes to buying almost anything:

- Join an online buying group such as Buying Groups (**www. buyinggroups.co.uk**) and Premier Purchasing Group (**www. ppg-uk.co.uk**), which help buyers to join forces and by buying in bulk get better prices and terms of trade.

- Negotiate better prices. Fewer than 1 in 20 owner-managers negotiate better deals from their suppliers. Companies such as Collective Purchasing (**www.collectivepurchasing.co.uk**) collect pricing information to help you negotiate without compromising on quality.

- Consider buying in bulk or on longer-term contracts, but only if the discount is higher than your cost of capital.

Don't leave any important area out when looking for lower costs. As well as suppliers of goods, service providers including insurance companies, utilities and banks are all well used to being negotiated with, as are accountants and lawyers.

Reduce the tax take

Tax on profits is often a small business's biggest single expense. All money that goes in taxes can be considered a waste as far as a business is concerned, as unlike individuals who may see something of value for their tax a business gets nothing back. So the rule here is to minimize tax within the law. These are some strategies for reducing taxes and so increasing retained profits, though some of that may not then be available as cash to the business:

- Check that you have charged all the allowable business expenses against profit. Bytestart, the small business portal, has a useful section on running a home office (**www.bytestart.co.uk**/home-office-expenses.html), dedicated to issues specific to businesses run from home.

- Top up or start a pension. If you take out a SIPPS (Self Invested Personal Pension Scheme), you can invest the proceeds in most types of business premises, a shop, warehouse, office or workshop. Before you take the plunge, get professional advice from a tax expert and a pension provider. To find out more about SIPPS, contact The Pensions Advisory Service (TPAS), an indepenent non-profit organization and a good place to head for general information (tel: 0300 123 1047; website: **www.pensionsadvisoryservice.org.uk**) and the Association of Independent Financial Advisers (tel: 020 7628 1287; website: **www.aifa.net**)

- Take advantage of your spouse's tax position, particularly if he or she has no other income from employment and is in a lower tax bracket than you.

- Invest in new equipment. Anything designated as energy saving or that reduces water use currently qualifies for a 100 per cent tax allowance.

Whatever you do make sure you keep within the law and take professional advice.

Bumping up sales

Generating more business is the most common strategy for growing a business, but it is not without risks. Igor Ansoff, a US academic, developed a way of categorizing strategies as an aid to understanding the nature of the risks involved. He invited his students to consider growth options as a square matrix divided into four segments. The axes are labelled, with products and services running along the 'x' axis, starting with 'present' and 'new', and with markets up the 'y' axis similarly labelled.

Ansoff then went on to assign titles to each type of strategy, in an ascending scale of risk (you can see the matrix at **www.strategyvectormodel.com** > Theories > Ansoff Matrix):

- *Market penetration* involves selling more of your existing products and services to existing customers – the lowest-risk strategy.

- *Product/service development* involves creating extensions to your existing products or new products to sell to your existing customer base. This is more risky than market penetration, but less risky than entering a new market where you will face new competitors and may not understand the customers as well as you do your current ones.

- *Market development* involves entering new market segments or completely new markets either in your home country or abroad.

- *Diversification* is selling new products into new markets, which is the most risky strategy, as both are relative unknowns. Avoid it unless all other strategies have been exhausted.

Milk your customer base

The greatest opportunities for rapid, profitable and low-cost growth lie in extending and developing your relationship with your existing customers. The following sections discuss some of the areas to explore.

Generate referrals

The chances are that your existing customers know others like themselves, who in turn know yet more potential customers. You will know from your own experience that, if anyone talks in glowing terms about a restaurant, cleaner, babysitter or website designer they have recently used, a long patient queue will form to get the contact details.

Where you don't actually see your customers face to face this is a little more difficult, but still possible. You can offer discounts, commission or prizes to induce satisfied customers to give you the contacts you need. The American Customer Satisfaction Index (**www.acsi.org** > Customer Satisfaction Benchmarks) measures satisfaction in 43 industries. Checking the score for your industry will give you a benchmark to aim for in order to increase your chance of improving the number of referrals you can secure.

Survey lost orders

There will be plenty of occasions when you don't get an order but that needn't be a dead loss. There is valuable information that can be gleaned from the experience if you take the time to find out why the order was lost. One company, an internet second-hand bookseller, discovered that the cost of shipping product was the single most important reason why an enquiry was not converted into an order. Their costs were out of line with others in the market because they had adopted a single price strategy that lumped heavy big books and small light ones together into a single price band; this was administratively easy but a marketing disaster, as a book costing less than a pound ended up costing five times that figure when delivery was taken into account. Once the firm knew why they were losing business they changed their strategy and started winning more business.

Win business from competitors

Having gone to all the trouble of winning and retaining customers it makes good sense to get them to buy more. Usually this brings you, the supplier, economies in administration costs and delivery charges, and as known entities existing customers can usually be relied upon to pay up.

But before you can get them to buy more you need to know how much they do or could buy and who else, if anyone, they buy from: in other words who you are in competition with. This is back to having good intelligence on your customers. You can find out who else supplies them by including a question on competitors in your next satisfaction questionnaire. As for how much they buy, usually you can rely on market averages. For example, if you are selling chemicals to swimming pool owners and they have to check chlorine levels daily and the useful season is 150 days a year, then you know they need at least three packs of 50 chemical testing strips. If they are only buying one from you, then they are buying up to two more from someone else.

Next you need to devise a strategy to win that extra business from them. Offering a three-for-two discount, free delivery if they order three or some such strategy will mean giving up some part of your additional profit, but still ending up with more profit than if you had settled for just a one-pack order.

Buy up competitors

If you have the cash then you can take over a competitor's business. You may not keep all their business, particularly if you are already supplying them; some businesses like to have at least two suppliers. Daltons Business (**www.daltonsbusiness.com** has guides on various aspects of buying a business. See also Chapter 1, 'Finding a business to buy', page 23.

Convert non-users

There are inevitably many non-users of whatever you and your competitors sell. So whilst the majority of the £1.8 billion annual sales of greeting cards are bought in bricks and mortar stores, rather than online, there is nevertheless an important and growing internet business to be tapped into. Companies such as Milkwood with a bricks and clicks model are developing ways to convert their non-user internet market, that is people who only buy in store to buying online too. Milkwood's 'refer a friend' strategy online and e-mail address capture initiative in store has played a major role in helping the business to double turnover from £2 million to £4 million in three years. (See the case study in this chapter.) You will receive £30 ($43/€35) FREE', AOL hope that, once they have broken their duck, a proportion will remain as customers.

Create new products and services

Most new product launches by big businesses don't succeed, and in the grocery business the failure rate is over 75 per cent. Whilst that figure may sound alarming you have to offset against that the cost of development, which if low may not be a problem, and the rewards of success. Google's two dozen new product launches, including Google Talk, Google Finance and Gmail, have yet to become serious players, ranking around 40th in their respective markets with no more than 2 per cent shares. Google's strategy of launching early and often mean that glitches are accepted, but their aim is to encourage their geeks to take risks and stay creative, knowing that the pay-off when they get a winner will be colossal.

These steps will help you get more new product winners:

- Review your competitors' products. To succeed, a new product has to be significantly better in some respect – price, performance, convenience, availability – to dislodge a well-entrenched rival.

- Test the market if development is going to be expensive.

- Ask your customers what they want. Samantha Burlton, founder of So Organic (www.soorganic.com), did lots of research on her customers in launching the 1,200 products they now sell online. Her website has an e-mail address and phone number for customers to contact the business with ideas or suggestions for products to be included in the range. Her product promise is that she will only list products she would be happy to recommend to her friends. (Burlton's use of public relations also makes for interesting reading – hit the 'In the press' tab at the top of the page.)

- Check out exhibitions where you will find out what competitors and customers are interested in (see also Chapter 7, 'Attending trade shows and exhibitions', page 119).

- Talk to anyone in your team who is in direct contact with your customers. They will be the first to hear complaints, niggles and ideas for improvements and additions to your activities.

Enter new markets

This strategy involves taking existing proven products and services into new geographic areas or new market segments. In Chapter 3 the market segmentation process was examined, and that is the starting point for researching new related market segments.

CASE STUDY   To begin at the beginning

Lyn Thompson, founder of Milkwood Publishing, started out in 1992 painting watercolour cards at her kitchen table in Cornwall and selling them at local craft fairs. Unable to keep up with demand she saw a business opportunity for original greetings cards. Her first step was to put together a business plan and with a loan of £3,500 from the Prince's Trust and six of her own designs, Milkwood Publishing was born! She quickly expanded into larger premises producing prints as well as cards and framing them myself. Quality at an affordable price is her USP.

Retailing was the next natural business opportunity that presented itself and Milkwood now have 10 successful retail outlets in Cornwall, The Whistlefish Galleries. The first Whistlefish Gallery opened in St Ives in 1998 followed by galleries in Falmouth, Padstow, Truro, Plymouth, Loo and Dartmouth. Lyn next developed a national and international chain of distributors and agents. Milkwood's UK agents sell into 1400 outlets in the UK and the company now export via distributors to France, Belgium, The Netherlands, Greece, Ireland Australia and South Africa. Dubai opened in 2016 and Korea in 2017. Another key step in business development was launching their online operation and via their website Whistlefish (www.whistlefish.com) they now generate significant over half their sales.

Lyn has also kept her eye firmly on cost. 'Our core strategy is to have the lowest cost operation in our very narrow market. In short we aim to be the cost leader focused in art based cards and prints sourced from original artists for which we alone have the reproduction rights. We don't necessarily compete on price but we use our cost advantage alongside tight cost controls and low margins to create an effective barrier to others considering either entering or extending their penetration of our market.'

The innovations that Lyn clams that have helped Milkwood grow include:

- 'Operating efficiencies: We have introduced and continue to introduce new processes, methods of working or less costly ways of working stripping out major elements of cost at every stage of our operation. For example we have stopped producing lines that are difficult to pack and bought in more efficient machinery.'
- Product redesign: 'We have rethought our product proposition fundamentally to look for more efficient ways to work. For example we ask artists to paint in such a way as to marry up with our standardization strategy.'
- Product standardization: Most of our competitors offer a near infinite range of cards and prints in many shapes and sizes. They claim that this gives customers a greater choice, but we believe they have to go this route because they just don't know their market. We have standardised our sizes having only two card sizes and a limited range of print sizes. This way we have a wide choice of what goes into our products but the manufacturing process itself is simple and efficient.
- Economies of scale: By putting our wide portfolio of designs into standardized sizes we can have longer production runs. Having streamlined our production means that our experience of making specific products is probably greater than a company ten times our size.'
  Lyn claims that 'the success of our company is because we take original artwork all the way through design, manufacture to point of sale using what I call in-sourcing'. This gives us certainty of quality and delivery, essential if global and online distribution channels are to be sustained.'

Diversification: the last resort

Selling things you know little about to people you know even less about can be the riskiest of growth strategies. Often diversification is founded on the concept of synergy, where two plus two equals five – or put another way where the whole is greater than the sum of the parts.

Unless you can quantify the value added in a diversification strategy, for example in better buying with quantity discounts or by being able to spread your costs over a bigger sales volume, stay away.

Key jobs to do

- Review your present pricing methods and test out the likely impact of selective price rises on revenues and profits.
- Examine cost reduction options.
- Check planned working capital ratios (use material in Chapter 9 too) and compare with past performance and competitors to identify opportunities for improvement.
- Review working methods to identify areas for improved efficiency.
- Launch a profit improvement programme.

Starting up overseas

If you are considering starting up overseas or expanding your existing business into international markets, whilst being adventurous you can be comforted in the knowledge that millions have been there before, over the years. The Institute for Public Policy Research (**www.ippr.org.uk**) Brits Abroad project shows that over 5.5 million British people live abroad, less than a fifth are retired, and a sizable minority of the rest have gone abroad to start a new business. The businesses started cover the whole spectrum: anything from a boatyard in France, a property agency in Spain, a bar in Crete, a boutique hotel in Bodrum, Turkey, a restaurant in Germany's Black Forest, to an English tearoom in Florida are prospering ventures started up by British people in overseas countries.

Whilst the basic rules of starting a business remain the same wherever it starts and whoever runs it, there are some specific country-related factors that come into play. With these in mind this chapter aims to augment the previous chapters for anyone with these particular purposes. See also the second part of Appendix 1, for general sources of help and advice for owner-managers in all the major overseas countries.

CASE STUDY

Pacific Direct (**www.pacificdirect.co.uk**) was started in her garage in Bedfordshire, England, by Lara Morgan as a means of supporting herself and her then husband-to-be whilst he went through business school. The niche she spotted was in providing hotel toiletries, an industry in its infancy 14 years ago when she started out. Soon she realized that to be competitive she would have to find low-cost manufacturing facilities. She identified China as the best place to get miniature plastic containers, disposable slippers, dressing gowns and other related products that go into a complete hotel bathroom package. As the contents of the toiletries bottles were supplied from the UK, France and the United States it made no economic sense to ship those out to China, so the bottles were brought back to the UK for filling. Soon Lara found a better solution, using a supplier in the Czech Republic who pitched a competitive price.

On the back of a competitive price structure Lara rapidly built up a unique offer, taking licences to fill hotel toiletry products with Penhaligon's, Nina Campbell, Floris, Ermenegildo Zegna, Elemis and the White Company brands. Starting with the Dorchester Hotel in Park Lane, Lara built up sales with international five-star hotels, cruise ships, airlines and resorts around the world. Both the Chinese and the Czech businesses needed money to expand to keep up with Lara's rapid growth, so she took majority stakes in both, offering credit to help them stay in the game. As well as running a multimillion-pound turnover business, Lara has ensured that Pacific Direct puts something back into the societies it impacts on. It works with local Bedford hospices and the Morning Star Orphanage in Nepal and does not test products on animals.

Choosing a business-friendly country

Finding the optimal country either to locate a new venture or to find suppliers and business partners involves researching the political and economic environment of the country concerned and its attitude to enterprise. You will also need to take stock of your own appetite for risk. Although, for example, buying into a factory in China and employing 400 staff sounds an adventurous, even dangerous, strategy for someone living in Bedford, as Lara speaks fluent Mandarin and spent her childhood in Hong Kong it was not as risky as it seemed.

Some regions and countries are probably just too risky for any but the desperate to try, though at the time of writing one enterprising Brit is setting up a property business in Kabul, Afghanistan. Apparently on the back of meteoric growth fuelled by the influx of aid workers and consultants, houses in desirable areas of town go for $500,000. Using the sources in this chapter you can keep track of the countries where you can have a reasonable chance of both being welcome and prospering.

Where enterprise is welcomed

Whilst some countries have restrictions on who can come into their country to do business, most do not. Where restrictions apply the most usual is the requirement that local directors or shareholders have to 'front' the organization. But these barriers are coming down, and even communist-leaning countries such as Russia, Cambodia, Vietnam and China are more welcoming to incoming entrepreneurs and business generally.

Some countries are more than just open. For example, the United States, Canada, Australia, Israel, Ireland, Italy and South Africa are amongst a growing band of countries that offer a fast track to citizenship for people who will bring money and innovative ideas. In the UK, for example, an investment of around £200,000 gives access to an entrepreneur or innovator's visa; in Canada C$300,000 gets an entrepreneur class visa; and in the United States the immigrant investor (EB-5) known as the 'Million Dollar Green Card' was introduced as far back as 1992. In fact the card can be had for as little as $500,000 in certain targeted areas of the United States. Surprisingly, only a total of 6,024 have been issued against an annual target of 10,000.

Doing Business (**www.doingbusiness.org**) is a free annual from the World Bank Group assessing and measuring business regulations and their enforcement across some 180 countries. Their indicators identify specific regulations that enhance or constrain business investment, productivity and growth and provide yardsticks to gauge how welcoming a country is towards entrepreneurs. The topics include: starting a business; closing a business; paying taxes; dealing with licences; employing workers; registering property; getting credit; protecting investors; trading across borders; and enforcing contracts. You can use the database to get a snapshot of each economy's aggregate ranking on the ease of doing business and on each of the 10 topics that make up the overall ranking. You can see that in 2010 Singapore was the best country to start a business in and Central African Republic the worst. In Australia an entrepreneur can start up taking just two days of paperwork, whilst in Suriname it will take 694 days and involve 13 separate procedures. These rankings are on the move as countries make major reforms. For example, in 2009 Belarus was languishing at 98th position, but by 2010 has risen to 7th. It achieved this by merging procedures, abolishing minimum capital requirements and removing basic bureaucratic matters such as the need to get company seals approved centrally. Data are also provided for each country for all the 10 topics covered in the database, and you can produce a tailored report on selected countries using specific measures for ease of comparison.

Reviewing the business climate

Finding a country that is welcoming to entrepreneurs is one thing, but it is equally important to establish whether the economic climate is likely to be favourable, whether or not business methods are corrupt and what the quality of life for you and anyone you may employ is likely to be.

There are a number of free or low-cost sources of background data on these subjects, which are discussed in the following sections.

The Central Intelligence Agency (CIA) *World Factbook*

The CIA *World Factbook* (**www.cia.gov/library**) has a wealth of information, sufficient to form a view on economic health or otherwise. The CIA keeps the *Factbook* up to date on a regular basis throughout the year, providing the most current information to hand. Once in the *Factbook*, you are offered a pull-down bar in the top left of the screen, which allows you to select any one of the 233 countries or regions afforded separate status for analytical purposes by the CIA. For each country there is a selection of basic economic, political and demographic information, as well as information on political or border disputes that may cause problems in the future.

The Rank Order Pages allow you to follow a number of analytical threads that let you compare and contrast countries with one another. Select 'References – Guide to Country Comparisons' from the central menu bar. These are lists of data from 80 fields in seven of the ten *Factbook* categories, given in descending – highest to lowest – order, with two exceptions: the unemployment rate and inflation rate, which are in ascending – lowest to highest – order.

Country Watch

Whilst the CIA *World Factbook* is backward looking, Country Watch (**www.countrywatch.com**) provides a five-year macroeconomic forecast, and a 20-year forecast of energy demand, supply and pricing is provided for each of 193 countries with 75 pages about each one. One-year online access to information on all countries costs from £50. You can get a free trial, which might be all you need to rule a country in or out of your search. Some libraries and colleges have this a free resource so if you are enrolled on a course or near a major library explore that before incurring any expense. It also provides demographic data on population size, education, political, economic, business, cultural and environmental information, as well as daily news coverage, and it has a substantial news archive.

NationMaster

This is a compilation of data from such sources as the CIA *World Factbook*, the UN and the OECD, aiming to be the web's one-stop resource for country statistics on everything. Using NationMaster (**www.nationmaster.com**) you can see the ranking at a glance for all of a country's key economic data, amongst other factors. So, for example, at a glance you can see that Zimbabwe has the highest level of unemployment at 95% whilst Qatar has barely 0.5%; perhaps not a great place to set up in business if you want to recruit staff. Using the tools provided you can generate maps and graphs using the site's statistics.

Transparency International (TI)

TI (**www.transparency.org**) defines corruption as 'the abuse of entrusted power for private gain'. Established in 1986, it is independent and impartial. It operates through a worldwide network of over 90 locally established organizations and is probably best known for its Corruption Perceptions Index (CPI). This is a composite of independent surveys studying 180 countries. In the latest survey they reported that sixty-eight per cent of countries worldwide have a serious corruption problem. Half of the G20 are among them. Denmark is the least corrupt country and the UK ranks 10th. Spain, however, comes in at 58th, just ahead of Malta, Rwanda and Jordan: you would be far less bothered by corrupt officials in Uruguay, Bhutan or Botswana than in Spain.

The Human Development Index

The HDI, published annually by the UN **http://hdr.undp.org/en**, ranks nations according to their citizens' quality of life rather than strictly by a nation's traditional economic figures. The criterion for calculating rankings is a summary composite index that measures 33 aspects of a country's average achievements in three basic aspects of human development: longevity, knowledge and a decent standard of living. From the main menu, choose 'Human Development Statistics' from the menu on the left of the page. Then select 'Get Data', from which you can choose the country you are interested in or you can 'Build your own table' and choose the countries and indicators you are interested in and download formatted tables, either on-screen or to an Excel file.

Researching international markets

The procedures of collecting market research and in many cases the sources of the data are the same for overseas markets as they are for your home market.

You need to identify specific customers, ideally by name, suppliers of materials and business equipment and some information on likely local competitors. Fortunately there is a reasonable degree of overlap in the sources of this information. These are the directories and other providers of such information on international markets:

- The British Franchise Association (**www.thebfa.org/international/franchise-associations-around-the-world**) has a directory of country franchise associations from which you can find information about franchising in each country.

- Chambers of commerce run import/export clubs, help with international trade contacts and provide market research and online intelligence through a 150-country local network of chambers. The international Chamber of Commerce (**www.iccwbo.org**) is the place to start.

- Corporate Information (**www.corporateinformation.com** > Tools > Research Links) is a business information site covering the main world economies, offering plenty of free information. This link takes you to sources of business information in over 100 countries. Their Industry Averages Reports are prepared on 28 industries with a total of 165 separate permutations (ie global, region and country). This contains a host of rations covering sales and financial performance.

- Research and Markets (**www.researchandmarkets.co.uk**) is a one-stop shop that holds nearly 1.5 million market research reports listed in a hundred or so categories across over 70 countries. Reports are priced from €20 upwards. For example a Medical Tourism report on India is priced at $32 whilst one on Targeting Medical Tourists from the UK costs $1,020.

- Thomas Net (**www.thomasnet.com**) is an online directory in 11 languages, with details of over 700,000 suppliers in 28 countries. It can be searched by industry sub-sector or name either for the world or by country.

- TranslatorsCafé (**www.translatorscafe.com**) is a database of over 4,000 linguists that can be searched by location, language, name and size of agency.

- World Intellectual Property Organization (**www.wipo.int/ directories**) is a country-by-country directory of the organizations responsible for intellectual property (patents, trademarks, logos, designs and copyright) around the world. From there you can find the rules and procedures for protecting IP.

- World Market Research Association (**www.mrweb.com**) operates its Blue Book (**https://bluebook.marketingresearch.org**) of people who conduct consumer, opinion and marketing research in almost every part of the world. Their database is searchable by country, business activity or type of research required.

People, property and professional advisers

Setting up a business overseas will, if not at the outset, once established involve employing people and finding premises. Any of these activities will have implications that may require the services of a professional adviser such as an accountant or lawyer. These international organizations provide advice and resources to help in these fields:

- Doing Business (**www.doingbusiness.org/data**) is a free resource from the World Bank Group giving information on the cost of hiring, paying and firing employees in 190 countries. For each country there is a wealth of information on working hours, severance pay, notice periods, redundancy and paid holiday periods.

- Global Property Guide (**www.globalpropertyguide.com**) is a guide to every aspect of buying and renting property in almost every country, with information on property price trends and finding a local lawyer and property agent.

- Martindale-Hubbell Lawyer Locator (**www.martindale.com**). This legal network is currently a database of over a million lawyers and law firms in 160 countries. On this page you can search for a lawyer by country and specialization.

- PayScale (**www.payscale.com/hr**) is a site where you can get accurate real-time information on pay scales.

- Worldwide-Tax (**www.worldwide-tax.com**), despite the name, is a very comprehensive site that deals with a host of taxation and financial subjects for some 70 countries. From the left-hand vertical menu bar headed 'World Directories' select the profession (lawyer, accountant, etc), from which you are directed to a country-by-country list of lawyers, who have usually been pre-qualified as having English-language websites and whose partners have a good command of English.

Money matters

Business wherever you conduct it means dealing with money; escaping your home country is unlikely to let you leave those concerns behind, far from it, and you may have a few additional subjects such as exchange rates and local wealth taxes to deal with too.

Getting funding

You will have some of the same options as in the UK, which were explained in Chapter 10, 'Raising the money', though in many countries your choice of provider may be limited to a handful of sound businesses, except where they are subsidiaries of the international major banks. Local banks will usually be quite secure for transferring money through and for handling small sums on an ongoing basis. It may not be prudent, however, to leave large sums either on deposit or even in the bank vaults. Unlike in the UK and Europe where the government in the case of default protects deposits of £75,000, that is rarely the case in less developed markets.

Banking options

It is highly likely that your own bank has either a foreign subsidiary or a partnering relationship with banks in overseas countries. If they don't, or seem reluctant for any reason, then consider one of the following two options.

Currently, opening a bank account in many other countries is a fairly relaxed process, but the procedures on monitoring for suspicious transactions are being tightened up. You need to be on your guard to see that you are not drawn unwittingly into a laundering activity. Worldwide-Tax (**www.worldwide-tax.com** > World Directories > Banks) has a directory to world banks, sorted by country, with the major banks in each country, including local banks and international banks having branches. Most have an English-language website that includes an explanation of how to open a bank account in their country as well as online application procedures.

Choose a bank with at least one person who speaks your own language, who is well versed in foreign transactions and ideally who knows something of the type of business you are starting or expanding into.

Equity providers

It may be possible to get financial backing from an investor willing to take a stake in your business, whether you are expanding overseas or starting up. Chapter 10 provides guidance on funding. Many of the private equity and crowd funding platforms provide access to international backers.

Dealing in foreign exchange

Running a business abroad means handling money in at least two currencies, your own and that of the country you will trade in or with. Many countries have their own currency, but not all currencies are equally stable. The less stable the currency the more cost and risk are involved in any transaction.

The key factors to find out about a currency are:

- Is it 'not fully convertible'? This means that the government of the country concerned exercises political and economic control over the exchange rate and the amount of its currency that can be moved in or out. China and India are amongst many countries that fall into this category. These currencies can be very volatile, and you will need permission to repatriate money.

- Is the currency 'pegged'? The most favourable way to obtain currency stability has been to peg the local currency to a major convertible currency, such as the euro or dollar. This means that, whilst the local currency may move up and down against all other world currencies, it will remain or at least attempt to remain stable against the one it is pegged against.

- Is the currency 'dollarized'? This is a slight misnomer, as the term is used to describe a country that abandons its own currency and adopts the exclusive use of the US dollar or another major international currency, such as the euro.

- Is the currency 'fully convertible'? If so, it stands on its own two feet and fluctuates as the country in question succeeds or fails. Russia, for example, lifted currency controls in July 2006 as a sign of economic confidence, making the rouble fully convertible.

These organizations can help you with foreign exchange matters:

- OANDA (**www.oanda.com**) were first to market in making comprehensive currency exchange information available over the internet, and now license out to hotels and airlines providing exchange rate information on their websites. From the left-hand menu bar you will find an extensive range of valuable tools, including Select FXConverter (foreign exchange currency converter) to access the multilingual currency converter with up-to-date exchange rates covering any of the 164 currencies used around the world. The date function is a neat addition, as you can see what rate you would have got in the past. For example, a British pound would have bought only $1.41 in 1985, whilst it bought $1.44 in May 2010 and by January 2017 the rate had dropped further to $1.22.

- The Financial Markets Association (**http://acifma.com**). From here you will find links to the websites of some 90 country-affiliated associations, listed by continent. The country associations contain directories of members.

Taxes

Most countries have some form of taxation, and the rules are often different for foreigners who invest in the country. There is usually no way of avoiding paying taxes somewhere, but you do have some choice as to where you end up paying it. The governing rule on who you pay your taxes to is not so much about where you live, nor necessarily where your income comes from, as where you are resident. The word 'resident' has a particular meaning when it comes to taxation and is not necessarily the same as having a residence card or living in the country.

Taking up residence

If you have been living and paying taxes say in the UK, then simply going overseas will not change the fact that you are 'ordinarily resident' in the UK. If you leave the UK to take up permanent residence abroad and so inform HM Revenue & Customs, they will normally accept this at face value and treat you as ceasing to be resident on the day following your departure. If you spend an average of 91 days or more per year in the UK, over any four-year period, you will be swept back into the UK tax net. You are, since a rule change in 1993, even allowed to have accommodation available for your use in the UK.

Double taxation agreements

It is possible to be tax resident in both countries if you meet both sets of rules. For example, if you spend 200 days abroad, 100 days in the UK and the remaining days elsewhere, both the foreign and the

British tax authorities or your home tax authority could reasonably lay claim to you. Most countries have 'double taxation' agreements that are designed to settle the argument. 'Tie-breakers', as the relevant clauses in the double taxation agreement are known, deal with such cases as those of people with homes, assets and income in roughly equal proportions in both countries. In those circumstances you are deemed normally to be a resident of the country of which you are a national.

The aim of double taxation agreements is to help make sure that you don't pay tax on the same taxable event twice, once in a foreign country and again at home. But you could well end up paying different taxes in each country.

The key taxes to consider

- *General income tax.* This is a tax on income earned in a particular country from employment or any profitable activity. Some countries operate a flat rate structure, such as Estonia, where 23 per cent is applied on all income. Other countries, such as New Zealand and Morocco, have a sliding rate with a 0 per cent band, whilst Thailand and Mexico tax even the lowest earners. The Netherlands, Denmark, Spain, Austria, Slovenia and China tax even fairly modest levels of income at between 45 and 59 per cent.

- *Income from investments.* In many countries, but not all, this falls into the same bands as for personal taxation.

- *Business tax.* The rates vary widely around the world. In Montenegro the corporare rate is 9 per cent whilst in india it is around 40 per cent. All business taxes are complicated, but in some countries they are more complicated than in others. For example, it takes over 1,000 hours to prepare and file all business taxes in countries such as Ukraine, Brazil and the Czech Republic, whilst in Singapore, Switzerland and the Seychelles the task can be completed in less than 70 hours.

- *Capital gains tax.* This is the tax charged against the profit made on the gain from investment in an asset, such as a business. As with other taxes there is a wide variety of rates and conditions to look out for. You can usually reclaim any capital gains tax paid if a reinvestment is made within a set period.

- *Value added and sales taxes.* These are taxes levied on transactions rather than on income earned. Within Europe these taxes are levied at widely different rates, anything between 15 per cent and 22 per cent being the norm. Canada's VAT rate of 5 per cent is one of the lowest, and Brazil's and Denmark's 25 per cent the highest. In addition some items are exempt from this tax in some countries.

- *Import duties.* Within the European Union import duties are largely a thing of the past. However, post Brexit and Trump this benign situation may change. Nevertheless many countries exempt personal effects brought into a country, including furniture, computers and even motor vehicles. But not all countries are equally forgiving. For example, you can import virtually anything into Iraq free of import duties, whilst taking anything into the Dominican Republic will be liable to a local tax of up to 40 per cent.

- *Tax holidays and inducements to invest.* Many countries offer individuals and businesses tax or grant inducements to buy business assets in certain areas. These are often short-lived opportunities and, like all such offers, are intended to encourage some risk taking. The degree of risk and reward varies enormously.

- *Annual property tax.* Simply owning a property usually lands either the owner or the occupants with a tax bill, which can be either nominal (Bulgaria) or prohibitive (Italy).

- *Wealth tax ('capital tax', 'equity tax', 'net worth tax' or 'net wealth tax').* Countries including Finland, France, Greece, Iceland, Luxembourg, Norway, Spain, Sweden and Switzerland levy a tax each year on the value of their citizens' assets. In some cases, the reach of the tax goes further still; in France, for example, anyone resident in the country on 1 January is taxable on his or her worldwide assets, and non-residents with assets in France are taxed on the value of their French assets as at 1 January each year. Spain abolished its wealth tax in 2009 only to reintroduce it 'temporarily' for 2012 and 2013. At the time of writing the tax is still in place and up for review sometime in 2017.

● *Inheritance tax and death duties.* You will have to consider who inherits when you or any joint owner of the business dies and set this out in a will. If you don't the death in question will be dealt with under the intestacy laws, which are a nightmare to deal with, especially if there is scope for ambiguity as to whether the matter should be dealt with under British law or the law of the country in question. Unlike the UK, certain family members under the law of many overseas countries have automatic inheritance rights. For example, spouses and children, even illegitimate ones, may not be cut out of a will. However, if you are still a British citizen, irrespective of your tax residency arrangements, your will, as long as you make one, will usually be dealt with under British law. Whilst a British will is usually valid under the law in most foreign countries it is advisable to draw up a will in the country in question to save time in being able to distribute the estate and the ensuing additional administrative costs. Your foreign and British wills must not conflict in any way; otherwise that will leave scope for interminable disputes, time delays and additional costs. You will need an executor for your foreign will. Whilst in the UK it is not uncommon for lay people to act as executors; proving a will abroad, especially for a foreigner, can be complex, so it may make good sense to appoint a local lawyer to steer the inheritors in the best direction.

Sources of help, advice and information on foreign tax

● Doing Business (**www.doingbusiness.org/data/exploretopics/ paying-taxes**). From there you will find the taxes that a small to medium-size business must pay or withhold in a given year, as well as measures of administrative burden in paying taxes. The opening table in this section shows the total number of taxes paid, the time it takes to prepare, file and pay (or withhold) the relevant tax, the value added tax and social security contributions (in hours per year), and the total amount of taxes payable by the business, except for labour taxes. To see the full details of the tax regime for a specific country, use the drop-down box on the top right of the screen or click on the relevant country link on that page. By clicking on the column headers you can sort the relevant data to show, for example, which country has the highest or lowest taxes, requires the most or least time to deal with or involves the most or the fewest separate tax payments.

- Worldwide-Tax (**www.worldwide-tax.com**). From the central menu on the home page select 'Tax Rates Around the World – Comparison' to find a quick summary of income and corporate tax levels as well as value added tax for all the countries covered. From the vertical menu bar on the left of the home page screen, select from the 'Shortcut to countries' section the countries you are interested in researching. Once in the country page, scroll down to the country taxes menu in the centre of the page and from there select the appropriate tax. At the bottom of that menu you can select 'Tax News' for the current year, where you will find the latest changes in tax rules for the country in question.

Key jobs to do

- Make a list of the countries you would like to live in and operate from.

- Assess the business environment and climate in each of those countries.

- Check the competitive situation in each of those countries in terms of customers, growth rates and numbers and strength of local competition.

- Review the banking, funding and foreign exchange risk profiles in each of those countries.

- Identify the most business friendly countries with the lowest cost of operations and a benign tax and legal regime. Work out why none of these will suit you and your business.

APPENDIX ONE
Home business help and advice

These are the principal sources of help and advice for anyone starting a business from home. Other important sources have been provided directly in each chapter throughout the book.

United Kingdom

ACCA (www.accaglobal.com/uk/en/research-insights). The accountancy body has information on planning, budgeting and forecasting, performance reporting and, profitability and cost analysis.

AfroCar (www.afrocar.co.uk) is an online directory for African-Caribbean businesses in the UK. They find and list small and medium enterprises (SMEs) of African-Caribbean businesses in the UK aiming to promote African-Caribbean businesses at no cost to listed business owners. Their stated goal 'is to elevate black businesses as a deprived community, one step at a time'.

British Association of Women Entrepreneurs (www.bawe-uk.org). For the past fifty years this association has acted as a peer group for 'women entrepreneurs who want to be challenged'. Associated Membership is open to those in business for less than three years at £80 per annum.

BSI (www.bsigroup.com/en-GB) provides information and resources to help small businesses introduce quality standards such as ISO 9000.

Business in the Community (tel: 020 7566 8650; website: www. bitc.org.uk) is The Prince's Responsible Business Network. They have a range of initiatives including Accredited Training, Arts and Business, Business Class, Business Connectors and The Access Programme that aims to create a level playing field for small and medium enterprises (SMEs) so they can grow, win business and create new jobs.

Department for International Trade (www.gov.uk/government/ organisations/department-for-international-trade) is the government agency charged with helping UK-based businesses succeed in 'an increasingly global world'. They provide information on doing business with every country and every business sector from aerospace to water.

eBusiness Clubs (www.ebusinessclub.biz) is a free service delivered through British chambers of commerce aimed at small businesses, offering access to a range of activities including events, ICT support and information from business experts. The strapline 'How technology can improve business performance' explains the central purpose of the clubs.

Every Woman (tel: 020 7981 2574; website: www.everywoman. com). They offer individual membership at £5 a month. That includes learning tools and content delivered through a variety of media, including webinars, workbooks, video and articles, and access to senior female role models, including advice, experience and thought leadership.

Federation of Small Businesses (tel: 0808 2020 888; website: www. fsb.org.uk) offers legal, environmental, fire and premises tips, as well as many other issues that small business owners may have to address as they grow. The Federation has the resources to take major test cases of importance to small business through the expensive legal process and has been particularly effective in dealing with taxation and employment matters. Amongst the benefits on offer are access to in-house solicitors, barristers and tax experts and provision of legal and taxation advice lines, including litigation and representation services. Membership is on a sliding scale dependent on number of employees, starting at *circa* £175.

First Tuesday (http://firsttuesday.org.uk) has 38,000 members with 10 branches across Europe and hosts networking meetings on the first Tuesday of every month. The idea is to bring entrepreneurs, investors and service providers such as accountants, lawyers and bankers together to create a 'circle of friends' who can help technology entrepreneurs get started or grow. Some events are free whilst most are modestly priced. Deloitte and Salesforce.com are sponsors of the initiative.

Forum of Private Business (tel: 0845 130 1722; website: **www.fpb. org**) is a membership organisation costing circa £175 to join, giving you information when you need and management tools to help your business stay within the law. By completing them you see how to comply with the regulations on employment, health and safety, bank finance and credit control.

Homeworking.com (**www.homeworking.com**), started in 1999, is a resource rather than a job directory and is full of useful tips and helpful warnings about the thousands of scam businesses on offer to would-be homeworkers.

Institute of Directors (tel: 0333 331 9905; website: **www.iod.com**) is the club for directors, membership of which costs £99 for IoD 99 membership which is open to anyone aged 18–40 who is a director or a founder of a business so long as your business has an annual turnover of less than £5m and has been established for 10 years or less. Expect to pay about double if you don't meet those criteria. For that you get access to a prestigious central London office and other offices around the UK and on the Continent, business information and research provided for you by the IoD's expert researchers and bespoke business advice on tax and law. It is also considered one of the best networking associations for entrepreneurs.

National Asian Business Association (tel: 0116 319 7413; website: **www.nabauk.org/**) sis a national voice for the Asian business community providing information and advice on anything from starting a business through to selling goods or services. Membership of NABA is free and comes with benefits such as free training on issues of interest such as exporting, financial planning and of course, a number of networking opportunities.

National Enterprise Network (tel: 01908 605130; **www.nationalenterprisenetwork.org/**). There are some 250 Enterprise Agencies in the UK that deliver business support services and directly or indirectly provide advice and information, counselling and training on a comprehensive range of business issues, to all types of owner-managed businesses, including pre-starts, start-ups, sole traders, partnerships, cooperatives and limited companies. The NFEA maintains a directory of English agencies on its website and links to Enterprise Agency networks in Northern Ireland, Scotland and Wales.

Prince's Trust (tel: 0800 842 842; website: **www.princes-trust.org.uk**) runs business programmes and provides low-interest loans for people aged 18–30 who want to start a business. Their *Support for starting a business* programme has helped over 80,000 young people to start their own business since it was started in 1983.

Telework Association (tel: 0800 616008; website: **www.tca.org.uk**) costs from £34.50 ($50/€41) a year to join the 7,000 other members who either work or are running a business from home. You get a bi-monthly magazine, a teleworking handbook with ideas for telebusinesses, and access to their help line covering all aspects of working from home.

Overseas agencies

Australia: Invest Australia (**www.investaustralia.gov.au**) is the central inform¬ation source for foreign investors; business.gov.au (**https://www.business.gov.au/Info/Plan-and-Start**) provides information, advice and contact points for all aspects of thinking about starting or a business.

Canada: Canadian Federation of Independent Business (**www.cfib.ca**) represents the interests of over 109,000 owner-managers across the whole of Canada. Industry Canada (www.ic.gc.ca) is the Canadian government's support agency responsible for all aspects of business and local support.

China: Invest in China (**www.fdi.gov.cn > English>Investment environment**) provides information and resources for investing in projects and joint ventures region by region.

Cyprus: Ministry of Commerce, Industry and Tourism (**www.mcit. gov.cy > English > Industrial Development Service > One Stop Shop for Setting up a Business**) has all the information on starting and running a business and accessing finance for a new or small business.

Developing countries: The International Finance Corporation (**www.ifc.org**), a member of the World Bank Group, provides advice, loans and equity to help foster entrepreneurship in the developing countries.

Europe: European Small Business Portal (http://ec.europa.eu/ small-business/index_en.htm) is the entry point to access all the EU's schemes to help small businesses and to a range of business tools and advice. There are direct links to a network of over 300 Euro Info Centres, 236 Innovation Relay Centres, 160 Business Incubation Centres and Your Europe – Business, a site with practical information on doing business in another country within the EU.

France: L'Agence pour la Création d'Entreprises (**www.apce.com**) is the French small business service. The website is in French and if that's a challenge Start Business in France (http://www. startbusinessinfrance.com) provides professional answers and advice on starting and running a small business in France. It costs €99 and for that you get a personal answer all your questions, clearly explaining your options in detail and give expert advice on your situation. Operating since 2009 they have 2,655 members and have answered about 56,175 questions.

Hong Kong: Hong Kong Trade Development Council has an SME Start Up Portal (**http://sme.hktdc.com/en/index.html**) which is a comprehensive resource for information, tips, seminars, events and online forums aimed at the small business community.

India: Indian Government National Portal (**https://india.gov.in/ topics/industries/micro-small-medium-enterprises**) covers all the regulatory issues about getting a business off the ground, hiring staff and raising money.

Ireland: Irish Small and Medium Enterprise Association (www.isme. ie) offers a comprehensive range of advisory services and training and development for new and small businesses.

Italy: The Italian Institute for Foreign Trade (**www.italtrade.com**) is the government agency that advises on information about the market and gives help and advice with starting a business in Italy. Using the 'Your Business Proposals' facility you can search for a compatible Italian business partner.

Malta: Malta Enterprise (**www.maltaenterprise.com**) is the government's site with information on inward investment, enterprise support and innovation and enterprise.

New Zealand: Ministry of Economic Development (http://www. mbie.govt.nz/info-services/business) is the agency responsible for ensuring that New Zealand is one of the best places in the world to do business in.

Portugal: Agencia de Inovaçao (http://ani.pt/en/) is the country's agency that supports innovative businesses. The Useful Links section connects to other useful organizations, including Invest in Portugal and Portugal in Business.

South Africa: The Small Enterprise Development Agency (**www. seda.org.za**) is the South African Department of Trade and Industry's agency for supporting small businesses. The site has all the information needed to start a business, find partners and access local regional support agencies throughout South Africa.

Spain: Invest in Spain (http://www.investinspain.org/invest), created in 2005 as part of the State Department for Tourism and Trade in the Ministry of Industry, Tourism and Trade, is the point of contact for all state, regional and local institutions helping businesses set up or expand into Spain.

Turkey: Turkish British Chamber of Commerce and Industry (http:// tbcci.org/starting-your-business-in-turkey) has all the information on starting a business in Turkey. Use the 'Business Partner Search' link in the Trade Services box, where you can state the type of business and relationship you are looking for and so find a partner in Turkey.

United States: Small Business Administration (website: **www.sba. gov**) provides financial, technical and management assistance to help Americans start, run and grow their businesses. Their website has a large quantity of information and business tools of value to business starters anywhere. Buy USA (**www.buyusa.gov** > Do you export U.S. products or services?) is the website of the US Department of Commerce from which you can select any country you want to do business in. Though aimed at US businesses the information is of value to anyone planning to start or grow a business anywhere in the world.

APPENDIX TWO

Directory of proven home businesses

Putting 'starting a home based business' into Google's search pane yielded 51,000,000 results when this edition was being written. Unfortunately most, perhaps as many as 95 per cent, of these are completely unworkable; try making money stuffing envelopes by hand in a world where even the smallest mailing house can buy equipment to fold, insert, seal and stamp at a rate of 10,000 per hour for about as many pounds. Or they could only appeal to a tiny minority who already have specialist knowledge: accountant, calligrapher, corporate art consultant and translator, all 'ideal home-based businesses' for which you are invited to buy ready-made business plans at £10 ($15/€12) a pop, are just a few of the hundreds of examples on offer. More sinister is the stream of venture propositions that are frankly little more than scams.

The internet has made scams easier to execute and less likely to be prosecuted. There are thousands of advertisements suggesting you can make a fortune from your sitting room by parting with just £9.99 ($14/€11.99), in return for which you get a dozen pages of trite, banal homilies, just enough for the vendor to avoid committing outright fraud. But even outright fraud has become tolerated. In the first instance the fraud is being perpetrated anonymously thousands of miles away in a manner that would require infinite courage were a shopkeeper trying to rip off a local customer. Secondly, the authorities are unlikely even to attempt to prosecute unless the fraud is large (over £500/$720/€590) and prolific.

These business ideas should be read in conjunction with Chapter 1, 'Finding the right business opportunity', Chapter 2, 'Picking the right business for you', and Chapter 3, 'Researching the market'.

You can check out the current scams on **www.scambusters.org**

Customers come to your home – all the time

This way of operating requires everyone in the family to be onside, and you need to be prepared to make some significant compromises in the way you live if it is not to become too oppressive. If you see your home as a refuge from the outside world and identify with the idea that 'an Englishman's home is his castle' then this may not be the way to go.

CASE STUDY

Niki and Miles Jameson moved to the edge of a market town in the West Country to escape the rat race. He had been a senior research director with an international pharmaceutical company and Niki was personal assistant to the company chairman. Marrying made their break with the company more urgent, and selling up their home near London gave them some spare cash for the transition. Niki trained as a beauty consultant at a local college and then worked for a period in a beautician's nearby to get some practical experience. Miles spent most of the first years renovating the house and converting an annexe into a holiday cottage. Niki, once their son was attending school all day, started her own beauty business, working out of a downstairs room at home. She took some clients with her from her employer, advertised in the local paper, registered with various online 'salon finder' websites and pushed her business card on to mums at the school gate.

Gradually her business built and she extended her skills, taking courses to allow her to offer bio-detox and electrolysis, whilst adding a small range of beauty products to sell to her customers after their treatment. She invested in improvements in her treatment room once she was sure she had a regular clientele. Initially Niki restricted client appointments to the hours when her son was at school, but as family life adapted to accommodate her business she took clients two evenings a week to fit in those with daytime commitments.

Business opportunities

These are some businesses you can run from home that require customers mostly to come to you. You will need to check with the various associations and bodies listed in Chapter 5 ('Checking out the rules', page 73), to make sure you comply with health, safety, fire and other associated risks.

- *Bed and breakfast.* There are tens of thousands of B & Bs, with anything from just one or two letting rooms up to a dozen or more, and most towns and villages in tourist areas have one or more. The Bed and Breakfast Association (**www. bandbassociation.org**) can help with all aspects of getting started. Bed and Breakfasts.co.uk (**www.bedandbreakfasts. co.uk**) is a good website to check out the competition and how much to charge and eventually to advertise on. Visit Britain (**www visitbritain.com**) provides a national star-rating standard for B & Bs, as well as advertising them on its website and in local Tourist Information Centres.

- *Childminding.* This is an increasingly popular business, particularly for people with young children of their own. It is a carefully regulated business, and all people working with children need to be registered with Ofsted **www.gov.uk/** register-childminder childcare-provider) The National Childminding Association (**www.ncma.org.uk**) has advice on getting trained, taking out insurance and getting qualified.

- *Home hairdressing, beauty therapy and related areas.* As the case study above illustrates, these types of business are relatively simple to operate from home, and by using an appointment system you can still maintain a degree of privacy. Organizations that can help and advise include: the Beauty Biz (**www.thebeautybiz.co/2/article/ jobs/setting-up-home-beauty-business**); the Hair Council (**www. haircouncil.org.uk**); the British Association of Beauty Therapy and Cosmetology (**www.babtac.com**); and the Hairdressing and Beauty Suppliers Association (**www.thehbsa.co.uk**).

- *Running a shop.* There are tens of thousands of premises comprising a shop with living accommodation either above or alongside. Although local shops are under pressure from big out-of-town shopping malls and precincts there are still over 32,000 small shops. These are mostly conveniently located near areas of population, selling a wide range of products in small quantities to people either without a car or between big shops. Alternatively they are in niche markets such as organic products, designer clothes and sports goods. Check out Living Over The Shop (**www.livingovertheshop.org.uk**) for general information, and the Association of Convenience Stores (**www.acs.org. uk**), where you can find information on market trends, supplier networks and even a business plan template.

- *Other services that can be run from home.* For those who have or are prepared to invest in acquiring the skills, these include: the British Wheel of Yoga (**www.bwy.org.uk**), Pilates (**www. pilatesfoundation.com**), home tuition (**www.thetutorsassociation. org.uk**), English conversation classes (**www.tefl.co.uk**) and language tuition (**www.alllanguages.co.uk**).

Customers come to your home – some of the time

Rather than having a steady stream of customers there are some businesses where most of what you do is out of the customer's sight and involves only periodic visits rather than having to be 'open all hours'. The dividing line between having customers come to your home all and just some of the time is not hard and fast.

CASE STUDY

Pete Leighton more stumbled into business than planned it. His ex-wife took their dog, a golden retriever, when they divorced, as she stayed in the country and he moved to a small flat in a town. When his circumstances changed and he moved back to living in the country he decided to get a dog again. To his shock he found that a dog with a good pedigree would cost between £250 ($361/€294) and £650 ($940/€765). The person he was buying from had a litter of 10, of whom eight had survived, and had a queue of willing buyers. The maths looked good: £650 ($940/€765) to buy a good bitch, stud fee £400 ($580/€470), feed and vet's bills of around £500 ($770/€600), making total cost £1,550 ($2,240/€1,825). Selling eight at £650 ($940/€765) each made £5,200 ($7,500/€6,120) income and £3,650 ($5,272/€4,295) profit. The next time round the profit would be even more, as he would already have the dog.

Pete discovered that it was not quite as easy as it seemed. The bitch needed special meals, plenty of walks and lots of attention and care. Then when the pups arrived their bedding had to be changed and washed several times a day, and carpeted floor had to be replaced with a hard floor that could be mopped frequently. His attention was drawn to the Breeding and Sale of Dogs (Welfare) Act 1999, which would require him to be licensed by the local authority if he planned to produce five or more litters a year.

Business opportunities

These are some businesses you can run from home that require customers to come to you only periodically. You will need to check with the various associations and bodies listed in Chapter 5 ('Checking out the rules', page 73), to make sure you comply with health, safety, fire and other associated risks, and see in Chapter 7 ('Getting a licence or permit', page 132) whether you need a licence to operate.

- *Animal breeding and grooming.* These associations can help with advice, information and further contacts: the Dog Breeders Association (**www.dog-breeds.co.uk**); the Cat Breeders Association (**www.cat-breeds.co.uk**); Pet Sitters International (**www.petsit.com**).

- *Clothes design, dressmaking, alterations, repairs and home sewing.* Savile Row Bespoke (**www.savilerowbespoke.com/training/srba-apprentice-scheme**) run an apprentice scheme for would-be tailors, and reading the Blooming Marvellous story (**www.bloomingmarvellous.co.uk**) will inspire you with just how far you can take a business starting out with only a pair of scissors and a kitchen table. Sewing.com (**www.sewing.com**) has a range of useful information for the home sewer, and Sew Essential (**www.sewessential.co.uk**) is a one-stop shop for everything in the sewing and needlecraft fields.

- *Home ironing.* Whilst launderettes have taken the slog out of heavy washing loads, and incidentally have proved a successful business to live above, ironing is still an undersupplied service. Allironedout (**www.allironedout.co.uk/agents**) are looking for people to work with them from your home, a shop or industrial unit, working flexible hours that fit around your family life.

- *Soft furnishings, curtains and upholstery.* Alongside the boom in the buy-to-let market has grown the need for high-quality but competitive home furnishings to make a property stand out from the herd. The products have to be durable as well as fashionable. The British Interior Design Association have a directory of all the training providers (**www.bida.org**).

Meet customers online

The internet is the classic business model for reaching the whole world with an extensive product range without necessarily leaving your home either to buy the products you are selling or to meet the customers face to face. It is also a business format that gives you maximum flexibility in the hours you work. For the most part, once established a well-built e-business will run itself, and where work has to be done it makes little difference whether you do it at 3 am or 3 pm.

Business opportunities

The internet is a highly competitive arena, and the days when just having a website was a USP are long since past. Functionality, design, speed and search engine visibility are all essential features whatever business you start in this sector. As well as Chapter 3, 'Researching the market', and Chapter 7 'Bringing your product and service to market', read Chapter 8, 'Building and using your website'.

eBay and other auction houses

There are dozens of auction houses you can plug into. The list below is indicative rather than exhaustive. Remember that all these sites are just windows on various worlds. You need unique products and services and competitive prices and attractive and compelling propositions to stand out in these very crowded markets:

- Abe Books (**www.abebooks.co.uk** > Sell Books) claim to be the worldwide number one among new, used and antiquarian book platforms and marketplaces, selling around 25,000 books worldwide. They will handle payment and have a free inventory management software package. It costs £17 a month to list up to 500 books and £200 for 15,000 and over. A fee of 8 per cent is charged on sales via their shopping basket payment and a further 5.5 per cent if Visa or MasterCard is used. You have to ship the books yourself.

- Amazon Services Europe (http://services.amazon.co.uk) will list, take payment, insure and if required pick, pack and deliver your products through their distribution system. Amazon provide tools to make it easy for you to upload inventory on to the website, and you can have an unlimited number of listings to sell to their millions of customers. There is no fixed-term contract, and charges start from £25 a month plus VAT.

- eBay Powerseller Programme (**http://pages.ebay.co.uk/help/sell/ sell-powersellers**). You may only know eBay as a place to pick up a bargain and sell on last year's ski gear when you move on to a snowboard. Certainly, that's one side of the business. The other is the PowerSellers as they are known, who make anything from a few hundred to tens or even hundreds of thousands of pounds.

General online selling businesses

- Etsy (**www.etsy.com**) is a creative marketplace where 24 million buyers around the world shop for unique items. Etsy's commission is 3.5% and they provide the Sell on Etsy app to manage orders, edit listings and respond to buyers instantly, from anywhere. Free social media tools and detailed stats about your shop's performance are on offer to help you increase your sales.

- Not on the High Street (**www.notonthehighstreet.com**) claim to be the UK's top curated market place with 39 million unique visitors every year. They are looking for 'innovative and original ideas; something a little different'. There is a joining fee of £199 and you pay 25% commission on sales (both sums are plus VAT). They have thousands of people selling through the site with some generating in excess of £1 million per annum.

Go out to sell – stay home to service

This business model keeps customers out of your home, but requires you to make periodic forays outside to drum up business. If you need to be on hand to look after children or elderly relatives full time, this may not be a way that will work well for you. In this sector you will need to hone your selling and promotional skills and drum up as much free PR as you can. Check out Chapter 7, 'Bringing your product and service to market', where these topics are covered.

Business sectors

- Bookkeeping is a service needed by small businesses. With 450,000 new businesses starting up each year, and few owner-managers with either the skills or the inclination to do this work, the potential is good. The Institute of Certified Bookkeepers (**www.book-keepers.org** > Where to Study) will point you in the direction of a course, which can be taken part time or by correspondence. From a standing start you should be able to do the books for a small business in three to six months. In Chapter 9 ('Keeping the books', page 152), you will see how the job is done and the range of inexpensive software that can make light work of big numbers.

- Business consultancy is a classic start-at-home business, and the range of options is enormous. The Institute of Management Consultancy merged with the Institute of Business Advisers in April 2007 to form the Institute of Consulting (**www.iconsulting. org.uk**), which is the industry professional body for all consultants and business advisers.

- Indexing. The Society of Indexers (**www.indexers.org.uk**) is the professional body that can inform you about training, pricing and finding work, though it has to be said this is not the best-paid work on the block.

- Market research and telephone selling are both sectors that pay on results, and as such measuring performance is relatively easy. The Direct Marketing Association (**www.dma.org.uk**) is the professional body and you can find out about training, competitors and fees from them.

- Online surveys are a way to make pin money, though the advertisements would suggest you could make more. Websites such as mysurvey (http://uk.mysurvey.com) and Opinion Outpost UK (**www.opinionoutpost.co.uk**) are good places to start your research and Money Saving Expert (**www.moneysavingexpert. com**/family) regularly provides a full rundown of the top paid survey sites.

- Property services such as holiday rentals, house hunting and property maintenance are increasingly popular home-start ventures. Examples include: Home Aways (**www.homeaway. co.uk**), which was started in 1996 by two Cranfield students, Ross Hugo and Trevor Barnes, and now has thousands of private owners signed up to let their holiday cottages anywhere from Australia to Wales.

- Small-scale food preparation can be carried out at home, making soups, jams, cakes and the like. One enterprising person decided that, rather than work downstairs in her father's Indian restaurant at night, she would use his kitchen by day to make and market a range of sauces to sell to local independent shops in the neighbourhood. Food and Drink Federation (**www.fdf.org.uk**) has as members everyone from long-established brands to small companies manufacturing organic products. They offer training, advice and facts and statistics on the sector.

- Typing, word processing and virtual office support are services in demand from other small businesses. Outsec (**www.outsec.co.uk**) founded in 2002, claims to 'combine technology and a global reach of sector-specific experienced British typists to provide industry with an online web-based secretarial facility of the highest calibre.' Their FAQ (http://dav.outsec.co.uk/faq/typistfaqs) covers all you need to know to get started working from home as a typist.

APPENDIX THREE

Home business information resources

Starting a business from home requires assembling an eclectic range of data and keeping it up to date. Not an easy task but with the sources below it should be possible to keep informed about most key business issues. For example, you can find out which country has the fastest improving business environment for new entrants (Rwanda, where new company law makes it possible to set up a venture in just two procedures and three days). Contrast that with Sierra Leone where it takes 1,075 days and it shouldn't be too difficult for an MBA to make an intelligent recommendation on where the best market expansion opportunities are likely to be found. Basic facts on which country spends the most on advertising – the United States, which outspends the next four countries on the list would be most people's educated guess. But appreciating that China ranks number two in this respect and advertising expenditure there is growing at 27 per cent per annum, whilst in the United States and United Kingdom growth rarely exceeds single digit levels is the intelligence an MBA needs to be able to dig up quickly.

Knowing where investors are best protected (New Zealand) or where it is hardest to fire employees (Venezuela); where the fastest growing economy, the best for quality of life, how much pay you should ask for if you are offered a job in the Kyrgyz Republic and how many companies make knitwear in Spain and how profitable they are all questions that can be answered in a few mouse clicks; and knowing the answers is what gives the home business starter a better chance of succeeding in their enterprise.

- Advertising Statistics Year Book (**www.adassoc.org.uk**) provides, in one volume information on almost every statistical fact on advertising industry trends covering the press, television, radio, outdoor and transport, cinema, directories, direct mail and the internet. Up to 30 years' worth of back data, together with trend analysis is available showing 'real' growth and share of advertising spend.

- The American Association of Advertising Agencies (**www2.aaaa.org**), usually shortened to 4A's produces annual and trend data on that market in much the same format as it is in the UK's Advertising Statistics Year Book.

- American Business Directory produced by InfoUSA (**www.infousa.com**) contains company address, current address, telephone number, employment data, key contact and title, primary Standard Industrial Classification (SIC) code, yellow pages and brand/trade name information, actual and estimated financial data on over 13 million US business establishments. A companion volume, Canadian Business Directory, covers over 1.5 million Canadian businesses.

- Applegate (**www.applegate.co.uk**) has information on 237,165 companies cross-referenced to 57,089 products in the UK and Ireland. It has a neat facility that allows you to search out the top businesses and people in any industry.

- Blog Directories: The information on blogs is more straw in the wind than fact. Globe of Blogs (**www.globeofblogs.com**) launched in 2002 claims to be the first comprehensive world weblog directory. Links up to over 60,000 blogs, searchable by country, topic and about any other criteria you care to name. Google (**http://blogsearch.google.com**) is also a search engine to the world's blogs.

- The British Library (**www.bl.uk** > Collections > Patents, trade marks and designs> Key patent databases) links to free databases for patent searching to see if someone else has registered your innovation. The library is willing to offer limited advice to enquirers.

- The British Library Business Information Service (**www.bl.uk/ services/information/business.html**) holds one of the most comprehensive collections of business information in the UK.

- The Central Intelligence Agency (CIA) World Factbook (**www.cia.gov/cia/publications/factbook**): This link will take you straight to the latest edition of the Factbook. The CIA keeps the Factbook up to date on a regular basis throughout the year, so you can be reasonably confident of having the most current information to hand. From the Factbook you are offered a pull-down bar in the top left of the screen, which allows you to select any one of the 233 countries or regions. For each country there is around half a dozen pages of A4 of basic economic, political and demographic information, as well as information on political disputes that may cause problems in the future.

- Chambers of Commerce (**www.chamberonline.co.uk** > International Trade > International Chambers) run import/export clubs, international trade contacts and provide market research and online intelligence through a 150 country local network of chambers. Their Link2Exports (**www.link2exports.co.uk**) website provides specific information on export markets by industry sector by country.

- The Chartered Institute of Patents and Attorneys (**www.cipa.org.uk**).

- Companies House (**www.companieshouse.gov.uk**) is the official repository of all company information in the UK. Their WebCheck service offers a free of charge searchable company names and address index, which covers 2 million companies listed by either name or unique company registration number.

- Copernic Agent (**www.copernic.com**) is an exceptionally useful free tool for web searchers. By using a meta search tool, capable of sending your query to multiple engines simultaneously it allows users to selectively search multiple sources and its powerful sorting and analysis tools can be customized to provide and rank sources of specific data.

- Corporate Information (**www.corporateinformation.com** > Tools > Research Links) is a business information site covering the main world economies, offering plenty of free information. This link takes you to sources of business information in over 100 countries.

- Desktop Lawyer (**www.desktoplawyer.co.uk**) has a summary of all the key issues from employing staff to health and safety and the pros and cons of partnerships as well as inexpensive partnership deeds.

- Doing Business (**www.doingbusiness.org**): This is the World Bank's database that provides objective measures of business regulations across 183 countries and produces occasional reports on major cities within those countries. You can find out everything from the rules on opening and closing a business, trading across borders, tax rates, employment laws, enforcing contracts and much more. There is a tool for comparing countries to rank them by the criteria you consider most important.

- Economics Network (**www.economicsnetwork.ac.uk**): This is a heavy-duty economics website supported by some thirty universities and business schools in the UK providing links to free data (mainly macroeconomic) on the UK and international economies at this link (**www.economicsnetwork.ac.uk/links/data_free.htm**). Valuable for helping sales forecasts and projections.

- European Patent Office (**www.epo.org**).

- FAME (Financial Analysis Made Easy) is a powerful database that contains information on 3.4 million companies for companies in the UK and Ireland. You can compare each company with detailed financials with its peer group based on its activity codes. The software lets you search for companies using your own criteria, combining as many conditions as you like. So, for example, you could identify competitors with the strongest and weakest financial position and so get an insight into how to compete with them. You can also identify those with the fastest and slowest rates of sales growth or best and worst profit margins, important facts to have to hand in any marketing armoury. FAME is available in business libraries and on CD from the publishers, who also offer free trial (**www.bvdep.com/en/companyInformationHome. html** > Company data – national > FAME).

- Corporate Reports (**www.corpreports.co.uk**) is an online service offering free instant downloads of financial reports from listed companies in the UK. Annual reports, balance sheets, profit and loss statements and interim reports are available from one of the largest databases of listed companies in the UK.

- Global Competitiveness Report (www.weforum.org/en/initiatives/gcp/index.htm). Produced by the World Economic Forum first published in 1979 covers 131 major and emerging economies providing an annual measure of a nation's economic environment and its ability to achieve sustained growth. This is a good starting point for identifying new geographic market segments to penetrate.

- Google News (www.google.com), which you can tap into by selecting 'News' on the horizontal menu at the top of the page under the Google banner. Here you will find links to any newspaper article anywhere in the world covering a particular topic. Using this you can keep track of press comment on say competitors to find out when, for example, they are recruiting for more staff, entering new markets or launching new products and services.

- Google Trends (www.google.co.uk > Labs > Google Trends) provides a snapshot on what the world is most interested in at any one moment. For example if you are trying to find out if consumers really care about green issues (useful to know when seeing how to pitch a new product) entering that into the search pane produces a graph showing how interest measured by the number of searches is growing (or contracting) since January 2004 when they started collecting the data.

- Human Development Index (www.undp.org): HDI is published annually by the UN and ranks nations according to a composite index that measures thirty-three aspects of a country's average achievements in three basic aspects of human development: longevity, knowledge, and a decent standard of living. From the main menu choose 'Human Development Statistics' from the menu on the left of the page. You can use this to get a quick appreciation of the prospects for your products and services. High-end cosmetic surgery, for example, is unlikely to find much of a market in countries at the bottom of the HDI index.

- The Institute of Patentees and Inventors (www.invent.org.uk) is a self help and networking association for inventors, with annual membership costing £70 a year, with a one-off joining fee of £15.

- The Institute of Trade Mark Attorneys (www.itma.org.uk) despite their specialized sounding names can help with every aspect of IP, including finding you a local adviser.

- The Internet Public Library (www.ipl.org) is run by a consortium of American Universities whose aim is to provide internet users with finding information online. There are extensive sections on business, computers, education, leisure and health.

- Kelly's (www.kellysearch.co.uk) lists information on 200,000 product and service categories across 200 countries. Business contact details, basic product and service details and online catalogues are provided. This is a good starting point for finding sales leads.

- Keynote (www.keynote.co.uk) operates in 18 countries providing business ratios and trends for 140 industry sectors providing information to assess accurately the financial health of each industry sector. Using this service you can find out how profitable a business sector is and how successful the main companies operating in each sector are, as a prelude say to considering expanding in those areas yourself. Executive summaries are free, but expect to pay between £250 and £500 for most reports.

- Lexis-Nexis (www.lexis-nexis.com) has literally dozens of databases covering every sector you can think of, but most useful for marketers researching competitors is Company Analyzer, which creates comprehensive company reports drawn from 36 separate sources, with up to 250 documents per source. So, when you get tired of scouring different databases to find out all there is to know about a competitor, customer or supplier, you could consider using Company Analyzer to access legal, business, financial and public records sources with a single search. Company Analyzer provides access to accurate information about parent and subsidiary companies and their directors, to highlight potential conflicts of interest.

- Librarians' Internet Index (http://lii.org): The mission of Librarians' Internet Index is to provide a well-organized point of access for reliable, trustworthy, librarian-selected websites. To be included the information must be freely available, have an identified and qualified site author and have current, accurate information about the topic concerned.

- LibrarySpot.com (www.libraryspot.com) is a free virtual library resource centre for just about anyone exploring the web for valuable research information. Forbes.com selected LibrarySpot.com as the Best Reference Site on the web and USA Today described it as 'an awesome online library'.

- MarketResearch.com (www.marketresearch.com) claims with some justification to be the world's largest and continuously updated collection of market research offering over 250,000 market research reports from over 650 leading global publishers. Whether you're looking for new product trends or competitive analysis of a new or existing market alerts from this source will keep you on top of the latest available intelligence.

- Microsoft (http://adlab.microsoft.com) is testing a product that can give you mass of data on market demographics (age, sex, income etc), purchase intentions and a search funnel tool that helps you understand how your market searches the internet. Using the demographics tool you can find that 76 per cent of people showing an interest in bay clothes are female and surprisingly 24 per cent are male. The peak age group is the 25–34 year olds and the lowest is the under 18s followed by the over 50s.

- The National Statistics (www.statistics.gov.uk) website contains a vast range of official UK statistics and information about statistics, which can be accessed and downloaded free.

- NationMaster.com (www.nationmaster.com): This provides compilation of data from such sources as the CIA World Factbook, UN, and OECD. Using the tools on the website you can generate maps and graphs on all kinds of statistics with ease. Their aim is to be the web's one-stop resource for country statistics on everything.

- Online newspapers (www.onlinenewspapers.com). Newspapers and magazines are a source of considerable information on companies, markets and products in that sphere of interest. Virtually every online newspaper in the world is listed here. You can search straight from the homepage, either by continent or country. There is also a separate site for online magazines (**www.onlinenewspapers.com/SiteMap/magazines-sitemap.htm**).

- Realtor.com (**www.realtor.com**): This is the website of the US National Association of Realtors. An MBA can use this site to work out the cost of living in 700 international cities across 162 different currencies. Invaluable either when moving job or advertising appointments. Select 'Moving' from the menu bar at the top of the screen, and then from the 'Moving Tools' menu in the middle of the left hand menu select 'Salary Calculator'. Once in the Salary Calculator tool select the term 'International Salary Calculator' highlighted in blue at the bottom of the first paragraph.

- Thomas Global Register (**www.thomasglobal.com**) is an online directory in eleven languages with details of over 700,000 suppliers in 28 countries. It can be searched by industry sub sector or name either for the world or by country.

- Trade Association Forum (**www.taforum.org** > Directories > Association Directory) is the directory of Trade Associations on whose websites are links to industry relevant online research sources. For example you will find The Baby Products Association listed, at whose website you can find details of the 238 companies operating in the sector with their contact details.

- Transparency International (**www.transparency.org**): TI established in 1986, is independent, impartial and operating through a worldwide network of over 90 locally established organizations, is probably best known for its Corruption Perceptions Index (CPI). This is composite of independent surveys studying 159 countries. In the most recent survey 70 countries were rated as having 'rampant corruption that poses a grave threat to institutions as well as to social and political stability'.

- UK Intellectual Property Office (**www.ipo.gov.uk**) has all the information needed to patent, trademark, copyright or register a design.

- UK Trade and Investment (**www.uktradeinvest.gov.uk**) is the government agency charged with helping UK-based businesses succeed in 'an increasingly global world'. They provide information on doing business with every country and every business sector from Aerospace to Water.

- US Patent and Trade Mark Office (www.uspto.gov).

- Warc (www.warc.com) claims to provide the most comprehensive marketing information service in the world. Their guide to world advertising trends covers latest annual advertising expenditure data across all main media for more than 60 countries, outlining key trends in media investment over the last 10 years.

- World Intellectual Property Organization (www.wipo.org > Resources > Directory of IP Offices) is a country-by-country directory of the organizations responsible for Intellectual Property (patents, trademarks, logos, designs and copyright) around the world. From there you can find the rules and procedures for protecting IP.

- World Market Research Associations (www.mrweb.com), whilst not quite the world does have web addresses for over 65 national market research associations and a hundred or so other bodies such as the Mystery Shopping Providers Association, which in turn has over 150 members, companies worldwide.

- Worldwide-Tax (www.worldwide-tax.com): This website is a very comprehensive site that deals with a host of taxation and financial subjects for some 70 countries. For each country there are a general and economic survey and links to providers of professional services such as accountants, banks, lawyers, government sites, as well as a complete and comprehensive section on the embassies in that country.

- Yellow Pages World (www.yellowpagesworld.com > Yellow Pages International) is an international directory of online yellow pages and white pages whose goal is to make it easy to find an online yellow pages or white pages provider in the country you want to search in. Currently 31 countries are covered.

INDEX

Italics indicate a table or figure.

CPSIA information can be obtained
at www.ICGtesting.com
Printed in the USA
LVOW13s1707190418
574120LV00020B/193/P